CAPTAIN

A Biography of Jerry Garcia

TRIPS

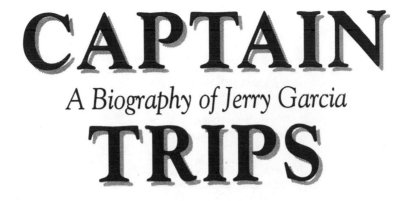

CAPTAIN

A Biography of Jerry Garcia

TRIPS

SANDY TROY

THUNDER'S MOUTH PRESS

First edition
First paperback printing, 1995

Published by
Thunder's Mouth Press
632 Broadway, 7th Floor
New York, NY 10012

LIBRARY OF CONGRESS CATALOGING-IN-PUBLICATION DATA
Troy, Sandy.
    Captain Trips : a biography of Jerry Garcia / by Sandy Toy. —
1st ed.
      p. cm.
    Includes index.
    ISBN 1-56025-090-9
    1. Garcia, Jerry, 1942- . 2. Rock musicians—United States
—Biography. 3. Drugs and popular music. 4. Grateful Dead
(Musical group). I. Title.
ML419.G36T76   1994
782.42166'092—dc20
[B]   94-21138
                                               CIP
                                              MN

Printed in the United States of America

For Miles Davis,
John Coltrane,
and John Lennon

CONTENTS

ACKNOWLEDGMENTS

Since I first got on the bus at Woodstock in the summer of 1969, I've met many people who have been involved with the Grateful Dead scene who graciously shared their memories, experiences, and insights with me. It would be impossible to name everyone I have talked to over the years, but I would like to thank all the individuals who provided me with information.

Special thanks go to Gene Anthony, Tom Constanten, Charlotte Daigle, John Dawson, Carolyn Garcia, Jerry Garcia, Dan Healy, Chet Helms, Jorma Kaukonen, Dick Latvala, Eileen Law, Stanley Mouse, Brent Mydland, David Nelson, Merl Saunders, Nicki Scully, and Rock Scully, who allowed me to interview them at length.

There were many Dead Heads who contributed their time to this project. I would like to give special acknowledgment to Steve Benavidez, David Dupont, Mark Fenichel, Brian Gold, Gigi Krop, Pat Lee, Tim Mosenfelder, Andy Sopczyk, and Steve Young.

I wish to express my gratitude to Gary Goldstein at Gary's Record Paradise for making his extensive collection of folk and old-time records available to me.

I am particularly grateful to my editor, Robert Weisser, for his guidance and help in shaping this book. I also wish to acknowledge the staff at Thunder's Mouth Press for their efforts on my behalf, especially Rebecca Corris.

Thanks to Tony Secunda for putting another book deal together.

To Debra, Anna, and Lindsey Troy, my eternal love for putting up with my endless hours at the computer. I couldn't have written *Captain Trips* without your support.

Finally, I would like to thank Jerry Garcia, whose music, art, and wit were the inspiration for this book.

FOREWORD

Jerry Garcia was a guy I knew in the "old days," the late 1950s and early 1960s when I was studying photography at the California School of Fine Arts on Chestnut Street in North Beach (now called the Art Institute) and Jerry was studying art. We didn't hang out together; I would see him from time to time in the coffee shop in the school's basement. Occasionally the school had Friday night parties that began in the drawing studios and painting galleries and then drifted into the school's courtyard, where students made music banging on guitars, makeshift drums, and other homemade instruments. In the middle of the courtyard there was a large octangular fountain, where occasionally I played bongos next to Garcia, who had a guitar. A couple of years later I saw him again, in a barber shop on Haight Street, being spun round and round on one of the chairs. Several guys were taking turns riding the chair, having a good time.

During 1966 I was "that photographer" who was around a lot, and I was tolerated as long as I didn't intrude at the wrong moment with my camera. As a freelance photographer, I sold my pictures to the newsmagazines who were falling all over themselves to get stories about the personalities and weirdness going on in San Francisco. Ken Kesey was part of it, as were the

Grateful Dead, who were the house band for Kesey's Acid Tests. The Acid Tests were made possible by the handiwork of Owsley Stanley, the notorious "King of LSD," who single-handedly manufactured millions of doses of acid and turned on a lot of people.

Going on a trip was very legal then. In fact, there was an aura about LSD that made it something most artists and free-thinkers wanted to experience: it was an all-new dimensional perspective on everything. Psychedelics were really *it*, an incredible perception for people. During those early days we thought we were on the road to changing the world. People talked about LSD with great reverence. Once turned on to acid, you couldn't wait to tell your friends. The nicest thing you could do for a friend was to turn him or her on in the proper environment: the music and incense and color and toys for one's trip. Tim Leary's League for Spiritual Discovery pushed acid as the sacrament of the cult he was creating, and his forty-six-room mansion at Millbrook in upstate New York was trip headquarters East. The Dead's old Victorian house at 710 Ashbury in the Haight became trip headquarters West.

Until LSD became illegal on October 6, 1966, Jerry Garcia and the guys sowed a lot of tabs. In fact, when the band came out on stage at the Fillmore, they showered their fans with handfuls of Owsley's latest brew—a lot of trips. Naturally the band had marvelous, great parties at 710 too, and although Jerry was never the spokesperson for the group, people selected him as the leader. Thus the name that went with his Uncle Sam hat: Captain Trips!

Gene Anthony

INTRODUCTION

Jerry Garcia is a special kind of person. Whereas so many of us tend to wander through life, searching for something that can hold our interest for a short time, let alone for a lifetime, Garcia has been devoted to music ever since he was a teenager. As his career developed, he became known best as a rock 'n' roller, one of the originators of the "San Francisco sound." However, his passion has been not only for one style of music, but for a whole range of genres, including folk, bluegrass, country, acid rock, rhythm and blues, gospel, and jazz.

Because of his passion, Jerry has never dabbled in these styles just to see what they could add to his rock repertoire. He has always plunged in, learning the instrument or style that fascinated him, practicing whenever he could (sometimes eight hours a day), and putting his reputation on the line by playing the new music before paying customers. And being the great technician that he is, Garcia is never completely satisfied unless his performances are top-notch.

Despite all this effort, Garcia has never thought of playing music as work. For him, it is an opportunity to have fun and take a permanent vacation from the dictates of straight society. This attitude partially explains the legions of die-hard fans who show up for Grateful Dead or Jerry Garcia Band concerts, or for shows by the other bands that Jerry has put together over the years. When Garcia is having fun, the music is great, and Garcia is almost always having fun on stage. This translates into continual good times for the audience.

Another reason for Garcia's popularity is that he is not afraid to experiment, to play a song differently each time out. In fact, the band doesn't necessarily know beforehand the order of the songs they will play at a concert—how they're playing and what improvisations they do are what determines which songs are played and when. And since his music is new each time he plays, Jerry is not jealous with it. When he is done playing it, the audience can have it, whether they want to trade tapes of it or just savor the sweet high of it.

This approach to music sets Garcia apart from most of the music industry. Jerry is not driven by money, nor does he desire fame. There is very little that is artificial about him, and he has no illusions about his place in history. Let others argue about who changed the course of rock 'n' roll; let others get out front of movements to change the world. These are by and large not Jerry's concerns, and he doesn't want people to look to him for leadership. What they *can* look to him for are more basic joys of life—a beautiful guitar riff, an exciting jam, an expressive lyric. For Jerry is the consummate musician; he's not playing because the audience likes the way a song sounds, he's playing because this is what he wants to do in life. Millions of people love his music, and many of these people see Jerry as an icon of the 1960s spirit. But Garcia is an independent spirit— the opinions and expectations of others do not affect him much. Listeners everywhere can be thankful for that.

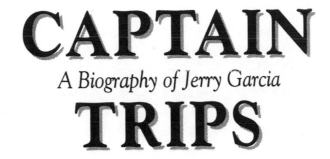

CAPTAIN
A Biography of Jerry Garcia
TRIPS

1

THE LONG, STRANGE TRIP BEGINS

Barely a decade removed from the catastrophic earthquake of 1906, San Francisco had totally rebuilt itself. It was a center for culture, business, and trade not only for the West Coast, but for the Pacific Basin as well. This was underscored in 1915 when San Francisco hosted the Panama-Pacific International Exposition to celebrate the opening of the Panama Canal. This once sleepy outpost of the Spanish Empire, a frontier town of no more than 200 inhabitants known as Yerba Buena until 1847, was now a cosmopolitan metropolis of almost 400,000 souls.

To this beautiful, exciting city by the bay came the teenaged Jose Ramon Garcia, who emigrated from La Coruna, Spain, with his entire family in 1919. The Garcia clan was well-to-do, and Jose had no need to take a laborer's job, as so many other immigrants of that era had to. He decided to become a professional musician, playing clarinet and other reed instruments in small Dixieland-style four-piece and five-piece bands. He eventually became an orchestra leader, conducting the big bands that were so popular in the 1930s.

In the early 1930s, while playing in the Bay Area, Jose met Ruth Marie Clifford, a strong woman of Swedish and Irish descent. Her family had come to San Francisco during the Gold Rush. Soon after Ruth met Jose, the two fell in love, and they got married in 1934. Staying close to their relatives, they made their new home in San Francisco, moving to a modest home at 121 Amazon Avenue, off Mission Street near Daly City and the Cow Palace, in the blue-collar Excelsior District.

Soon, however, their lives took a radical turn. Before their third anniversary, Jose's music career came to an end. During the Depression, the musicians' union had what was called the Seven-Day Law, which prohibited members from working seven nights a week in order to spread the scarce work to as many members as possible. Typically, those who had steady jobs would play five nights a week and have two free nights. To supplement his income, Jose had been working a second job on his off-nights, and when the union found out, Jose was expelled. He was then unable to find work, for other union musicians were forbidden from working with non-union players. Since all of the good musicians were in the union, Jose's opportunity to play music with other quality players was gone.

Rather than leave their home town for the sake of Jose's calling, the Garcias looked for other work. Jose took up bar tending, and in 1937 he bought a tavern in downtown San Francisco at 400 First Street, at the corner of Harrison near the

Bay Bridge, which had been completed only the year before. The Four Hundred Club had a terrific location, across the street from the merchant marine local, the Sailors' Union of the Pacific. The bar was filled with sailors who had traveled to the South Pacific, the Far East, and other exotic ports. Often the sailors would bring in arcane mementos of their travels to the far reaches of the world.

In the same year that they bought the Four Hundred Club, Jose and Ruth had their first child, Clifford. Five years later, on August 1, 1942, their second and final child, Jerome John, was born at Children's Hospital. Jose's genes were apparent in his youngest son's dark curly hair, high forehead, and thick eyebrows. The unusual name came about because of his father's fondness for the great Broadway musical composer Jerome Kern. Jerry was raised a Roman Catholic and received early religious training, but was never confirmed.

Garcia was surrounded by music as a child. His father would play him to sleep at night, the clarinet's lovely, woody melodies echoing in Jerry's dreams. His mother listened to opera, and his maternal grandmother loved country music. Family gatherings tended to be musical, too, for his father's side of the family would gather round and sing songs together.

Garcia's own passion for music manifested itself early. When Jerry was little more than a toddler, the family would go to the Santa Cruz Mountains in the summer. One of his first memories of those vacations was of having a 78-rpm record and playing it over and over and over on a wind-up Victrola, until he drove his parents crazy and they gave him something else to play with. At home, Ruth Garcia played some piano, and Jerry took lessons as a young child. However, he never advanced very far with piano because he couldn't or wouldn't learn how to read music. Ruth insisted he keep at it, though, so Jerry would bluff his way through his lessons, learning the music by ear rather than reading the notes on paper, and developing an ability to discern how a song should be played. Perhaps this was the first improvisation he did in his musical career, a skill for which he would become famous later.

Another trip to the Santa Cruz Mountains, when Jerry was four, was more pivotal. Jerry and his brother, whom he called Tiff, had the job of splitting wood for the fire. Jerry would place a piece of wood, take his hand away, and Tiff would chop. By bad timing, Tiff lopped off half of the middle finger of Jerry's right hand. Hearing the screams, Ruth comforted Jerry as best she could, and wrapped his hand in a towel. Jose then drove Jerry to a hospital in Santa Cruz, some thirty miles away over mountain trails and back roads, where Jerry's hand was bandaged. Subsequent checkups resulted in smaller and smaller dressings, with the reassuring doctor commenting on the good progress of the healing. Then the final bandage was unwrapped—and Jerry saw that his finger was gone! It appears that Jerry quickly adapted to this, however, even turning it to his advantage. Rather than being self-conscious about the missing digit, he got a lot of mileage from displaying it to the other kids around the neighborhood.

The next year saw a loss that would take Jerry and his family much longer to overcome. The Garcias were on a camping trip and Jose was fly-fishing, wading in a river that may have been too treacherous to get into. Suddenly he slipped and went under, and he was swept away by the raging water. Jerry was playing on the bank of the river near his father and saw what happened, and the death of his father crippled him emotionally for a long time. "I couldn't even stand to hear about it until I was ten or eleven," he recalled. "I didn't start to get over it till then, maybe because of the way it affected my mother."

The loss of Jose traumatized the Garcias, irrevocably affecting Jerry's childhood. Ruth, who had been staying home to take care of the family, was now compelled to work full-time at the bar. Handling the business, her children, and her widowhood was too much for the grief-stricken Ruth. She decided that it would be best for the whole family if Jerry lived with her parents, William and Tillie Clifford.

Jerry's grandparents, who owned a small house at 87 Harrington Street in the Excelsior District a few blocks from Ruth's home, raised him for the next five years. Both grandparents worked, William as a driver and Tillie as the secretary-treasurer of the Laundry Workers Union Local 26 in San Francisco.

Living with his grandparents changed Jerry for life. "I think that probably ruined me for everything," he said. "It made me what I am today. I mean, they were great people, but they were both working and grandparently and had no stomach for discipline." He was able to do as he pleased pretty much without constraints. Jerry would explore the Excelsior District after school or spend time at his mother's bar listening to the sailors tell their exotic tales of the world beyond San Francisco. He gained a sense of independence that set a precedent for his later life.

Tillie's fondness for country music also made a lasting impression on her grandson. She was a big fan of the Grand Ole Opry, and listened regularly to the Saturday night radio broadcasts from there. Jerry soaked it all in, hearing the likes of the Carter Family, Bill Monroe, and Flatt and Scruggs. "I probably heard Bill Monroe hundreds of times without knowing who it was," Garcia later said. "When I got turned on to bluegrass in about 1960, the first time I really heard it, it was like, 'Whoa, what is this music?' The banjo, it just made me crazy."

In 1950, when Jerry was eight years old and in the third grade, his teacher enlarged the world for him as the sailors at his mother's bar had. Miss Simon was a bohemian, and she was the first person to let Jerry know that it was all right for him to draw pictures and do other artwork. She encouraged him to paint murals and to make things out of ceramics and papier-mache. All of a sudden, being a creative person was a viable possibility in life. Jerry was taken with the idea of becoming a painter, and began drawing and painting constantly in sketchbooks. This fascination with art became a guiding interest throughout his life.

In 1952, when Jerry was ten, his mother married Wally Matusiewicz. Wally helped run the Four Hundred Club, and this gave Ruth more time to devote to her sons. She reclaimed Jerry from her parents, and along with so many other

Americans in the 1950s, decided to move out of the city and raise her children in a "better" area. The family moved to a middle class neighborhood in Menlo Park, a suburb on what is called the Peninsula about thirty miles south of San Francisco, near Palo Alto and Stanford University. Their house at 286 Santa Monica Avenue was across the street from St. Patrick's Seminary, and the quiet, peaceful surroundings were a sharp contrast to the rough-and-tumble Excelsior District in San Francisco where Jerry had been living without much parental supervision. "I was becoming a hoodlum, so my mom moved us from San Francisco to this new, ranch-style 1950s house in Menlo Park, a real nice place," said Garcia. "My mom made a lot of money, and the thrust of her thinking was to get us out of the city."

Having asthma as a child, Jerry spent a lot of time at home in bed. "I was a reader because I was a sickly kid," Garcia recalled. "So I was in bed reading. It probably was a boon to me." His stepfather introduced him to EC comics, and as with thousands of other kids, these helped him get even more into reading. *Tales from the Crypt*, *Vault of Horror*, *Haunt of Fear*, and *Shock Suspense Stories* were early lessons in literacy for him. He was fascinated by EC's horribleness, tongue-in-cheek humor, and graphic illustrations, and started a collection of comic books that he continued as an adult. He also got excited by science fiction, reading *The Martian Chronicles* by Ray Bradbury, who was his favorite author, and books by Edgar Rice Burroughs and others. Marshall Leicester, a friend of Garcia's since they were both ten years old in Menlo Park, recalled that Jerry had a "great head for words and wordplay. There was a lot of wit-play between us, that old *Mad Magazine* satirical outlook that was so liberating for American kids in the 1950s."

As Garcia advanced through school, he got a reputation as a notorious underachiever. To some of his teachers, there was merit in this evaluation, for Jerry stopped doing homework in the seventh grade because he thought it was a waste of time. However, he did well in subjects in which reading was of primary importance—art history, English, and spelling—and he had the advantage of elaborate and accelerated classes, which were offered as part of a program sponsored by Stanford University, which conducted educational pilot programs in the public schools.

Jerry's seventh-grade teacher, Dwight Johnson, made a lasting impression on him. Johnson drove an old MG and also had a vintage Black Shadow motorcycle. He was a wild, controversial guy who eventually got fired for stirring up the students. Garcia recalled, "When we went down to the Peninsula, I fell in with a teacher who turned me on to the intellectual world. He said, 'Here, read this.' It was [George Orwell's] 1984 when I was 11 or 12 . . . that was when I was turning on, so to speak, or became aware of a world that was other than the thing you got in school, that you got in the movies and all that; something very different. And so right away I was really a long way from school." Johnson opened lots of doors for Garcia and got him reading deeper material than science fiction. He taught him that ideas were fun and gave Jerry the sense that there were radical possibilities and other life-styles. In a way, Johnson was partly responsible for Garcia turning into a freak in the 1960s. "I was encouraged to be an artist, and my time on the Peninsula nailed that down real well." (Amazingly, despite being an inchoate nonconformist, Jerry did earn three merit badges in the Boy Scouts, for knot tying, compass reading, and life-saving.)

Looking back on this period in Jerry's life, it is ironic that in her flight from the city to suburbia, Ruth Garcia may have inadvertently guaranteed Jerry's future as a nonconformist. His penchant for doing as he pleased, reinforced by his time living with his grandparents, didn't sit well with officials at his junior high school in Menlo Park. His grades were bad, his attitude toward school officials was worse, and he was forced to repeat the eighth grade. Instead of helping him become a better student and making him toe the line, it probably confirmed his opinion of how little schoolwork and the rules of society meant to him.

During the family's time on the Peninsula, rock 'n' roll music made its initial impact on the national music scene. In 1953, "Crazy Man Crazy," a recording by Bill Haley and His Comets, became the first rock 'n' roll song to make Billboard's national best-seller charts. Rock 'n' roll soon staked out its place in American popular music and emerged as a new art form that appealed to the hearts and minds of the youth. In July 1954, Elvis Presley released his first 45, his rendition of Arthur Crudup's blues tune "That's All Right," and rockabilly took off. In 1955, Chuck Berry and Bo Diddley, perhaps two of the greatest talents of early rock 'n' roll, released "Maybellene" and "Bo Diddley," respectively. This Chicago rhythm and blues sound was the nearest equivalent to rockabilly among black styles, and it appealed to young white adolescents, who responded to the rock 'n' roll beat.

Garcia's brother began listening to rock 'n' roll and rhythm and blues. Tiff was a big influence on Jerry, and Jerry listened to the music that Tiff listened to. Tiff and Jerry would harmonize to the popular tunes of the day. Jerry recalled, "He was into very early rock 'n' roll and rhythm and blues. I remember the Crows—you know, 'Gee.' . . . It was basically black music, the early doo-wop groups. Hank Ballard and the Midnighters were a big early influence for me. My brother would learn the tunes, we would try to sing them, and he would make me learn harmony parts. In a way, I learned a lot of my ear training from my older brother."

The Garcias lived in Menlo Park for about three years. During that time Jerry's stepfather was managing the Four Hundred Club, commuting each day in the family car, until the bar was sold to the state, which had chosen that block as the site of a freeway entrance. When Garcia was thirteen or so the family moved back to San Francisco and he began going to Denman Junior High School, a tough city school in comparison to Menlo Park. There, he became what his mother had tried to prevent—a hoodlum, if only for self-preservation. "Either you were a hoodlum or you were a puddle on the sidewalk. I was part of a big gang, a nonaffiliated gang. . . ." But Jerry wasn't really cut out for this role. "It was a state of war, and I didn't last long in that. I spent a lot of time in Mission Emergency Hospital on weekends, holding my lip together, or my eye, because some guy had hit me with a board."

After graduating from Denman, he went on to Balboa High School, which was another roughneck school. On the weekends he'd go out with his friends and do a lot of drinking and partying. When he was fifteen, he got turned on to marijuana. "Me and a friend went up into the hills with two joints, the San Francisco foothills, and smoked these joints and just got so high and laughed and roared and went skipping down the streets doing funny things and just having a helluva time." Marijuana was just what Garcia was looking for to have fun, because he never really liked drinking.

Although he hung out with his high school buddies during the week, Jerry the hoodlum was secretly leading a double life. On weekends and during the summer, he was reading all the books he could get his hands on and attending sessions at the California School of Fine Arts in the North Beach section of San Francisco, which was the center of the local Beatnik movement during its heyday in the late 1950s.

The San Francisco Beatnik scene can trace its beginnings to the literary parties that radical poet Kenneth Rexroth had been having in the city since the 1940s. In the early 1950s poet Lawrence Ferlinghetti moved to San Francisco. In 1953 he became a partner in the City Lights Bookstore and by 1955 he was its sole proprietor. City Lights, open seven days a week from morning until midnight, soon became the heart of the artistic and intellectual community. Its late hours, relaxed atmosphere, and alternative point of view made the bookstore attractive to nonconformists who rejected the materialism and conformity of the Eisenhower years.

A watershed in San Francisco's literary and Beatnik scene occurred at the poetry reading at the Six Gallery in San Francisco on October 7, 1955. Allen Ginsberg organized the gathering, which consisted of poets Philip Lamantia, Michael McClure, Gary Snyder, Philip Whalen, Ginsberg, and Rexroth, the papa-critic of avant-garde San Francisco. The Six Gallery was an old garage with white walls, a dirt floor, and a stage, and for this event it was filled with more than one hundred people. The standing-room-only crowd was primed for the occasion courtesy of Jack Kerouac, who had collected money and brought jugs of wine to the reading. Kerouac wandered around the room offering everyone a swig of wine, continually muttering "Wow!" and "Yes!" in harmony with his buddy, Neal Cassady. It was Ginsberg's first public reading, and he read from his poem "Howl" as members of the audience shouted, "Go! Go! Go!"

No poem reflected the spirit of the Beat movement better than "Howl." The Beats thumbed their noses at mainstream culture, and "Howl" expressed their alienation, their restless search for spiritual fulfillment, their experimentation with drugs and sex, their nomadic life-style, and their rejection of Cold War politics. "Howl" made a palpable impact on the audience that night, and the next day Ferlinghetti offered to publish it. When customs agents seized a shipment of copies entering the country from the English printer, Ferlinghetti was arrested as the publisher, and the ensuing media attention put the City Lights Bookstore and the San Francisco Beatnik scene on the map.

San Francisco had a number of places, like City Lights, the Place, and the Coexistence Bagel Shop, which offered haven for Beatniks, poets, and artists. In the midst of this artistic renaissance in San Francisco, Jerry Garcia was taking art classes, and when not in class he would roam the streets checking out the sights and sounds of the Beat movement. Garcia remembered, "I was going to the art institute on Saturdays and summer sessions. This was when the Beatniks were happening in San Francisco, so I was in that culture. I was a high-school kid and a wannabe Beatnik. The art school I went to was in North Beach, and in those days the old Coexistence Bagel Shop was open, and the Place, notorious Beatnik places where these guys—Lawrence Ferlinghetti, Kenneth Rexroth would get up and read their poetry."

The California School of Fine Arts offered a painting class for high school students taught by Wally Hedrick and Elmer Bischoff in which Jerry and his friend Mike Kennedy enrolled. They threw themselves into painting and became part of the underground social scene at the school. During class the instructor would play records while the students painted. One record that particularly struck Jerry was a Big Bill Broonzy album. Broonzy was a strong singer and was widely recognized as one of the great folk bluesmen of the era. It was the first time Jerry had heard anybody play acoustic blues, and he was fascinated. As soon as he had the extra money, he ran out and bought a Big Bill Broonzy album.

Impromptu parties were held in the social hall of the art

school, where the Studio 13 Jass Band, consisting of several of the art instructors, would play a mixture of traditional New Orleans jazz and lots of blues. Garcia showed an affinity for the blues, and he went to see black rhythm and blues shows. "Me and a couple of friends used to go out to black shows, not only at the Fillmore, but also at Roseland over in Oakland. I'd usually hear about the shows on the radio. . . . I'd sometimes go down and stand on the corner at some barbecue place or something and just stare at the posters, just to see the guys. Because you couldn't see them on radio, and there wasn't much in the way of album covers back then."

Garcia watched intently as the musicians performed and wondered whether he could do that. He had been tinkering around playing rock 'n' roll on his mother's piano, but he desperately wanted a guitar, and he spent a good deal of time at the pawnshops on Market and Third streets in San Francisco looking at the electric guitars. Then, on his fifteenth birthday in 1957, his mother gave him an *accordion*. "It was a beauty. It was a Neapolitan job. My mother bought it from a sailor at the bar." Appreciation of workmanship notwithstanding, Garcia wanted only a guitar. "When I first heard the electric guitar, that's what I wanted to play. I petitioned my mom to get me one, so she finally did for my birthday. Actually, she got me an accordion, and I went nuts—'Aggghhh, no, no, no!' I railed and raved, and she finally turned it in, and I got a pawnshop electric guitar and an amplifier. I was just beside myself with joy."

His guitar was a Danelectro electric with a tiny Fender amplifier. His stepfather tuned it for him, and he ended up playing in a weird open tuning for about six months. He taught himself to play and picked up a few tricks from his cousin Danny, who knew some rhythm and blues. Garcia said, "I was fluid in a primitive way . . . but the most important thing I learned was that it was okay to improvise: 'Hey, man, you can make it up as you go along!'"

Garcia's first idol on the guitar was Chuck Berry. "When I was a kid I got all his records and I'd just try like crazy to learn how to play them. I'd listen to a record and I'd try to figure out what the guy was doing, and it was virtually impossible to do because of the way I had my guitar tuned."

Finally Garcia met a guy in school who showed him the right way to tune the guitar and the basic first-position chords. While still in high school in San Francisco he met some other musicians—a piano player and a drummer—with whom he began playing, but then his mother moved the family out of the city to a small town on the Russian River in an attempt to keep Jerry out of mischief. "In high school, I fell in with some other musicians—Beatnik types, the pot-smokers. My only other option was to join the beer drinkers, but they got into fights. I kept getting into trouble anyway, so my mother finally moved us out of the city to Cazadero." He went to Analy High School in Sebastopol and started playing guitar in a group that had saxophone, piano, and bass, playing easy-listening saxophone tunes that were big in those days. "I hated it there. I had to ride a bus thirty miles to Analy High in Sebastopol. I played my first gig at Analy. We had a five-piece combo—a piano, two saxes, a bass, and my guitar. We won a contest and got to record a song. We did Bill Doggett's 'Raunchy,' but it didn't turn out very well."

*   *   *   *

It wasn't long before Jerry was cutting school, sneaking away in his mother's car, and going down to the Peninsula to visit a girl-friend. He dropped out of high school at the end of his junior year. "I was a fuck-up in high school. When I was a kid, I was a juvenile delinquent. My mom even moved me out of the city to get me away from trouble. It didn't work. I couldn't stand high school. . . . I was involved in more complex ideas. I start-ed reading Schopenhauer, Heidegger, and Kant when I was in the seventh grade. After that, school was silly. I couldn't relate to it. Not only that, I was a teenager, so I had an attitude. I kept saying, 'Why should I be doing these dumb things?' So I failed school as a matter of defiance."

The free rein Garcia had been given as a child by his grand-parents had developed into a fierce independent streak. As a teenager he couldn't abide by his mother's rules, and he was having a hard time staying out of trouble. His escapades were beginning to catch up to him, and his mother's patience was wearing thin. At seventeen, Garcia decided to enlist in the military. "It was either that or jail." "At the time I thought, 'Well, I'll show 'em; I'll join the Army.'" His mother signed the papers, and away he went.

Jerry broke off all communication with his family when he joined the Army. His home life hadn't been working out, so he took his guitar and tried to get away from it all. After finish-ing basic training at Fort Ord he was transferred to Fort Winfield Scott in the Presidio, overlooking the water and the Golden Gate Bridge. He was assigned to a headquarters com-pany, which is one of the easiest duties in the Army. Garcia was in the motor pool and also went to missile school, but he last-ed only nine months. "Basically, the problem with the Army was they didn't get me far enough from home. I got stationed in San Francisco, so it was easy for me to skip out." True to his nature, Garcia treated the Army like it was school or a bum job. He was always late and a fuck-up. "I would miss roll call. I had seven or eight or nine or ten AWOLs, which is a pretty damn serious offense in the Army." As a result, he was court-martialed twice, restricted to barracks, and given extra duty. Finally the commanding officer had enough of his antics and he was dishonorably discharged.

Garcia's brief hitch in the service did have its upside. While stationed at the Presidio he met a country guitar player who got him into finger-picking. "I was just a three-chorder then. I was self-taught, and I had never met another guitar player, actually, until I got into the Army. Then I met this recruit who played a little bit of finger style, and I was totally fascinated by it." When he joined the Army, Garcia had been playing an electric guitar and was into rock 'n' roll, but this encounter got him interested in acoustic guitar, which blossomed into his fascination with folk, bluegrass, and banjo music.

After he got out of the Army in 1960, Garcia went to the Art Institute in San Francisco to study painting for a short time, then gravitated to the coffeehouse scene near Stanford University back in Palo Alto. Palo Alto offered the perfect environment for Jerry to nurture his interest in music and art. He had no desire to be on the fast track to a job, a career, and the American dream. Rather, he epitomized the Beatnik dropout who refused to bow to authority or conform to society's norms. "Y'see, my personal code of ethics is all based in 1950s artists' evaluations, which were pretty much characterized by a disdain for success." "As soon as *On the Road* came out, I read it and fell in love with it, the adventure, the romance of it, everything."

Jack Kerouac's novel had been published at the beginning of September 1957. Critic Gilbert Millstein of the *New York Times* called it "the most beautifully executed, the clearest and most important utterance yet made by the generation Kerouac himself named years ago as 'Beat,' and whose principal avatar he is." Millstein predicted *On the Road* would become the credo of the Beat generation. Other reviewers weren't as impressed. *Time* magazine charged Kerouac with creating "a rationale for the fevered young who twitch around the nation's jukeboxes and brawl pointlessly in the midnight streets." *On the Road* became the book that shocked straight America with its chronicles of two dropouts trekking across the country from New York to San Francisco, Mexico to New Orleans, in search of kicks, pleasure, and truth. The book's protagonist, the fictional Dean Moriarty, was based on Kerouac's friend Neal Cassady, who would soon become a major influence in the life of Jerry Garcia, who was embarking on his own hip odyssey.

2

FROM ACOUSTIC BLUEGRASS TO ELECTRIC ROCK

G arcia's interest in the philosophy of life expounded by Jack Kerouac in *On the Road* dovetailed perfectly with the development of the folk music scene in the Bay Area. Such music had been recorded in the United States for several decades, and its centuries-old roots were in the music that the "common folk" played in their homes, around fires, and for small groups. Woody Guthrie, ranked as the most influential songwriter on the American political left from the 1930s through the 1950s, wrote hundreds of songs about the American situation. He composed songs about ordinary people who were casualties of the Great Depression, about migrant workers who were victims of discrimination, as well as lyrical depictions of the Dust Bowl in America's heartland. Guthrie, one of the most important names in the history of American music, inspired not only his peers, such as Pete Seeger and Ramblin' Jack Elliot, but also the Beats.

The sudden craze for folk music began around 1958, and with it came a new social venue: the coffeehouse. These usually small, intimate rooms catered to a youthful clientele who were alienated from the straight, social-climbing mores of the Eisenhower years. Rather than have a highball and discuss sports, hairdos, business, children, and the missile gap, these young people preferred to get together over a cup of espresso—considered a more intellectual drink—and discuss radical politics, civil rights protests, and the emptiness of bourgeois society. Early on, these spaces were not the trendy cappuccino bars of today. They were more often than not a basement, a loft, or a back room that could fit perhaps a dozen tables, a small stage, and a serving area with a few coffee pots. They might be open only Friday and Saturday nights.

The coffeehouse provided the perfect forum for young people to hang out in a stimulating intellectual environment, to exchange new ideas, and to raise their consciousness on a number of issues. Folk music was the ideal vehicle to express these issues, for it often included topical compositions that addressed social and political concerns of the day. Aspiring musicians would sit around the coffeehouses, playing their guitars and banjos, and singing songs by the masters or their own local lyrics.

The folk music revival led to an upsurge of interest in old songs and forgotten performers, an interest that was not lost on the major record labels. They began to groom polished folk acts whose emphasis was less on the message of the lyrics than on the sound of the music. These groups appealed to mainstream audiences who did not like the liberal views of musicians such as Guthrie and Seeger, but who enjoyed the soft acoustic sound of the songs. Artists like Seeger took umbrage at the capital and publicity behind these groups, for most of America was getting the idea that they were what folk music was all about. Notwithstanding this rift in the folk community, in October 1958 the Kingston Trio's version of "Tom Dooley"—a far cry from the type of social or political commentary that the "pure folk" artists espoused—became the number-one hit in the country.

Despite the sanitized folk songs that were getting radio airplay, folk music continued to be the music of choice for those rejecting the values of straight America. And a case could be made that the commercial folk music brought new members to the counterculture, many more than the pure folk artists could have garnered at that time. The new listeners wanted to hear more of this music, and they had to go to the coffeehouses where it was being played. Not only did this demand enrich the coffeehouses and provide new places for artists to perform, but it brought mainstream people into contact with distinctly nonmainstream ideas.

Not surprisingly, the coffeehouses that attracted this crowd were concentrated near colleges, as the campus was the center of intellectual and social ferment of the time. It was no accident that Greenwich Village in New York City became the mecca for folk artists on the East Coast—its clubs were no more than a short subway ride from tens of thousands of college students, faculty, Beatniks, and free-thinkers. In California, near Stanford University, places like St. Michael's Alley in Palo Alto and Kepler's Bookstore in neighboring Menlo Park provided settings where students could get their intellectual kicks and where musicians could perform.

These two establishments were at the center of Palo Alto's fledgling folk music and bohemian scene. St. Michael's Alley, located at 426 University Avenue, was Palo Alto's first European-style coffeehouse, and it became the coolest place in town to hang out at. The atmosphere was free and open, as was the owner, Vernon Gates, an easygoing guy who let people do their thing. You could sit around all night over coffee talking with friends, meeting people, and listening to music without being hassled. Though the entertainment was casual, it was a good place for a young musician to develop his chops.

Kepler's Bookstore offered a different type of space. Opened in the mid-1950s by Roy Kepler, a social activist and peace advocate, the place *was* a bookstore. Kepler's goal was to promote the public interchange of ideas, and his store stocked the works of authors from the entire political spectrum. Kepler also encouraged the free verbal exchange of ideas, and he welcomed the artists, musicians, and bohemians who started frequenting his establishment in the early 1960s. Like Gates, Kepler didn't mind the unconventional young people who congregated at his bookstore, and musicians would show up and play music informally inside, or outside in the parking lot.

*   *   *   *

It was in this fertile environment that Jerry Garcia found himself after his discharge from the Army in 1960. Jerry was a Beatnik-wannabe who shunned the conventional attitudes of his parents and the conservative 1950s, and he decided not to go back to his mother's home. Army life—or maybe it was just Army food—had toughened his body somewhat, and he was almost skinny. Around that time he also began to sport a trim mustache and beard that made him resemble a Spanish duke. You could tell by looking at him that he was not part of mainstream America, but he was a far cry from the long-haired freak appearance that characterized him only six years later.

Almost naturally, he drifted into the Palo Alto coffeehouse scene. Although Jerry had no visible means of support for quite a while after leaving the Army, he found sustenance in Palo Alto. The Stanford University community was an integral part of the developing coffeehouse scene, and Palo Alto provided the perfect mix of students and intellecuals to support a struggling artist or musician. "When I got out of the Army I went down to Palo Alto and rejoined some of my old friends down there who were kind of living off the fat of the land, so to speak, a sort of hand-to-mouth existence . . . ," Jerry recalled. "There would be various households that we would hang out at and get a little something to eat." Students living in Stanford's Roble Hall would occasionally sneak dorm food out to him, and the teenagers from the middle-class neighborhoods of Palo Alto and Menlo Park were more than willing to let an aspiring artist/musician raid the pantry and refrigerator for a no-parents-allowed lunch or dinner.

Shortly after Garcia moved back down to Palo Alto, he met his future songwriting partner, Robert Hunter, first at the

Comedia Theatre and then repeatedly at St. Michael's Alley, where they both hung out. Hunter had also just gotten out of the Army, and they both ended up living in their broken-down cars in an empty lot in East Palo Alto. Garcia reminisced, "Hunter had these big tins of crushed pineapple that he'd gotten from the Army, like five or six big tins, and I had this glove compartment full of plastic spoons, and we had this little cooperative scene, eating this crushed pineapple day after day and sleeping in the cars."

Hunter played some guitar, and the two friends began singing and playing together, learning songs by the Kingston Trio and other mainstream folk acts. The two aspiring folkies started performing around town, and eventually got their first paying gig as "Bob and Jerry"—five bucks apiece. They played songs like "Heave Away Santy Ano" and "Down by the Riverside" at gigs at St. Michael's Alley, Stanford University, and a local Quaker school. For Garcia, this period was "just enormous fun." He hung out at St. Michael's Alley at night and Kepler's Bookstore during the day. "That was my 'day job': I practiced guitar and read books at Kepler's."

Despite spending hours each day practicing, Jerry did not ignore the social aspect of his situation. As he said, "You can think of the inside of Kepler's as the Greenwich Village part of the scene and the parking lot to the beach as the California experience." Although he was by no means the tanned hunk the rest of the country associated with California because of the prevalent rock 'n' roll beach movies of the time, he was a good-looking guy with thick, dark, curly hair and an intriguing face. He had been reading voraciously since seventh grade, and he had great wit and a keen intellect. This, and the fact that he was a performer, made it easy for him to meet girls, and he enjoyed the action.

Jerry dated a number of women, but it was not in his nature to have several girlfriends at one time. When he found someone with whom he connected, he stayed with her. Interestingly, this is a trait that he seems to have maintained to the present, even though he will never be seen as an example of marital longevity. He has been married three times and has had a number of affairs, but when the relationship has been right, he has stuck with it.

An early serious relationship was with Charlotte Daigle, who was a senior at Palo Alto High School when she met Jerry in 1960. She was about Garcia's age, and they dated for more than a year. "I used to hang out at Kepler's Bookstore and I met Jerry there. Jerry would sit around inside playing guitar or hang out in the parking lot, and we'd talk. I remember he had a good sense of humor." Daigle's girlfriend Chris Mann dated Hunter, and the two couples would go out together.

> We had a foursome: Jerry and I, and Chris and Bob. Jerry and Bob were performing folk songs at various places in the area, and we'd go and listen to them play. They didn't have a following, and they were trying to make it as a folk act in local clubs. They were good, and I remember what a thrill it was to hear Jerry play the twelve-string guitar. He was very proud of the fact that he could play it well even though he was missing a finger. However, I was very worried about his ability to sing. People would kid him about his voice, and said he played a better guitar than he could sing. But he wasn't put off by it. When all these people were

telling him, "You can't sing," and he kept singing, it showed determination and confidence in himself.

The way I see him, he really did things on his own terms, the way he wanted to, without a lot of concern about what he should do or what people wanted him to do. He listened to his inner voice. It was one of the reasons I liked him. I thought of him as a cool guy who had a different way of looking at things. The 1950s was a time of such conformity, and people were beginning to break out of molds. Jerry was in the forefront of that and was doing it seriously.

Though Garcia was actively trying to make it in local clubs as a folk musician, he was torn between music and art because he still fancied himself a painter. "I hadn't decided I was really going to play music. I was oscillating between the art world and music." Then something happened that gave him a sense of purpose and direction. In February 1961 Jerry was involved in a tragic automobile accident. Jerry, his close friend Paul Speegle (an accomplished artist whose painting *The Blind Prophet* hung at the Peninsula Peace Center in Palo Alto), and some other guys were in a Studebaker Golden Hawk roaring through the country when the driver lost control and the car careened off the road. "All I know is that I was sitting in the car and there was this disturbance and the next thing, I was in a field." The car was just a crumpled mass. Garcia had been thrown out of his shoes, through the windshield, and clear of the wreck. Not so with Paul, who was dead.

Charlotte vividly remembered that Jerry talked about the crash a lot. "It was a traumatic event that seemed to really affect him—that Paul Speegle had died in his place. Apparently Jerry had traded places with him in the car right before the crash. At the time it was a really big thing in his life—'There but for fate go I.'"

The incident had a profound effect on Garcia and put his life in focus. "That's where my life began. Before then I was always living at less than capacity. I was idling. That was the slingshot for the rest of my life. It was like a second chance. Then I got serious." Realizing that he couldn't concentrate on two art forms at the same time, Jerry decided to put his painting on hold (although he continued to sketch privately in his own books) and get serious about music.

He chose music because he liked the interaction with other people that it provided. While painting was the solitary endeavor of an artist alone with brush and canvas, the music that Jerry liked to play involved the creative effort of several individuals working together. The dynamics of a musical performance involved not only musicians but audience as well. A musician could respond to positive feedback from the audience with an inspired performance, which could never happen with painting. Later in his career, Garcia would comment that the symbiotic relationship of band and audience was integral to his musical experience, what made it come alive for him.

Having made up his mind, Garcia began hanging out with Marshall Leicester, his childhood friend from Menlo Park. Garcia recalled, "After I got out of the Army, I fell in with Hunter, and we were influenced by the folk scare—the Kingston Trio and that kind of stuff. I didn't know how to find my way into that music till I met some people who were more involved with it, like Marshall Leicester." Leicester turned Garcia on to bluegrass music and old-time string band music, reintroducing Garcia to the music of Flatt and Scruggs, Bill Monroe, and the Carter Family, and introducing him to the New Lost City Ramblers. Garcia remembered, "The first time I started to study what was going on in [bluegrass] music was 1961. I heard bluegrass music, and there was something about that music that was very familiar to me. I think that it was speaking to my memories of listening to the Grand Ole Opry every Saturday night when I was a small kid. Something about the sound of it, the harmony, the way the music works. Then I decided I had to learn how to play five-string banjo."

No doubt Garcia's fascination for bluegrass and old-time music was attributable to his grandmother's love of country music. During the time that Tillie Clifford raised her grandson after his father's death, Garcia was in an emotionally sensitive state and the sounds of the Grand Ole Opry made a lasting impression on him. When he heard the music as an adult, it struck a sympathetic chord in his heart and soul. There are serious ballads full of tragedy and despair in this music, yet the music also evokes a feeling of hope in the midst of the hard times. Perhaps when young Jerry was experiencing his own personal loss, the music inspired a sense of optimism and well-being in him.

The New Lost City Ramblers was one of the most important groups in the folk revival of the late 1950s and early 1960s. The group specialized in old-time music and concentrated on older, less well-known traditional songs rather than the more standard material developed by the Carter Family and other groups of that genre. They made every attempt to perform the old-time folk songs in their original form to preserve the authentic folk style and tradition. Garcia especially liked their repertoire, and their faithful rendition of traditional folk music would later find an echo in the various bluegrass projects that Garcia would undertake in his career. Charlotte Daigle recalled Jerry's excitement when he discovered the music of that group: "I remember him coming to visit me, discussing the New Lost City Ramblers and saying that was the direction he wanted his music to go in."

Another early influence on Garcia was Joan Baez, one of the leading "uncommercial" folk artists. Baez was a year older than Garcia, and coincidentally also had a Hispanic background—her father was born in Mexico. While her father was teaching physics at MIT in the 1950s, folksinger friends taught the teenaged Joan to sing ballads and folk songs from all over the world. After appearing at the Newport Folk Festival in Rhode Island in 1959 and again the next year, Baez released her eponymous debut album in December 1960. Riding the folk revival wave, it was an immediate hit, becoming the number-three best-selling album in 1961.

Partly because of the success of Baez's album, "uncommercial" folk music was now commercial, too. Baez went on a national tour in 1961 to promote her album, and Garcia had to go see her. He had lost interest in the "dippy folk songs" he had been playing at small gigs with Hunter, and Baez's sound enthralled him. "What first attracted me was the sound of it—those kind of modal changes and the sound of Joan Baez's voice and the sound of her guitar." During that summer Garcia went with Charlotte to a Joan Baez concert in the auditorium at Palo Alto High School. "Jerry wanted to go to the Joan Baez concert and sit in the front row so he could watch her," Daigle said. "He watched her intently, commenting, 'This is great, I can out-guitar her.' Jerry wanted to see what kind of musician she was. He wasn't making light of what she was doing; rather, he was terribly excited that she was well-known and he was as good on guitar or better."

Garcia was totally into the music in a unique way—he was artist, technician, and fan all rolled into one. With Baez, as with the New Lost City Ramblers and his other early influences, Jerry went to school on her style and technique, incorporating them into his repertoire and expanding them with his own artistry. Yet he was not fool enough to think that he was "better" than these other performers; his ego was in check. He acknowledged his roots, and never lost his love of listening to other musicians do their thing.

During that important summer of 1961, Garcia met David Nelson, who became one of Jerry's closest friends. (Nelson later played lead guitar in the New Riders of the Purple Sage, a group that toured and worked with Garcia many times.) Nelson, who grew up on the Peninsula, first met Garcia at Kepler's Bookstore. Nelson was helping Rodney and Peter Albin set up the Boar's Head Coffeehouse. "It was summer," Nelson remembered, "Gar's Levi shirt was open, and he was wearing finger picks, playing a Stella twelve-string guitar. Rodney asked him if he would play at the Carlos Bookstall in San Carlos. I was surprised that Garcia knew exactly what he was talking about, and all of a sudden they were a couple of businessmen talking about this. Garcia says, 'Yeah, I could do that.' And Rodney was saying, 'Bring all your friends, and we could have a good party.'"

The Boar's Head was set up in an upstairs loft at a bookstore on San Carlos Avenue on Friday and Saturday nights. It was very informal and had an open-mike policy. Garcia and Leicester played there in July 1961, performing songs by the Carter Family, the New Lost City Ramblers, and other traditional folk and old-time music. Rodney Albin had the foresight to bring a reel-to-reel recorder to the Boar's Head, and so some of the earliest Garcia performances were captured on tape. Garcia played acoustic guitar and Leicester played banjo, and the influence of the New Lost City Ramblers was evident. Garcia performed his repertoire in an authentic manner faithful to the tradition. Though his vocals were weak on some of the tunes, Jerry displayed his skill on the guitar and his ability to bring emotion to a song, especially when he sang about lament and lost love in a number like "Wildwood Flower."

Although he was a month short of his nineteenth birthday at the time, Garcia shows great stage presence on these tapes. Several times, he got the audience singing along with him. Other times, he was the witty master of ceremonies, introducing the songs and making comments from the stage: "Now we are going to have a lot of fun, which will be something different for you all, I guess. Okay, what we are going to do now is tune, see, 'cause we are going to play this next thing with the guitar in D tuning, which is notoriously difficult to tune into. So if any of you have any long-distance phone calls to make, any parking tickets to pay, or anything like that, you can do it now. The song we're gonna do now is one that's done by the New Lost City Ramblers. If you ever heard the New Lost City Ramblers, you know they play mostly old-time music. This is an approximation of the same sort of thing, except that we're not the New Lost City Ramblers, contrary to popular opinion. They don't look like us."

Garcia had turned a corner when he hooked up with Marshall Leicester, and his change of direction into traditional old-time music inspired him to take up five-string banjo, his first serious instrument. As determined to learn bluegrass banjo as he was to get his first guitar when he was fifteen, he taught himself by slowing down old-time country records, borrowing instruments until he could afford his own. One day he borrowed Nelson's banjo: "I put my money together to get a five-string banjo one time. Garcia hears about this. He wanted to play a five-string banjo. I'm hangin' at the house one day and Garcia calls and says, 'I hear you got a banjo. Can you bring it down to St. Michael's Alley?' And I said, 'When?' He says, 'Now, tonight, and bring your guitar.' So I went down to St. Michael's Alley and brought my guitar and banjo. Of course, Garcia puts on finger picks and he's just tryin' that Scruggs stuff on the banjo."

Garcia took up the banjo with a vengeance, and just a short time later he was recognized as *the* banjo picker in Palo Alto. This distinction was perhaps not so difficult to achieve, for there were actually very few banjo players on the Peninsula; even so, Garcia's outstanding abilities on the instrument were apparent to all.

In retrospect, Garcia was not just learning an instrument;

he was bringing a new sound to an audience who had never heard anything like it. The old-time folk music was almost exclusively a back-East country affair. It made few in-roads on the urban scene. In a sense, by virtue of practicing and playing as much as he did, by letting the music be heard, Jerry helped create an awareness of old-time folk music in the Bay Area.

His mastering of the difficult-to-play banjo was clearly an indication that Garcia had the discipline to become a professional musician. This fact was not lost on Philip Chapman Lesh, a serious musician who had played classical music since the third grade, studied theory and harmony in high school, taken up the trumpet at age fourteen, and played in the College of San Mateo's jazz band. Lesh was a music student when he met Garcia in 1961 at the Palo Alto Peace Center, a gathering place for students, Beatniks, and other intellectuals.

Despite being in "two different worlds musically," as Garcia described them, Lesh appreciated Garcia's home-grown talent. Lesh was astounded by Jerry's playing—"I'd never yet heard anyone play the banjo like that. It was the most inventive, most musical kind of banjo playing you could ever imagine." The esteem was reciprocal. Garcia was blown away when Lesh demonstrated that he had absolute pitch. They were at Kepler's Bookstore when Lesh challenged Garcia to play any chord on his guitar, and he would identify it. Garcia agreed to a round of "Name That Chord," and Lesh correctly called every one. Jerry and Phil became fast friends, and their relationship broadened Garcia's musical horizons to include jazz and classical music.

In September 1961 Garcia decided he had to go to the Monterey Jazz Festival, which was held outdoors at the Monterey County Fairgrounds. The festival featured some of the biggest names in jazz: John Coltrane, Dizzy Gillespie, Duke Ellington, Dave Brubeck, George Shearing. Perhaps no musician typified the improvisational direction of modern jazz more than saxophonist Coltrane. A significant portion of the festival program was devoted to stimulating and unusual avant-garde music, which delved into new areas of jazz. Jerry was fascinated by this sort of playing.

Charlotte Daigle accompanied Garcia to Monterey. "It was Jerry's idea to go to the festival. He bought the tickets for us, and we went two days. We had reserved seats, and Jerry took it very seriously. Jazz fans were very formal at the time, and other people were dressed up. Our crowd from Palo Alto was very Beatnik looking and we stood out from the rest of the audience. It created something of a stir."

One place that welcomed the Palo Alto Beatnik crowd was the Chateau, located at 838 Santa Cruz Avenue in Menlo Park. The Chateau was a large house owned by artist Frank Seratone. It was set back from the street, which afforded it a degree of privacy. It had extra rooms that people could rent or stay in, and the house became a crash pad for the Beatnik hordes. Garcia camped out in the pumphouse in back for a while, and Hunter lived there on and off.

The Chateau became the scene of endless parties and jam sessions. "I remember sneaking out of my parents' house late at night to go to parties at the Chateau," Charlotte Daigle said. "I would go there at midnight and all sorts of people would be hanging out there partying—drinking wine, listening to music, dancing. It was an all-night party and at the time it seemed wild and crazy—the excitement of being with your peers, where anything goes. There was some pot smoking going on, but it wasn't in the open yet, and people would go out back. In retrospect it doesn't seem like what we were doing was that unusual, but at the time we were rebelling from the social conservatism of the 1950s. I remember that someone taught us the Twist, and we all thought it was really far out."

Starting on November 18, 1961, the residents of the Chateau put together a not-to-be-forgotten event they called the "Groovy Conclave." Hundreds of tickets were printed and distributed within the folk and Beatnik circle. It was a colossal party that lasted several booze-soaked days without any bad vibes or trouble from the law. Hunter estimated that three or four hundred people showed up, and the house was packed to the rafters. Phil Lesh showed up with Tom Constanten, his new roommate at Berkeley, where they were both enrolled as music majors.

Like Lesh, TC was something of a musical genius. He was a classically trained pianist who debuted on May 28, 1961 at the Las Vegas Convention Center, performing his own "Conversation Piece" with the Las Vegas Pops Orchestra. He was only seventeen. The roommates discovered they shared an interest in avant-garde music, and spent endless hours studying and writing together. They took numerous trips to the

Peninsula, where Lesh introduced TC to Jerry Garcia, Robert Hunter, and other folk musicians and Beatnik types who were hanging out in Palo Alto.

Constanten described the Groovy Conclave: "Hunter greeted us with 'Why the hell don't you get drunk?' It was an event to relive, a movie to tape again. I remember going out back to the pumphouse, where Garcia lived for a time, and smoking dope with at least eleven people who were crammed in there passing joints. This was during the era when people were paranoid and didn't smoke inside the main house because smoking dope wasn't out in the open yet."

The Chateau's main house was filled with music, dancing, and good old-fashioned partying. Constanten remembered Garcia playing guitar and singing in the front room, and gave this account of what he sounded like and how he looked: "Jerry was playing acoustic guitar and singing songs like 'Matty Groves,' 'Long Black Veil,' and 'I Was Born in East Virginia.' He was very much into his folk thing, the oral tradition of folk music where songs are passed on and consequently there are different versions of the same tune. He did the Greenback Dollar version of 'I Was Born in East Virginia.' Garcia was a serious folkie who looked like a coffeehouse folksinger. He was part of the Vitalis/Brylcreem crowd and wore his hair brushed back."

A few months later, Lesh was at another party at the Chateau where Garcia was playing, and he got the idea to make a tape of Garcia's music to audition for a spot on *The Midnight Special*, a folk music show on KPFA in Berkeley. At the time, Lesh was working as a volunteer engineer on the show. "I was at a party and Jerry was playing and singing, and I asked him if I could make a tape of him to play for Gert

Chiarito, who was the host of *The Midnight Special*. I just had this flash—'God, this guy sounds really good; he makes the music live.'" Garcia was all for the idea, and the two of them immediately drove over to Berkeley to Phil and TC's apartment on Durant Avenue to get Constanten's tape recorder to make a demo. Phil recorded Garcia doing a number of songs. "I played the tape for Gert and asked her if she thought he was good enough to play on *The Midnight Special*. She said, 'This guy could have a show all to himself.'"

Garcia's episode of the show was called "Long Black Veil"—one of the songs he was playing at the time. It was his first appearance on the airwaves. The hour-long show was broadcast live all over the Bay Area, with Garcia performing several songs and talking music with Chiarito. The show went so well that Gert invited him back often, and Jerry almost became a regular.

The renown Garcia gained from the KPFA shows led to appearances at coffeehouses throughout the Bay Area. He played at the Coffee and Confusion Gallery in North Beach in San Francisco, the Offstage in San Jose, the Jabberwock in Berkeley, and the Tangent in Palo Alto. While playing this circuit, he met some of the musicians who, along with him, developed what would come to be known as "the San Francisco sound"—Jorma Kaukonen, Janis Joplin, Paul Kantner, and David Freiberg.

During the summer of 1962, Jorma Kaukonen, who later became the lead guitarist for the Jefferson Airplane and Hot

Tuna, moved to the Bay Area to attend the University of Santa Clara. Jorma had been playing guitar since 1956 and had taken a serious interest in acoustic-style blues guitar. He began appearing at coffeehouses around the Bay Area, performing acoustic blues tunes of musicians like Lightnin' Hopkins, the Reverend Gary Davis, and Blind Boy Fuller. It wasn't long before Jorma became recognized as one of the best finger-picking acoustic blues guitarists on the coffeehouse scene, and he soon developed a friendship with Garcia. Jorma remembered how their relationship started:

> There was a place called the Folk Theatre that was the precursor to the Offstage, which was on First Street in San Jose, and the first weekend that I was in California there was a hootenanny. Many of the people who became 'somebody' later on were at this particular hootenanny, and that was my welcoming my first weekend in the Bay Area. As I recall, Jerry was there and a bunch of Palo Alto people. After we met, Jerry and I would occasionally play together because I knew a lot of old-timey songs and I liked to play rhythm guitar behind people like Jerry who were playing that stuff. It wasn't my forte, but everybody did everything at one time or another. In those days, really up until the period of time when we all became sort of quasi-adult musicians, working full-time in bands, there was a lot of interaction between musicians.

David Nelson recalled when he and Garcia went to see Jorma (then called Jerry) Kaukonen play at the Tangent: "Garcia grabbed me and said, 'You gotta hear this guy, you gotta hear this guy.' I said, 'Who is he?' Garcia said, 'Jerry Kaukonen, he plays that Reverend Gary Davis and Blind Boy Fuller stuff, he does it right.' I remember going to the Tangent and peering out from the back room, which is where we put our instruments, and hearing him play and looking at Garcia who is looking at me, and we're just going 'Wow!'"

Jorma impressed Garcia not only because he was an excellent guitarist, but because they were kindred souls. Kaukonen was a blues purist who played acoustic blues in a manner that was faithful to the source, just as Garcia played old-time folk music. Though both were urban kids from middle class families, they were able to play traditional music in an authentic manner that gave it a legitimacy that other musicians were not able to achieve. Each was a disciplined devotee of his musical genre who had the talent and dedication to master an idiom that he loved. Jorma spent hours listening to the blues in order to learn how to play blues guitar, just as Jerry spent hours listening to old-time folk music in order to play in the tradition.

In June 1962, Jerry, who was always looking for a place to play, got a gig at the new Boar's Head, which had relocated to the San Carlos Jewish Community Center. The group he put together—the Sleepy Hollow Hog Stompers—featured Garcia on guitar and banjo, Marshall Leicester on banjo and guitar, and Dick Arnold on fiddle. They played a selection of traditional folk and old-time music. The tapes of these performances show that Garcia was in good form, often injecting humor into the evening's proceedings:

GARCIA: If you're wonderin' why in an old-timey band you can't understand the words very well, it's because we don't know them, and we can't figure them out off the records, so we make up our own as we go along.

LEICESTER: The records are scratchy.

GARCIA: The fact is we don't have any records, it's our voices that are scratchy.

GARCIA: If you're wonderin' about our fiddle player and why he doesn't say much, it's because he doesn't speak a word of English. You see, we found him accidentally in a little Hungarian restaurant, playing sweet tunes to the elderly matrons that would come in and sit down.

LEICESTER: That explains his romantic, violent hair and burning eyes. He's a passionate gypsy violinist. Actually, we found him in a pizzeria in San Pablo.

GARCIA: Playing in the background to curdle the mozzarella cheese. It makes for better pizza.

GARCIA: Listen, for you people who really want more, we'll be back later with a hundred more songs, and they'll all be the same song and you won't know the difference. We'll just change the words a little each time. So we'll be back if any of you have the stamina.

GARCIA: We're back again to do a little of the old-time hill music that we stole from the Ramblers, and they stole from old records, and the musicians that were on the old records stole them from their fathers, and things like that. So it's all part of the oral tradition, and that's your lesson in folklore for tonight. Now I would like to do an interesting song that has a rather interesting background—none. It doesn't have

any background at all that I know of. Perhaps it has a background—it might be true or it might be a lie. I'm leaving
that up to your judgment if you care that much. [To
Leicester] Are you finished tuning yet? I can't think of anything else to say.

Garcia had been playing music with his friend Marshall for
more than a year, building up a repertoire of old-time songs and
improving his technique on the five-string banjo. His love of
the instrument inspired him to organize a bluegrass band.
Though Palo Alto was not a hotbed of bluegrass music, Jerry
was able to recruit the musicians he needed. David Nelson
remembered, "Garcia decided to put together a real bluegrass
band. It was the Hart Valley Drifters before I was playing with
them—Garcia on guitar and banjo, Marshall Leicester on
banjo and guitar, Eric Thompson on guitar, and Ken Frankel
and Worth Hanley on mandolin." The formation of the Hart
Valley Drifters helped develop a bluegrass scene in the Palo
Alto area. As had happened with old-time folk music, Garcia
and his bandmates created an awareness of bluegrass in a community that ordinarily would not have had much interest in
that type of music.

This facility for bringing musicians together and creating
public interest in his music is a major part of Garcia's success in
music. He is able to do this for a number of reasons. First, he is
a gifted musician whose talent cannot be contained by any one
genre; thus, he is always sincerely reaching out in different
musical directions to expand the boundaries of what he brings
to performances. Second, Jerry has confidence in his own abilities and a sense of purpose in his endeavors. Third, he is gen-

uinely enthusiastic about his music, which is an inspiration to musicians and audiences alike.

In the fall of 1962, when he was only twenty, Garcia had to regroup the band. (Leicester had gone off to college.) He had an offer for the Hart Valley Drifters to play at an art gallery in San Francisco, so he asked David Nelson to play guitar for the group. Nelson recollected, "Garcia called me and said, 'Believe it or not, I've got somebody interested at this art gallery that will hire us to play if we put a band together. What you'll have to do is come over a couple of nights for a few hours and we'll have a rehearsal. We'll run it down and get it all together about what material we want to do.' I said okay, I would do it." In his best showman style, Garcia added, "Nelson, you've got to let your hair grow longer. You'll look anemic on stage if you have short hair, so let it grow out."

Before they could play the art gallery, Pete Albin invited the Hart Valley Drifters to perform at the College of San Mateo Folk Festival, which was scheduled for the same day as the art gallery engagement. Garcia decided that the band should play both gigs. They did the art gallery first and then the festival. Nelson described the folk festival: "It was righteous . . . because there were lectures that went into the musical history of folk music, and there were also three sections of the show. Garcia was fantastic. He played in all three sections. In the first segment he played by himself, singing ballads with just a banjo. Then I came on the stage and joined him for the second segment, which was old-time string band music, and after that the rest of the band came out for the last segment, which was the bluegrass stuff." Garcia's three-part performance at the festival was an early indication of his musical genius. Though it had only been a couple of years since he had been playing "dippy folk songs," he was now able to perform a full slate of authentic folk ballads, old-time songs, and bluegrass music at a legitimate folk festival.

Although they were serious musicians who would go far in their careers, they were still just young guys at this time, dealing with the mores of the day, as this quote from David Nelson shows:

> After the festival, the band headed over to Susie Woods's house to unwind. This tradition had evolved at the Boar's Head where after the gig we would all go to Susie Woods's house. It was like a cast party after a play. We'd go get some wine and everybody would get mellow. Rick Melrose, who was the emcee at the folk festival, came up to me about twenty minutes into the party and wanted me to get Hunter and ask him to go buy some wine because we were underage. So I went over to Hunter and put forth the idea that we go out and get loaded. I got this weird look from him like "I don't know," but he goes over to Garcia, and Garcia looks at me too, and says to Hunter, "Well, I guess he said that, so that's cool, I wanna get loaded too." So we all go out to the car and Hunter pulls out of his pocket what looked like a restaurant toothpick and lights it up. Melrose looks at me and says, "What's that?" but I keep my mouth shut because it suddenly dawned on me what they were doing.

So not only did Nelson play his first gig with the Hart Valley Drifters that day, he also had his first Hart Valley drift.

Smoking marijuana was soon to become a part of the cultural milieu of the 1960s. The dramatic increase in the use of marijuana began when large numbers of young people started questioning the social values of their parents. The use of marijuana altered perception and could change the way a person felt about life. Experimentation with drugs—marijuana and also LSD—brought a change of consciousness that embraced peace, honesty, equality, individuality, and sensuality.

Marijuana use was quite common in the music world—jazz artists had been smoking it for decades. Many musicians felt that marijuana improved their ablity to play and write music because it heightened their senses and made them more open to what the music held. They could hear and feel the music differently, enabling them to be more creative. Garcia had been smoking marijuana since he was fifteen, and it became an integral part of his life-style.

On February 23, 1963, the group, now called the Wildwood Boys, played the Tangent in Palo Alto. They were well-received by the crowd who enjoyed the music and had a few laughs, too. This is how Hunter introduced them:

> Our little group is called the Wildwood Boys. On banjo we have honest Jerry Garcia, who tunes quite incessantly. We have simple Dave Nelson, our sphinx who never says anything and wants more than anything in the world to be a real boy, and back here we have our bass player, whose name is Norman [Van Mastricht], and he loves you all, but

I don't. They tell me not to say this because you are supposed to establish immediate rapport with your audience—infinity, reality, and communications, et cetera, so I guess I'd best. I'll just say whatever comes to mind until I finish tuning. This next song is one that Jerry wrote, who alternately named it after a friend of ours in the audience, "Vilma Gefilte Fish." We don't call it that now. We did call it "Sweatshirt" for a while. We don't call it that anymore. We've decided to call it "Jerry's Breakdown," because it sounds ever so much more nice, like Earl Scruggs and "Earl's Breakdown," and things like that.

In those days, the band did a lot of tuning on stage. Mostly it was because of Garcia. Nelson discussed Garcia's penchant for incessant banjo tuning:

Garcia had a stress thing about tuning and ended up tuning too much. That was one of the things that was a problem. He'd get stressed and nervous about playing. The stress would work itself out in tuning. Then he wouldn't be able to hear. His ears would get locked into the nervousness and he wouldn't be able to tune. I remember giving him a note and thinking, "Please hear this!" I'd say, "Jerry, Jerry, you're not listening, listen to your tuning." He'd be tuning—ding, ding, ding, ding, ding, ding, ding, ding, ding, ding, trying to tune. The best way to deal with it was to say, "Fine, fine, calm down," and not pay any attention to it and play when we could. Then we would try to keep him playing so he couldn't get into that ding, ding, ding, ding, ding thing again. It was a problem for a while, but he was such a good banjo player.

In addition to his passion for bluegrass music, Garcia also took time to pursue another of his interests in life—women. Garcia had an affinity for females who were unconventional and who could relate to his bohemian life-style. Charlotte Daigle talked about this. "After I had gone off to college for a while, we went our separate ways. We would see each other occasionally, but it was my impression that Jerry didn't have a real interest in pursuing a traditional one-on-one relationship. He was a free spirit who wanted to experience life on his own terms. Jerry was a social rebel, and my relationship with him was typical of the way he was. I was attracted to people who were on the edge, and so was he."

Another woman Garcia dated at that time was Diane Huntsberger, a classmate of Daigle's at Palo Alto High. She was a nonconformist who wore black clothes and no makeup. Karen Huntsberger remembered the day Diane, her older sister, brought Garcia home to meet her parents: ". . . my parents weren't too happy. She and Jerry were going to run away, become beachcombers, and play guitar. At the time Jerry was playing music and roaming around town in a truck. He used to come over and play guitar in our living room." Mr. and Mrs. Huntsberger were no doubt relieved when Garcia met another Palo Alto High graduate, Sarah Ruppenthal, and began dating her.

Sarah grew up in the Palo Alto area and was a friend of Joan Baez, who also went to Palo Alto High. (Baez's family had moved to Palo Alto when her father got a job teaching at

Stanford.) Garcia met Sarah in early 1963 when she was at Stanford University studying communications. Sarah was into film, and Garcia spent a lot of time with her learning about filmmaking at the school and working on soundtracks for other students' films. Sarah was also a musician, and she and Jerry spent hours listening to music.

It was just a matter of time before Jerry and Sarah started performing together. As the duo "Jerry and Sarah," they played acoustic string-band music from the 1920s and 1930s, as well as other folk and country songs. They performed at St. Michael's Alley and the Tangent in the spring of 1963. Sarah would sing and play guitar, and Jerry would sing and accompany her on guitar, banjo, or fiddle.

The pair got married in May 1963 after Sarah became pregnant. Garcia recalled, "Well, I got married back there somewhere and it was one of those things where she got into trouble, you know, in the classic way—'I want to have the baby.' I was tryin' to be straight, kinda." And Nelson, the best man at the wedding, recalled the conversation he and Jerry had about it. "Jerry had been going with Sarah for a while. Before he was going to marry her he took me to a coffee shop in Palo Alto and he lays it on me. He said, 'I've got to tell you something: I'm thinking of getting married.' He wanted to sound me out on it, to get my reaction. I just thought, 'Oh, no, that's it, man, the scene is over.' I said, 'Nothing is going to be the same.' Garcia said, 'Oh, you watch—it will be the same, man.'"

It was a traditional ceremony held at a church in Palo Alto. Sarah's parents were there, and so was Jerry's mom, Ruth, with whom Jerry had had little contact since he'd left home. Phil Lesh summarized the affair. "I made it to Jerry's wedding, which

was a classic—especially the reception. I don't think I made it
to the wedding, actually. It was priceless at the reception: All of
her friends were at the booze; his friends were all at the food."

With the birth of his daughter Heather on December 8, 1963,
Garcia had a family to support. To make ends meet, he began
teaching music at Dana Morgan's Music in Palo Alto. Dana
Morgan observed, "[Garcia] and another fella came in to see if
I could use a guitar teacher, and it just so happened that I did
need them. After all, teachers and salesmen like Garcia used to
sell carloads of guitars in the early 1960s. Every damn fool had
to have a guitar and walk around strumming it. But Garcia
didn't look like a fool. He was a very immaculate, tall, thin boy.
He had coal-black hair and a little mustache. He looked like a
Spanish gentleman."

Garcia had by no means joined the nine-to-five rat race,
but he managed to eke out enough money to survive without
abandoning his bohemian code of ethics. "When I was teaching music, I was doing it because it was a way to exist without
having to do a work thing—put on a collar and go do eight
hours a day and all that stuff. I'm not interested in doing that."
"I was working in the music store in earnest now, and our baby
was born and it was okay and all that, but it wasn't really
workin'—I was really playin' music. I was playin' music during
the day at the music store, practicing, and at nights I would go
out and gig."

Garcia was by all accounts a good guitar teacher. He was
passionate about the music and never stopped learning new

techniques and styles, and he passed this excitement along to his students. Since he was unable to read music, his students learned to play music the way he had—by ear and by feel. And his teaching didn't stop at the doors of the store. He was not a jealous person, so he could help other musicians without having problems with whether they would become better than him. Part of Jerry's ethic was to play great music, and that included helping others to play as well as they could. Nelson commented that Garcia was always willing to give pointers on the guitar. "I'd ask Gar a few questions at parties, about pickin' and stuff like that, and he was more than happy to tell me about finger-picking styles, who to listen to and where to research it. I remember one time I asked him where he got songs like 'Days of 49' that nobody had recorded, and Garcia replied, '*Putnam's Golden Songster*; check it out, man.' To this day I've never found *Putnam's Golden Songster*."

As Garcia got more and more into the five-string banjo, he built up a repertoire of bluegrass tunes, breakdowns, ballads, mountain tunes, rags, and country blues that he performed in a variety of groups—the Thunder Mountain Tub Thumpers, the Sleepy Hollow Hog Stompers, the Hart Valley Drifters, the Wildwood Boys, and the Black Mountain Boys—groups that existed for only a gig or two, several weeks, or several months. Jorma Kaukonen reflected, "I remember Jerry being a consummate bandleader at an early stage when most of us [folk musicians] were really playing solo. His forte was always putting groups together. And really, whether it was an old-timey band, a bluegrass band, or whatever, he put bands together and did a great job."

Although none of these bands stayed together for very long, Kaukonen's assessment that Garcia did a "great job" still applies. Longevity is only an issue in hindsight. Garcia was thinking in groups of players, a much more complex situation than being a soloist. What Garcia was showing were leadership skills: evaluating talent, knowing which musicians could play together, and keeping groups together through hours of practice and gigs without being dictatorial. He was also doing the advance work for the bands—talking to coffeeshop owners, booking performances, getting the band known. This was a commitment not only to his music, but to other people, that is rare in a person so young.

As a result of Garcia's serious attitude about bluegrass music, the Wildwood Boys won the amateur bluegrass open contest at the Monterey Folk Festival in the summer of 1963. David Nelson explained, "At the Monterey Folk Festival the band consisted of Garcia on banjo, Hunter on bass, Ken Frankel on mandolin, and little Davey Nelson on guitar. We played 'Nine Pound Hammer,' and we won for best amateur band. What drew us to that particular festival was that it was bluegrass-heavy. There were many bluegrass bands—the Country Boys with Clarence White and Roland White, Bill Monroe and the Bluegrass Boys, the Osborne Brothers, and Doc Watson, who played old-time music. It was dazzling stuff."

Soon after Monterey, the Wildwood Boys evolved into the Black Mountain Boys. The band was losing Eric Thompson, one of its guitar players, and Garcia was looking for someone else who could take his place. Knowing the area talent as he did, Jerry soon found the right man—Sandy Rothman. Sandy described their first meeting. "I remember Jerry coming into the store [the Campus Music Shop in Berkeley, where Rothman was working], pointing his finger at me, and saying, 'Are you Sandy Rothman? We want you to be our new guitar player.'" Rothman joined the group and played with them until the spring of 1964.

Before Rothman left the band, he and Garcia took a spring road trip back East to study bluegrass music. They drove across country in Garcia's 1961 Corvair, touring the South with a tape recorder and collecting live performances of bluegrass music, which would provide great material for their repertoire. Garcia was after every bit of 1950s bluegrass he could lay his hands on. Though there were a few bluegrass albums available on Folkways Records, real bluegrass music was still hard to come by in the Bay Area. So in order to perfect the sound of his band, Garcia also relied on field recordings, and he became an avid tape collector.

One stop was at the Union Grove Fiddlers Competition in North Carolina, which attracted some 6,000 bluegrass fans on Easter weekend. It was there that Garcia first met mandolinist David Grisman. Garcia remembered, "I had my banjo; he had his mandolin. We cranked a little bit and he kind of tested me. I guess he wanted to see if these guys from the West Coast could play." Though they didn't know it at the time, the two musicians would develop a lifelong relationship based on their shared love of acoustic music.

Garcia and Rothman also spent some time near Bloomington, Indiana, because a friend of theirs, Neil Rosenburg, was managing Bill Monroe's country music park, the Brown County Jamboree. Here they had an incredible stroke of good fortune—a chance meeting with a man who had a tremendous collection of live tapes that he'd made at the Jamboree Barn throughout the 1950s. Rothman commented, "To us, that was like finding the end of the rainbow, and we ended up staying there for a couple of weeks in his basement— you know, a couple of weirdos from the Bay Area copying all his tapes."

Another dream—Garcia's and Rothman's fantasy to play with Bill Monroe in his band—didn't come true. The dream was too big, and when presented with an opportunity to make it happen, their nerve failed them. As Rothman told it, "That was the fantasy of country boys into bluegrass—get in the Bluegrass Boys and then play the Grand Ole Opry. Well, why couldn't that be a city boy's fantasy, too? I have [a] mental snapshot of one day when Jerry and I were standing around at Bean Blossom, about ten feet from Bill Monroe, leaning on our instrument cases, trying to vibe this thing to happen. We wanted him to come over and invite us to play in his band. But we were too scared to even say a word."

Though Garcia didn't get to play with his musical idol, his trip back East had been worthwile. He'd seen some great live bluegrass music, and had a fresh batch of tapes to dissect when he returned to the Bay Area. Jerry packed the Corvair and drove back to California to be with Sarah and Heather, while Rothman stayed in Indiana for the summer.

*   *   *   *

Upon his return, Garcia began playing in Mother McCree's Uptown Jug Champions, a band that got its start at the beginning of 1964. Garcia had met a young musician named Bob Weir when he was giving music lessons at Dana Morgan's Music. Weir grew up in the well-heeled community of Atherton, which is on the Peninsula a few miles north of Palo Alto. Bob got his first guitar when he was fourteen and spent his last year of formal education at the progressive Pacific School in Palo Alto, skipping classes and learning to play the guitar. He hung out in the coffeehouses in Palo Alto and watched guitar-pickers like Jerry Garcia and Jorma Kaukonen playing folk music, bluegrass, and blues.

On New Year's Eve, 1963, Weir and a friend were roaming the streets of Palo Alto looking for something to do. They were too young to get into any clubs, so they wandered over to Dana Morgan's Music, where they heard banjo music. They knocked on the door, and it opened. Weir recalled, "It was Garcia. We recognized him from the numerous bands that he was in at the time. . . . He was the local hot banjo player. He was in there playing banjo, waiting for his students to show up. Of course, it was New Year's Eve, and absolutely none of them were coming." Weir talked Garcia into letting them use a couple of guitars from the store, and they started jamming.

By the end of the evening they decided to assemble a jug band. They rounded up a bunch of old jug band records and started working on songs in Garcia's garage and at the music store. Weir played washtub bass, jug, and some guitar. They enlisted another young musician, a local harmonica player named Ron McKernan, known as "Pigpen." His father, Phil McKernan, had been a blues disc jockey who went by the name

"Cool Breeze" on KRE, Berkeley's progressive radio station. Pigpen grew up listening to his father's huge collection of blues albums and learned to play blues piano and sing the blues. At fifteen he had already quit school, and was hanging out at the various Palo Alto scenes musicians frequented. At sixteen, he was playing harmonica in his first band, the Zodiacs, and Garcia would occasionally sit in on bass when they had paying gigs, in order to bolster his income.

Garcia remembered the young Pigpen: "He'd come around to these parties and I'd be playing blues and he'd watch very carefully and he'd go home and learn things, all on the sly . . . he'd been playing harmonica secretly, and one time he got up on stage at a folk music place and I backed him on the guitar— he played harmonica and sang. He could sing like Lightnin' Hopkins, which just blew everybody's mind!" Garcia and Pigpen became close friends, spending hours at the McKernans' listening to old blues records.

In addition to Garcia, Weir, and Pigpen, Mother McCree's Uptown Jug Champions also had David Nelson on guitar and David Parker and Bob Matthews sharing duties on washboard and kazoo. Nelson detailed the origin of the band:

> Hunter and I came up with the name for the jug band. We named it together—Hunter came up with Mother McCree's, and I added Uptown Jug Champions. The jug band's first rehearsals were at my room at 431 Hamilton Street in Palo Alto, which is where Hunter, our friend Willie Legate, and I lived after Frank Seratone disbanded the Chateau. The Hamilton Street house was a big house that we sublet from some college kids and slowly took over. I

rented this little eight-by-ten room in the basement for fif-
teen dollars a month. It had a dirt floor with boards over it,
and the ceiling consisted of the beams from the floor above.
The rehearsals for the jug band were down there. I remem-
ber Weir, Pigpen, Garcia, Bob Matthews, Dave Parker, and
I had to straddle the boards on the floor to get a solid foot-
ing. We rehearsed songs like "Deep Elem Blues" and the Jim
Kweskin Jug Band songs "Washington at Valley Forge,"
"Beetle Um Bum," "K.C. Moan," and "I'm Satisfied with
My Gal."

In one respect, the jug band represented a major departure
from the kind of music Garcia had been performing. Mother
McCree's featured a lot of Pigpen, who was seriously into the
blues. Garcia relished the fact that Pigpen could play and sing
the blues like an old black southern bluesman. Pigpen brought
his own style to the band, which was radically different from
the bluegrass and old-time music Jerry was playing with his
other group, the Black Mountain Boys. Far from being a conflict, this dichotomy became a source of Garcia's growth as a
musician.

Mother McCree's Uptown Jug Champions played anyplace
that would hire a jug band, and they started getting popular
around the mid-Peninsula area. Garcia remembered, "Our jug
band was complete and total anarchy. Just lots and lots of people in it, and Pigpen and Bob and I were more or less the ring-
leaders. We'd work out various kinds of musically funny
material. It was like a musical vacation to get on stage and have
a good time."

Garcia was the de facto leader of the band, although he

publicly eschewed the role. It was not Jerry's style to name himself leader of anything, although people often tended to follow him. And the interactions within the group made the designation unnecessary. However, as the group evolved, Garcia's decisions were crucial in selecting personnel and the direction of the music. An early example was recalled by Bob Matthews: "I think I only lasted [in the jug band] about six months. I went from washboard to first kazoo, to second kazoo, to being out of the band. I think I was out of the band the night we were playing and Jerry leaned over to me in the middle of a tune and said, 'Why don't you take a break,' and I got off the stage."

Mother McCree's stayed a jug band for almost a year. Then, at Pigpen's urging, the band went electric. Pigpen had been after Jerry for some time to start up an electric blues band because he was totally into his blues trip. Garcia agreed that a transition to electric instruments was a logical next step in the evolution of the band since they were already playing a lot of blues and some rock 'n' roll tunes. They patterned themselves along the lines of the early Rolling Stones, who were also playing a lot of blues songs. Garcia said, "Me and Pigpen both had that background in the old Chess Records stuff—Chicago blues like Howlin' Wolf and Muddy Waters and people like Jimmy Reed, Chuck Berry."

With the core band in place—Garcia on lead guitar and vocals, Weir on rhythm guitar and vocals, and Pigpen on harmonica, keyboards, and vocals—all they needed was a bass player and a drummer. Back they went to Dana Morgan's Music, where they found a bass player in Dana Morgan, the son of the owner, and a drummer in Bill Kreutzmann, who taught music at the store with Garcia. The elder Morgan supplied all the equipment the band needed.

Kreutzmann was a local kid who grew up in Palo Alto. His mother was a choreographer who taught dance at Stanford, and as a child his mom would have him pound out the beat on an Indian drum while she worked out her steps—he even did it at some of her classes. He began taking drum lessons when he was twelve and as a teenager played in a Palo Alto rock band called the Legends. Bill's dad William recalled when his son first hooked up with Garcia's new electric band: "I remember they would occasionally bring their equipment over to our house and practice in our garage. They were real young then, especially Weir, who looked like he was fifteen." In fact, both Weir and Kreutzmann got fake IDs so they could play in clubs that served liquor.

Ostensibly the electric band was to be a blues band, but Garcia saw it differently: ". . . theoretically it's a blues band, but the minute we get electric instruments it's a rock 'n' roll band. Because, wow, playin' rock 'n' roll, it's fun."

Although collectively the bandmembers had been playing for a long time, they were still basically teenagers. They were serious musicians, and Garcia even had a wife and child, but they were into the music scene because it was fun. It was that attitude that made the group exciting to watch and to perform in, and it was that attitude that propelled the group into rock 'n' roll when the Beatles took American culture by storm.

David Nelson remembered, "Garcia came over to my house

and said, 'Let's go down to St. Michael's Alley, they have an album by this group, the Beatles, from England. Teenage girls like them, and I'd like to hear them.' So we went down to St. Michael's Alley and sat at a table, and the owner put the album on their system. We sat there and drank coffee and listened to it. Garcia and I would look at each other after every song, and I remember the verdict was iffy. Little did we know that these guys were heads too! It wasn't until *A Hard Day's Night* came out three or four months later that it turned our heads around."

Garcia recalled, "I'm a cinephile, and I remember going to see a Richard Lester film one night—*A Hard Day's Night*—and being blown away by the Beatles. 'Hey!' I said to myself. 'This is gonna be fun!' The Beatles took rock music into a new realm and raised it to an art form." What Garcia saw the Beatles doing was new and exciting to him. The Fab Four not only changed the course of popular music with their unique brand of rock 'n' roll, but they inspired Garcia to transform his obscure jug band into a rock band that would become one of the greatest in history.

3

THE GRATEFUL DEAD ARISE

It was around New Year's Eve 1964 when the jug band went electric, changing their name to the Warlocks. The Warlocks rehearsed in a small room at Dana Morgan's Music, using equipment they borrowed from the store. They began to develop a repertoire of cover tunes by playing 45s over and over on the store's phonograph until they got them right. David Nelson was at some of the first rehearsals. "Weir was just a green kid, unbelievably green, and Garcia would stop everything and just rail on Weir: 'No, no, no, chowderhead, knucklehead, idiot goon child! No, no, no, I told you a thousand times!' He'd be yelling about some passage in the song. 'Let's try it again.' But it was all very good-humored. Eric Thompson and I would watch, and it was hilarious. I've got to hand it to Weir, he hung in there and got better and better."

Garcia started playing a red Guild Starfire guitar because he liked the feel of it and the thin body sound, and he also used a Fender Twin Reverb amplifier. As always with a new instrument, Jerry concentrated on developing his technique by listening to musicians he admired. He especially liked the instrumental work of Freddie King. King was a big influence on Garcia when he picked up the electric guitar again with the Warlocks. Jerry acknowledged that he got many of his ideas about playing guitar off of the album *Here's Freddie King*, and that his approach to lead guitar was derivative of King's style. Some of the first songs the band started doing were rock 'n' roll tunes like Chuck Berry's "Promised Land" and "Johnny B. Goode"; the Rolling Stones's versions of "King Bee," "Little Red Rooster," and "Walking the Dog"; Bob Dylan's "It's All Over Now, Baby Blue" and "She Belongs to Me"; and adaptations of some of the jug band material, "Stealin'" and "Don't Ease Me In."

As the Warlocks, they had a hard time getting work at first. They didn't get hired anywhere for a long time, but they finally started landing some club dates. Their first gig was at Magoo's Pizza Parlor in Menlo Park. They played three nights over a three-week period, and word about their brand of electric blues and rock 'n' roll began to spread. Garcia described what transpired. "The first night at the pizza parlor, nobody was there. When we played there again, it was on a Wednesday night; there [were] a lot of kids there. And then the third night there [were] three or four hundred people, all up from the high schools—and in there, man, in there was this rock 'n' roll band. We were playing; people were freaking out."

Phil Lesh recounted the details of the night that he went to see Garcia's band play at Magoo's: ". . . whenever it was that they were playing, we took acid and went down there. . . . We came bopping in there, and it was really happening. Pigpen ate my mind with the harp, singing the blues. . . ."

The original configuration of the Warlocks didn't last long, because Garcia asked Lesh to join the band to replace Dana Morgan on bass. "During the set break," Lesh recalled, "Jerry took me off to a table and said, 'How'd you like to play bass in this band? Our bass player is not a musician, and we have to tell him what notes to play.'" No matter that Phil had never played a bass guitar; Garcia never had a doubt. "You know the strings on a guitar," Garcia instructed. "Well, the bass is the bottom four strings tuned one octave down." Though Lesh had not been a big fan of rock 'n' roll, he liked the music the Warlocks were playing and agreed to join the band.

Garcia's experience putting bands together made him realize that he couldn't pass up the chance to bring a major talent into his newest group. Though it might have been very practical to have Dana Morgan in the Warlocks because his father provided the equipment the group needed, Jerry saw the limits for the band if Dana stayed in. Lesh, on the other hand, was a serious musician whose jazz and classical background broadened the musical possibilities for the Warlocks, and his interest in avant-garde music would ultimately be a major influence on the direction the band would take. Garcia's decision to invite Lesh into the group was a significant step in the evolution of the band, and demonstrated Garcia's ability to evaluate talent and to recognize what was most important for the band.

*   *   *   *

After Lesh became a member of the group, the Warlocks moved their rehearsals from Dana Morgan's Music to a place called Guitars Unlimited in Menlo Park, where Phil borrowed a bass guitar to practice and perform with. (With Dana Morgan gone from the Warlocks, the group had to return most of their equipment to his father's music store. Garcia's mother, Ruth, later came to their rescue, loaning the band the money to purchase the equipment they needed.)

Within two weeks of acquiring a bass, Lesh was playing in the band. He practiced more with the group than on his own, because he felt that he could get his chops down better if he received input from the others. They spent a lot of time—about four hours a day—practicing in the back of Guitars Unlimited.

If Guitars Unlimited was not available to them, they would rehearse at any location they could find. Sue Swanson, Connie Bonner, and Bob Matthews, all of whom went to Menlo-Atherton High School with Weir, became the Warlocks' first fans and would let the band rehearse at their homes when their parents were out of town. Swanson remembered, "When Phil came on board he was just learning to play the bass and to sing. I used to hold his music. I think the first song he ever did with the Warlocks was 'Do You Believe in Magic.'"

The Warlocks' first club gig with Lesh on bass was a three-night stand in June 1965 at Frenchy's in Hayward. However, their sound didn't go over big, and when they showed up for the second night, they found that they had been replaced by an accordion-clarinet-bass trio. Undeterred, the Warlocks picked up an extended engagement at the In Room in Belmont, playing regularly for a month and a half. During their engagement they had the good fortune to open for the Coasters. In later years, the band (or one of its spinoffs) would perform the Coasters' songs "Searchin'," "I'm a Hog for You Baby," "Poison Ivy," and "Youngblood."

TC recalled seeing the Warlocks in Belmont: "The In Room was a lounge in a hotel. Oftentimes there wouldn't be much of a crowd, which was okay because the band was woodshedding their material, and if you are going to embarrass yourself it is good that there are few people out there. When the Warlocks first started as a rock 'n' roll band they jumped in with both feet doing quintessential rock 'n' roll songs like 'Woolly Bully.' It seemed like a right-angle turn when Jerry went electric. It was a real different direction for him to go in."

In actuality, however, it was not such a divergence for Garcia. Both he and Pigpen had heavy backgrounds in rhythm and blues, and Garcia easily made the switch from performing bluegrass and jug music to rock 'n' roll. The early band did a lot of Chicago blues with Pigpen singing lead vocals. Garcia explained, "When we first started the Warlocks I thought, 'Wow, Pigpen's this guy who can play some keyboards, some harmonica, and he's this powerhouse singer." As usual, with his wide-ranging musical interests and penchant for adventure, Jerry wasn't scared to play a fascinating new style that was seemingly beyond whatever he had been doing.

The Warlocks played six nights a week, five sets a night, for six weeks at the In Room, and it was there that they developed a unique brand of rock 'n' roll that would become nationally popular only when FM stations caught on and started playing long record cuts a year or so later. The usual path for emerging bands was to play bars and small clubs, and to play songs as they were played on the Top-40 stations—three minutes and out. The hope would be to attract a following, and then to attract a Hollywood-type promoter to manage them, book their dates, and get a record contract. Garcia, a determined nonconformist in other aspects of his life, was not about to take this slick approach to making it in the music business. He wanted to play his music, and he wanted to do it according to his rules. The Warlocks' days as a straight rock 'n' roll band were short-lived, as Garcia noted: "[We] developed a whole malicious thing, playing songs longer and weirder and louder, man. For those days it was loud, and for a bar it was ridiculous. People had to scream at each other to talk, and pretty soon we had driven out all the regular clientele."

The management apparently didn't mind how the band played, or perhaps they were just somewhat nonconformist themselves. The bartenders that they hired were also outlandish. As Weir noted, they added their own weirdness: "The bartenders were crazy; they were potheads and, like, we'd be playing and they'd line the bars with ashtrays, fill them with lighter fluid and then light them. The whole bar would seemingly go up in flames and the place would get pretty crazy for a minute, so we'd pick louder and more intense." It was no coincidence that it was at these gigs where the band first played music on LSD. Garcia reminisced, "We were playing in the bar in Belmont. . . . One of those days we took it. We got high, and goofed around in the mountains. . . . We went to the gig and we were all a little high and it was all a little strange. It was so weird playing in a bar being high on acid."

*   *   *   *

LSD had entered the picture in the early 1960s because the United States government was conducting psychological experiments with psychotropic drugs at the Veterans Hospital in Menlo Park, and had advertised for volunteers to test a range of hallucinogens for twenty dollars a session. These experiments were part of Operation MK-ULTRA, a supersecret CIA program whose purpose was to test the use of psychedelic drugs as an espionage tool to modify an individual's behavior by covert means. But like a virus from some wild chemical warfare laboratory, it got out into society and had absolutely unexpected effects. One of the inadvertent consequences of the escape of this drug, which was intended as a mind-control weapon to be used against the enemies of the country, was that it ushered in the 1960s psychedelic revolution and accelerated the flowering of the American counterculture.

When Garcia and Hunter were living at the Chateau, Hunter participated in the drug tests. After Hunter had experienced his first trip, it was just a matter of time before his good buddy Garcia tried the drug. Garcia recalled, "When he came back with his reports of what it was like, I thought, 'God, I've got to have some of that.'" He continued, "When I was in junior high school, I saw a documentary showing a bunch of people taking LSD. The film showed this artist who was just drawing lines, and he was obviously very moved—like a peak ecstasy experience. I thought, 'God, that looks like such fun!'" The unconventional Garcia obviously missed the point of the antidrug film.

Garcia did his first LSD trip sometime in 1964. He recounted his first experience on acid: "All of us people who'd been takin' various kinds of drugs together . . . we got this LSD,

we all took it, glop, glop, here in Palo Alto, and we just wandered round and round the streets bumping into each other and
having these incredible revelations and flashes, it was just
dynamite . . . we were playing around in this house, we had a
couple of Superballs . . . we bounced them around and we were
just reading comic books, doodling, strumming guitars . . . we
were rediscovering the world."

The first time that LSD and music interacted in a way that
changed the band's life was when they went to see the Lovin'
Spoonful at the Longshoremen's Hall in San Francisco on
October 24, 1965. This was one of the early dance concerts put
on by the Family Dog, a concert-promoting group whose nucle-
us was Luria Castell, Ellen Harmon, Jack Towle, and Alton
Kelly. They had a profound effect on how people experienced
rock 'n' roll in concert. Beginning with the first rock 'n' roll
shows put on in the 1950s by Alan Freed, concerts were strictly sit-down affairs where people were ejected for getting out of
their seats and dancing. The Family Dog felt that this was
ridiculous. Castell, a young woman from San Francisco, felt
that "San Francisco could be the American Liverpool" and
that "rock 'n' roll [was] the new form of communication for our
generation." They decided to put on rock 'n' roll shows so that
the people of San Francisco could dance.

At a Family Dog concert, the hall was filled with people
who were dancing and grooving with the music in an unre-
stricted environment that encouraged spontaneity. Often, long
lines of dancers would snake through the crowd holding hands.

When the Warlocks, who had been taking a group LSD trip in Marin County on the day of the Lovin' Spoonful concert, arrived at the Longshoremen's Hall, the place was packed with smiling concertgoers who were dancing uninhibitedly. It became clear to Garcia that he was witnessing a fantastic thing and that working in bars was not the way for the band to expand into this new idea. Lesh was so taken by it all that he told Ellen Harmon, "Lady, what this little seance needs is us."

Garcia and Lesh both recognized that the dynamic represented by the dance concert was something the band should be part of. Garcia, having disdain for the "Hollywood hype scene, booking agents in flashy suits, gigs in booze clubs," was ready to abandon the bar scene. The Family Dog concert opened Garcia's eyes to what a total musical experience could be for an audience and a band, but it was Ken Kesey and the Merry Pranksters who precipitated the Warlocks sudden break with the straight music scene.

Kesey had also volunteered in the name of science to be a guinea pig for the United States government. A University of Oregon graduate, he was attending the Stanford University Creative Writing Program in hopes of becoming a novelist and was living on Perry Lane, Stanford's bohemian quarter. Perry Lane consisted of barely a dozen cottages that rented for sixty dollars a month; though small, it was a hotbed of cultural rebellion. Kesey's experiences with LSD at the Veterans Hospital proved to his liking, and he took a job there as a psychiatric aide. Working the graveyard shift when the hospital was fairly deserted, he was able to avail himself of whatever drugs the medicine cabinets had to offer.

Under Kesey's tutelage, the government's experiments were expanded on Perry Lane in the form of LSD chili and other concoctions. Word began spreading that Kesey had found some sort of creativity pill that was helping him work madly on his novel *One Flew Over the Cuckoo's Nest*, which was more or less based on his experiences as an aide at the VA Hospital. Kesey finished the book in only ten months, and it was published in February 1962, with Kesey receiving a $1,500 advance from the publisher and later another $20,000 for the movie rights.

The Chateau and Perry Lane were in close proximity to each other, and there had been some intermingling of the two scenes. Garcia remarked, "At the time our headquarters were very close together, so to speak. Kesey used to live on Perry Lane, which is just down from Stanford, and we lived over at the Chateau, which was maybe two or three blocks away, and we would stumble over to their parties and some of them would spill over to our parties. But we really were different scenes because we were much younger. . . . We were all just dropouts and they were college people."

Perry Lane was a scholarly world of talented writers who were at the center of a vibrant literary scene. Kesey's house would often be the site of after-hours intellectual discussions that included some of the most talented people in the Stanford writer's program—Larry McMurtry, Ed McClanahan, Gurney Norman, Peter Beagle, Ken Babbs, and Robert Stone—many who would go on to become successful novelists. Kesey's literary soirees came to an end in 1963, when much of Perry Lane was bought by a developer who planned to bulldoze the cottages and replace them with tract homes.

After a final dinner of spiked venison chili, Kesey bid farewell to Perry Lane and headed to La Honda, which was up in the mountains fifteen miles west of Palo Alto. With some of the money from the sale of his book, he bought a piece of land with a cabin on it and set up camp for his band of psychedelic adventurers, who became known as the Merry Pranksters.

One such adventurer was Neal Cassady, who had turned up at Perry Lane after reading *One Flew Over the Cuckoo's Nest.* Cassady, the real-life model for Jack Kerouac's Dean Moriarty in *On the Road,* was an unconventional dropout who shocked straight America in the 1950s and became a hero to the Beats. Cassady and Kesey had an affinity for each other, and Cassady became a fixture at La Honda. Another inhabitant of La Honda was Ken Babbs, Kesey's best friend on Perry Lane, who was the one who came up with the idea of pranks, the cosmic put-on; hence the name "Merry Pranksters."

In 1964 the Merry Pranksters headed across country in a 1939 International Harvester bus that had been outfitted on the inside with the basic necessities for life on the road and changed on the outside into an ever-evolving multicolored psychedelic mural. They painted the word FURTHER on the front of the bus, and CAUTION: WEIRD LOAD on the back. The bus had a sound system so that the Pranksters could broadcast from inside the bus to the outside. With Cassady at the wheel, they tripped across country on LSD causing intentional scenes wherever they traveled. The Merry Pranksters rode through the United States taunting straight America with their bizarre behavior and dress, while filming their pranks for a movie they hoped to produce called *The Merry Pranksters Search for a Cool Place*.

Returning to La Honda, the Pranksters lived communally and stayed high on LSD much of the time. Fascinating individuals kept arriving at Kesey's place: Owsley Stanley, the "Acid King," who produced millions of doses of LSD and almost singlehandedly turned on a generation; and Carolyn Adams, known as Mountain Girl, who later became Jerry Garcia's wife. Kesey recalled, "There were no rules for those who wanted to get 'on the bus.' There was no official period of probation, and no vote on is he or isn't he one of us, no black-balling, no tap on the shoulder. And yet there was a period of proving yourself, and everyone knew it was going on and no one ever said a word about it."

The use of LSD had given the Pranksters a feeling that they were acquiring new powers and that together they could form a group mind. The appearance of Owsley on the scene was fortuitous, because it gave Kesey a virtually unlimited supply of LSD and enabled him to bring this new consciousness to many more people. In December 1965 Kesey decided to further his mission of altered consciousness by going public with a series of "Acid Tests." Mountain Girl outlined it: "We had this idea to give LSD free to people at events that we were going to set up. It grew out of a party idea, a Saturday night party. Every Saturday night you have a colossal party and you invite anybody and everybody you can think of to invite and turn them all on and have a good time and show weird movies, light shows, or anything we could think of at the time to do. The early Acid Tests were at Kesey's place, and there was also one at Babbs's place. We did them for three or four weeks before we took it to San Jose." "It was a total experience," Kesey explained to writer Tom Wolfe, "with all the senses opened wide, words, music, lights, sounds, touch—lightning." This was just the sort of experience that Garcia was looking for in his music.

The first public Acid Test was held on December 4, 1965, in San Jose at the home of a bohemian named Big Nig. Page Browning, one of the Pranksters, was a friend of Garcia's from the Chateau and knew that Jerry would do something just for kicks. He called Garcia and told him about what was going down in San Jose and asked if the band would come. Garcia observed, "One day the idea was there: 'Why don't we have a big party, and you guys bring your instruments and play, and us Pranksters will set up all our tape recorders and bullshit, and we'll all get stoned.' That was the first Acid Test."

Mountain Girl described what happened: "San Jose was the first public Acid Test in 1965. It was a complete blowout— manic bash. Nobody forgot it—it was cataclysmic! The band played, everybody got high, weird and strange. LSD was legal then and people were taking big doses. Some people took their clothes off and it spilled out into the street."

It was a watershed event that drew the public into the psychedelic adventure that Kesey and the Pranksters had begun. The San Jose Acid Test was on the night of a Rolling Stones concert in the Bay Area, and the Pranksters had passed out handbills at the concert that read: "Can YOU Pass the Acid Test?" and giving the location of the event. About four hundred people showed up, and the psychedelic revolution had begun.

After that, the Pranksters got the idea to do it regularly. Garcia remembered, "After that first one we all got together, us and Kesey and everybody, and had a meeting about it, and thought, well, you know, that first one there had all those people there, but it was too weird 'cause it was somebody's house. . . . We decided to keep on doing it, that was the gist of it . . . the idea was to move it to a different location each week."

With the advent of the Acid Tests, the Warlocks dropped out of the straight music scene and became psychedelic explorers destined to become innovators of the so-called "acid rock." Garcia explained, "The Acid Test was the prototype for our whole basic trip." He commented, "We were lucky to have a little moment in history when LSD was still legal and we could experiment with drugs like we were experimenting with music." When LSD entered the scene "the whole world just went kablooey."

The Acid Tests: to go where no human had gone before—a psychedelic journey combining LSD, rock 'n' roll, light and movie projections, tapes, strobes, and black light that took the explorer on a trip with no reservations. "Okay, so you take LSD and suddenly you are aware of another plane, or several other planes, and the quest is to extend that limit, to go as far as you can go," said Garcia. "In the Acid Tests that meant to do away with old forms, with old ideas, try something new."

*   *   *   *

The San Jose Acid Test was the Warlocks' first appearance as the Grateful Dead. The metamorphosis occurred when Lesh discovered that another band was already calling itself the Warlocks and that they would have to change their name. Lesh reflected, "I often wonder if I hallucinated that record, because I never saw it again. I was just thumbing through 45s, you know, in a record store. . . . I went back and told the boys that I'd seen a record with the name 'The Warlocks' on it and if we were serious and wanted to make a record we ought to start thinking about changing our name." For several weeks they mulled over different names but nothing fit—Mythical Ethical Icicle Tricicle; Bimini and the Vivisectionists; Nonreality Sandwich.

Garcia remarked, "We discovered there was a band back East recording under that name [the Warlocks]. We decided, 'Oh, no, we can't have that, we can't be confused with somebody else.' So we were trying to think up names, and for about two or three weeks we went on the usual thing of coming up with thousands and thousands of very funny names, none of which we could use."

They used the name Emergency Crew when they cut a demo on November 3, 1965, in San Francisco for Tom Donahue's label, Autumn Records. Later that month the band was sitting around on High Street in Palo Alto trying to come up with a suitable name when Garcia happened upon a phrase that stuck. He explained how they finally found their name: "One day we were all over at Phil's house smoking DMT. He had a big Oxford dictionary, I opened it, and there was *grateful dead*, those words juxtaposed. It was one of those moments, y'know, like everything else on the page went blank, diffuse,

just sorta oozed away, and there was GRATEFUL DEAD, big black
letters edged all around in gold, man, blasting out at me, such a
stunning combination. So I said, 'How 'bout Grateful Dead?'
and that was it." Garcia added, "It was funny because we didn't
really like it at first and it kind of made us shudder. We were
worried that nobody was going to go for it—it's too weird."

David Nelson remembered: "I was at home at the house on
Waverly Street that day when the band was having a meeting
at Phil's place in Palo Alto, a few blocks away. Garcia came
back to our house where he lived with his wife, Sarah, and
grabs Sarah and me in my room, and closes the door. 'OK,
we've been thinking about the new band name ideas'—and this
is after all the jokes have died down, Mythical Ethical Icicle
Tricycle, etcetera—'we've got a serious name idea here, and I
just wanted to try you out because it's not like any other kind of
name.' I remember going 'Uh, oh!' and I looked at Sarah, and
she was going, 'Yes, dear,' to her husband, and he said, 'The
Grateful Dead,' and he looked as frightened as we did. He was
looking off into space, he wasn't looking at either one of us, and
he again said, 'The Grateful Dead,' and looked at us and said,
'What do you think?' Sarah and I are looking at Jerry, thinking,
'Oh, my God!' I remember I couldn't say anything. I fended off
his glance, thinking, 'Don't look at me for a reaction.' I
couldn't handle it for a few seconds. Then I said, 'I don't know,
you think you want something that bad-sounding?' Then Sarah
said, 'I think I like it. I think it would be a good idea.'"

Though the name had a definite resonance, it took some
getting used to. The band had a hard time getting promoter Bill
Graham to use the name for the Mime Troupe Benefit at the
Fillmore Auditorium in San Francisco. Bob Weir recollected,

"Our drummer, Billy Kreutzmann, got on the phone to him to get us on the bill. We had just changed our name from the Warlocks to the Grateful Dead. But Bill Graham didn't like the idea. He was going to put Warlocks on the poster. And we had a long hassle with him and he finally put 'Grateful Dead—formerly the Warlocks.'"

Two years later, when the band was well-known nationally, they met the Maharishi Mahesh Yogi, who commented that he didn't like the band's name and suggested that they call themselves "Everlasting Life." He gave everyone in attendance a personally selected mantra and, as he made his grand exit, handed them each a rose. The Dead didn't take his criticism—or criticism from other sources—seriously, because their name worked. The juxtaposition of the words had a shock value that made the name memorable. As Robert Hunter so aptly put it, "Once heard, the name is not forgotten." Things would just not have been the same musically had the band been called something like the Psychedelic Cowboys, which is what they were.

Another eventful Acid Test was at a nightclub in Palo Alto called the Big Beat, a plushy club in an L-shape with a stage in the angle. The Grateful Dead had their equipment set up on the stage, and the Pranksters had their gear set up on the other side of the room on tables—a Day-Glo organ, tape recorders, microphones, and a strobe light. The strobe light, in between the two setups, would flash the whole room.

Rock Scully, who had worked with the Family Dog, met

the band at this gig. Scully remarked, "Ken Kesey was lecturing around the Bay area at that time, and I went and saw him. Owsley had shown up at the lecture and he told me about this band, the Grateful Dead. I went to an Acid Test down on the Peninsula [the Big Beat] and heard them and thought they were great."

Scully also recalled, "I was standing by the bar and [Pigpen] walked up to me wearing his biker jacket with all the medals on it and he says, 'Owsley told me to come over and talk to you. He says you're gonna manage us or something.' I said, 'Yeah, I'd like to. I don't know what we're gonna do, though—you guys are ugly as sin.' He said, 'Yeah, aren't we?' I said, 'Yeah, that's neat! The Rolling Stones are ugly, too!' He said, 'Yeah, we do the same kind of music, except we do it better!'"

Stewart Brand was at the Big Beat Acid Test with his side show of taped music and slides of Indians, a multimedia presentation that was a total environment where you could see the sights and hear the sounds of Indian life. Brand had fallen in with the Pranksters around the time of the Big Beat Acid Test and before long was organizing an even larger version, which became known as the Trips Festival. The Trips Festival was held the third weekend in January 1966 at the Longshoremen's Hall in San Francisco. The festival lasted three days and was a multimedia event that included Brand's "America Needs Indians Sensorium," the Pranksters, the live music of the Grateful Dead as well as Big Brother and the Holding Company, light shows, and LSD. Booths were scattered throughout the hall offering incense, psychedelic literature, and political leaflets.

Another individual who helped organize the Trips Festival

was Bill Graham. Graham had some experience organizing concerts, having set up the benefits for the Mime Troupe, and his talents were utilized to run the business end of things. Mountain Girl remembered, "Bill Graham had control of the door at this event. He was a maniac. He sold tickets and insisted people have tickets. He was like the antagonist for the free trip, but at the same time he was on our side, working for us."

The Trips Festival was where Garcia met Graham. "Here's this guy running around with a clipboard . . . in the midst of total insanity. I mean total wall-to-wall gonzo lunacy. Everybody in the place is high but Bill. And I was having the greatest time in the world. . . . It was a great, incredible scene, and I was wandering around. I had some sense that the Grateful Dead was supposed to play sometime maybe. But it really didn't matter. We were used to Acid Tests where sometimes we'd play and sometimes we wouldn't. . . . Anyway, I was out there wandering around and my attention was drawn to this opaque projector projecting onto one of the many screens in the place. And the screen said, 'JERRY GARCIA, PLUG IN!'"

Garcia headed to the stage where the Grateful Dead's equipment was set up and discovered that somebody had knocked over his guitar and broke the bridge off. Strings were sticking out everywhere. Graham appeared and told him to start playing, but Garcia was just sitting on the floor, looking down at his guitar and holding it like a baby. "I gesture to the guitar and I say, 'It broke. Broke, you know?' And Bill looks down at it. Immediately, without saying a word, he falls down onto the ground and starts picking up pieces. He fumbles around with them trying to fix it for me. I thought, 'What a

nice guy.'" Despite Graham's best efforts, neither Garcia nor
the Grateful Dead played again that night.

In 1965 and 1966 approximately a dozen Acid Tests were
held up and down the West Coast: San Jose, Palo Alto, Muir
Beach, San Francisco, Portland, and Los Angeles. Thousands
of people turned on to LSD and became part of the Pranksters'
multimedia experience. Garcia recalled the Acid Tests during
a radio interview:

> For sheer unmitigated total all-out craziness you
> couldn't beat the Acid Test. Nothing has ever been like
> those. They were really the most fun of any of those kinds
> of things. I remember the one at the old Fillmore was
> tremendously successful because they had all those little
> cubbyholes. . . . It had that segmented thing going—the big
> room and lots of little rooms. There were microphones dis-
> tributed all over the place, and all different people with mix-
> ers and tape recorders, and speakers all over the place. And
> so somebody might say something in the corner and it would
> go through a delay and you might hear it up in some other
> room completely unrelated, but there would be this incred-
> ible timing thing that would be happening so that every-
> thing that happened would sort of fit right in perfectly. . . .
> Somebody would find a microphone on the floor and say,
> "Hey, is anybody there?," and all of a sudden they would
> hear their voice, huge, coming from all over. And they
> would start raving, and it would go away, and something else
> would come up. . . . Then the cops came and busted that
> one. That Acid Test was a good one for the whole cop show.
> The cops came in, and they looked around. Here's one of

Ron Boise's big sculptures, the big thunder machine is there—[freaks] banging on it, pouring Day-Glo paint over it, and it's making this incredible din, resonating, and weird tapes and weird sounds going on, and people running around, and all this just totally bananas shit going on. Here's these straight good old four-square San Francisco Irish cops, a whole bunch of them, a dozen or so of them. And they're in there—"Who's in charge here?" The limit of the absurd, you know, "Who's in charge here?" There's cops standing in the middle of the floor with half a dozen freaks around them raving at 'em, raving strange things at 'em. . . . and here's this cop, like a lieutenant up there, trying to make an announcement over the microphone while the dials are being run by some madman up in the balcony somewhere, so the cop's voice is coming in and out, and Kesey is raving some semi-patriotic slogans over the top of the cop's rap about it—"We have to clear the place out." And the thing would cut off right in the middle of his rap. Phil and Weir are there arm in arm around each other, and they're singing the "Star-Spangled Banner" real loud in the cop's ear, and some big bear of a freak is banging his hand with a tambourine. It was so funny, really hilarious. All this funny stuff for timing. It was like a huge Marx Brothers movie. . . . That's what I loved about those things. There was absolutely no paranoia—there's no law against being weird. The police were like big buffoons, some kind of dog police or something.

. . . Then the cops were up in the balcony. They were going around in a little official knot, sort of inspecting. All of a sudden these freaks are there with this ladder, and they're putting this ladder up to the balcony and they're climbing it, and they're hollering, "Hug the heat! Hug the heat!" It was amazing!

Part of what made the Acid Tests work were the pranks of Kesey and Babbs and the antics of Neal Cassady, who would rave over the microphones or wander around blowing people's minds. Mountain Girl remarked, "Neal Cassady was the main announcer, the mad commentator who gave the blow-by-blow. His entire life force was behind him. He was beautiful at the Trips Festival and the Acid Tests. We'd give him the microphone and a spotlight and some brilliant piece of clothing to shred. He'd do weird scat singing if the music wasn't happening. He'd talk or give commentaries on the girls. Just constant entertainment. He moved fast and loved dancing in the strobe light babbling all this comic rap stuff."

Garcia credited Cassady with inspiring him to stick with music. "It wasn't as if he said, 'Jerry, my boy, the whole ball of wax happens here and now.' It was watching him move, having my mind blown by how deep he was, how much he could take into account in any given moment and be really in time with it." Garcia elaborated: "Neal represented a model to me of how far you could take it in the individual way, in the sense that you weren't going to have a work, you were going to *be* the work. Work in real time, which is a lot like a musician's work. I was oscillating at the time. I had originally been an art student and was wavering between one-man/one-work or being involved in something that was dynamic and ongoing and didn't necessarily stay any one way. And also, something in which you weren't the only contributing factor. I decided to

Jerry Garcia, 1969. (BARON WOLMAN)

In 1950 Jerry Garcia posed outside his mom's bar, "The Four Hundred Club," located at 400 1st Street in Downtown San Francisco. (GRATEFUL DEAD ALBUM: WARNER BOOKS, NYC 1989)

Jerry and his first wife Sarah performing folk and old-time music at The Tangent in Palo Alto, CA in May, 1963. (ARCHIVE PRESS)

The Wildwood Boys won the Amateur Bluegrass Open Contest at the Monterey Folk Festival during the summer of 1963. Playing, from left to right: Ken Frankel, mandolin; Jerry, banjo; Robert Hunter, bass; David Nelson, guitar. (ARCHIVE PRESS)

*Charlotte Daigle dated Jerry in the early sixties when he first
arrived in Palo Alto after being discharged from the army.*
(COURTESY OF CHARLOTTE DAIGLE)

David Nelson; one of Garcia's closest friends who played in Jerry's early acoustic bands and later played lead guitar in New Riders of the Purple Sage, a group that toured and worked with Garcia many times. (COURTESY OF DAVID NELSON)

Jerry hamming it up for the camera in the Panhandle, San Francisco, 1967. (GENE ANTHONY)

Jerry Garcia in the recording studio in the 1960's (MICHAEL OCHS ARCHIVES)

Haight-Ashbury's Community Band. The Grateful Dead, 1966: Left to right—Bill Kreutzmann, Phil Lesh, Bob Weir, Jerry Garcia, Ron "Pigpen" McKernan. (GENE ANTHONY)

The Grateful Dead, 1960's.
(MICHAEL OCHS ARCHIVES)

Jerry rolling a joint in The Dead's business office at 710 Ashbury Street. Sunshine, (Ken Kesey and Mountain Girl's daughter) dancing around the room, stops to peer at the camera.
(GENE ANTHONY)

Mountain Girl (one of The Merry Pranksters and Jerry's second wife) is all smiles hanging out with friends at 710 Ashbury Street in 1967. BELOW, LEFT, *Jerry's room at The Grateful Dead's far-out hippie pad at 710 Ashbury Street, 1967.* RIGHT: *Jerry Garcia, 1966.* (PHOTOS: GENE ANTHONY)

The Grateful Dead, 1966.   (GENE ANTHONY)

Jerry Garcia, 1966.   (GENE ANTHONY)

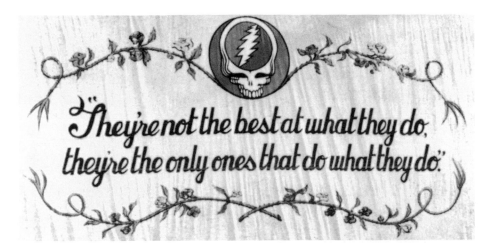

"They're not the best at what they do, they're the only ones that do what they do."

The Grateful Dead, 1966.

The Warlocks, 1965. Jerry, Bill Kreutzmann, Bob Weir, Phil Lesh, and Ron "Pigpen" McKernan. (HERB GREENE/MICHAEL OCHS ARCHIVES)

Jerry Garcia pauses in Back Bay, 1972.
(MICHAEL DOBO/MICHAEL OCHS ARCHIVES)

Ken Kesey. (GENE ANTHONY)

The Bus. (GENE ANTHONY)

Kesey became a hero to the restless youth of America when he helped launch the sixties counterculture with his series of acid tests, 1965.
(GENE ANTHONY)

Rock Scully. (GENE ANTHONY)

Garcia on Baker Street, San Francisco, 1967.
(HERB GREENE/MICHAEL OCHS ARCHIVES)

Pigpen, 1967. (GENE ANTHONY)

*Wavy Gravy, Merl Saunders and Jerry Garcia play a free concert
with The Legion of Mary band at Marx Meadows in Golden Gate
Park, San Francisco, September 2, 1974.* (GREG GAAR)

Heliport practice studio, 1966. (GENE ANTHONY)

The Dead in 1966. (HERB GREENE/MICHAEL OCHS ARCHIVES)

go with what was dynamic and with what more than one mind was involved with."

At the Acid Tests there were no demands made upon the musicians. Garcia stated, "There were no sets. Sometimes we'd get up and play for two hours, three hours; sometimes we'd play for ten minutes and all freak out and split. We'd just do it however it would happen. It wasn't a gig, it was the Acid Tests, where anything was OK. Thousands of people, man, all helplessly stoned, all finding themselves in a roomful of other thousands of people, none of whom any of them were afraid of. It was magic—far out, beautiful magic."

As Kesey's Acid Tests gained notoriety, increasing numbers of people began experimenting with LSD. The Acid Tests, which had furthered Kesey's mission of altering consciousness, were not just attracting nonconformists, but were creating them. LSD was a mind-expanding chemical that opened up the doors of perception and allowed one to view the world with a fresh perspective. Many LSD users began to question their basic value system and priorities in life. Some users felt that an acid trip was a mystical experience that enabled them to see God, and they touted LSD as a religious experience. These facts were not lost on the authorities, who were looking for any justification to throw the book at Kesey. Sensing that jail was inevitable, Kesey missed a court hearing for a marijuana bust, and fled to Mexico at the beginning of February 1966.

With Kesey on the lam, the Bay Area Acid Tests petered out. Fortunately for San Francisco bands and audiences, two new sources of music and dance opened at that time. Inspired by the thousands of people who had turned out for the Trips Festival, Bill Graham began to book his own concerts at the Fillmore Auditorium, starting the first weekend of February 1966. For a short time he shared bookings at the Fillmore with Chet Helms, who had taken over the Family Dog. Helms, a Texan, had brought to San Francisco a young blues singer named Janis Joplin, who was soon to become famous singing with Big Brother and the Holding Company, the band Helms was managing. Helms soon took the Family Dog shows to the Avalon Ballroom, and he and Graham started producing concerts every weekend. A considerable rivalry developed.

Jorma Kaukonen remarked, "The competition between Chet and Bill was a healthy thing for the San Francisco music scene. It was a shame when Graham eventually eliminated the competition. Both promoters put on a good show, but their styles were different. Chet was a hippie who was part of the Haight-Ashbury scene, and he knew the musicians. Though Chet wanted to make a profit, the Avalon was much more psychedelic and a hippie scene. Bill was a money-sucking capitalist pig who had real security, and you could get your ass kicked there."

The idealistic Helms and the hardass Graham were as different as night and day, and the atmospheres at their respective venues reflected this difference. Helms tried to create a safe environment, a sanctuary for evolving rites of passage that fit the hopes, dreams, and ideals of the hippie community. Graham was a businessman whose main concern was the bottom line. His security force, recruited from the mostly black

Fillmore district, wore green-and-yellow uniforms and were instructed to keep the audience in line.

Jann Wenner, who later founded *Rolling Stone* magazine, was a student at UC Berkeley when he wrote the following in the student newspaper, the *Daily Cal:* "When these things were originated by the Family Dog, they were meant to present local rock groups and generally provide everyone with a good time, as little hassle as possible, and just be a gas for the performers, participants, and spectators. Graham has turned these dances into money-making schemes first and foremost. Whatever fun one has is strictly incidental to, almost in spite of, Bill Graham."

The concert scene at the Avalon received more favorable reviews. "The Avalon at its finest was like a continual party," said Garcia. "Everybody that was going to it was aware that the whole money thing—the way it was being distributed—was ultimately for the good of the community."

Graham and Helms became the two top promoters in San Francisco, and the competition between the Fillmore and the Avalon provided a continual schedule of good music for the people of the city. As a consequence, local bands like the Grateful Dead, the Jefferson Airplane, Quicksilver Messenger Service, Big Brother and the Holding Company, the Great Society, Country Joe and the Fish, and the Charlatans were given a great opportunity to get steady work. And that was what the local bands were really concerned about.

Besides local groups, national acts were booked, and Graham in particular brought in older blues and jazz musicians who were largely unknown to the white audiences. He often paired up the black blues and jazz acts with the local San

Francisco groups, whose music had often been inspired by some of these veteran musicians. San Franciscans got to see seminal performers like Miles Davis, Elvin Jones, Charles Lloyd, Howlin' Wolf, Muddy Waters, Sonny Terry and Brownie McGhee, Bo Diddley, Lightnin' Hopkins, James Cotton, Otis Redding, B. B. King, Albert King, Chuck Berry, Albert Collins, Freddie King, and John Lee Hooker, as well as national acts like the Paul Butterfield Blues Band, the Blues Project, the Mothers, Love, the Byrds, the Doors, the Young Rascals, the Buffalo Springfield, Steppenwolf, Blood, Sweat, and Tears, and English groups like the Who, Cream, the Yardbirds, the Moody Blues, Eric Burdon and the Animals, Pink Floyd, and Procol Harum.

Psychedelic posters designed by artists like Wes Wilson, Stanley Mouse, Alton Kelley, Rick Griffin, and Victor Moscoso were used to promote the shows at the Fillmore and the Avalon, with each concert having its own original poster. Almost immediately after the posters for an upcoming concert were put up, they would be taken down by people who wanted to collect them or to hang them on their walls at home. The Fillmore and Avalon posters took on a life of their own, and before long they were considered works of art that were framed and hung in museums and galleries.

In order to take best advantage of the opportunity to play before larger audiences, Garcia and the Dead decided to move down to Los Angeles to rehearse and work up some new songs. Though they had about four sets of material, it was mostly old cover tunes. Owsley, who had befriended the band at the Acid Tests, became their financial backer. He rented them a house on the fringes of Watts and bought them sound equipment. Garcia noted, "We were living solely off of Owsley's good graces at that time. The Pranksters were on their way to Mexico, and we were living at a house that Owsley had rented. We had no money, of course, no furniture, no place to sleep, or anything like that. Owsley's trip was he wanted to design equipment for us, and we were going to have to be in sort of a lab situation for him to do it."

At this time, Rock Scully became the band's manager. With Owsley on hand and the band itchy to play, several Acid Tests were set up in Los Angeles. But it just wasn't the same with Kesey gone. At the Watts Acid Test the vibes were intense, and several people freaked out. Garcia remembered it as "the night everybody was terribly overdosed."

After the Los Angeles Acid Tests in February and March 1966, the band moved back to San Francisco and found a place to live at Rancho Olompali, a secluded ranch off Highway 101 in Novato with a big Spanish-style two-story house, a swimming pool, barns, and a lot of land around it. There was a creek in the back, and out front there was a big lawn. Word spread about the Dead's new digs and soon a good portion of the San Francisco music scene was partying at the ranch. Members of the Jefferson Airplane, Quicksilver Messenger Service, Big Brother and the Holding Company, the Charlatans—many of the players had known each other since their folk music days—and other bands would get together and jam. The Dead would set up their equipment between the house and the pool. Whatever musician felt like playing would go at it during the day before two or three hundred people—some of whom were high on LSD—lounging around in the sun or swimming naked in the pool. Garcia remembered, "Novato was completely comfortable, wide open, high as you wanted to get, run around naked if you wanted to, fall in the pool, completely open scenes." It was an oasis of rock 'n' roll.

Tom Constanten recalled visiting Olompali. "Bill Walker [a mutual friend of TC and Phil Lesh] and I drove from Vegas to see Phil, who was living at Olompali at that time with the whole band. There was a sign out front that read 'No Trespassing—Violators Will Be Experimented Upon.' Page Browning was walking around the property with several copies of the *San Francisco Chronicle* hawking them like a newsboy. That paper, the Monday, May 30, 1966, edition, had a headline article called 'Inside Report on LSD Journey,' which discussed a fantastic account of an LSD trip. The article was a big hit at Olompali. . . ."

With all that was going on—the Trips Festival, the burgeoning San Francisco music scene, the contact between the bands, there was a feeling in the air that big things were set to happen for the musicians. Jorma Kaukonen reminisced about one particular conversation at Olompali: "Jack [Casady], Janis [Joplin], Jerry, and myself were just talking one day, and one of the things we were talking about was how long it would take before we [musicians] would be considered the real thing." At that point, it was a matter of only a year or two before these purveyors of what became known as the "San Francisco sound" would be recognized as legitimate national artists. Janis Joplin, the Jefferson Airplane, and the Grateful Dead would all receive acclaim for being in the vanguard of a new style of music.

The good times at Rancho Olompali were short-lived because the Grateful Dead had to move out after only eight weeks. The band stayed in San Francisco for a brief time, getting a room at 710 Ashbury Street, an old Victorian house in the middle of Haight-Ashbury. It was a boarding house where Rock Scully lived with his friend Danny Rifkin, who was managing the house at the time. Rifkin had gone to Los Angeles when the band was woodshedding there and had been helping Scully and Owsley set up gigs. He got on well with the band, and Scully asked him to help manage them.

Though 710 would eventually become their home, when the Dead left Olompali there was only one vacant room in the house. The group used it as a business office and found another place to live—Camp Lagunitas in the San Geronimo Valley in western Marin County. Camp Lagunitas had cabins and a swimming pool, and a dining hall with a piano where the band would rehearse. While they were at the camp the band got into archery. One night, for a lark, they decided to dress up like Indians and raid the nearby ranch of their friends, Quicksilver Messenger Service. In full Indian regalia and war paint, the Grateful Dead burst into Quicksilver's house, whooping it up with bows and arrows. Quicksilver got caught with their pants down, and they surrendered.

John Cippolina of Quicksilver recalled, "You know how it started: They were sitting around their camp and they were on this big Indian trip, naturally, because they had camp crafts, they had an archery range, and they were the Grateful Dead. One night they were sitting around with makeup. Jerry Garcia was beautiful. He had 'Tippecanoe and Tyler Too' written across his nose. They got themselves all done up, and worked themselves up into a frenzy doing a war dance, and they said, 'Let's go get the Quicksilver,' and they really got us." To get even, Quicksilver decided to stick up the Dead when they were performing at the Fillmore, handcuff them to their microphones, and play a tune through their equipment. On their way over to the Fillmore, however, a police officer saw them in the street with their plastic guns and hauled them off to jail.

In June 1966 the first Grateful Dead record was released on the Scorpio label. It was a 45 of "Stealin'" with the flip side "Don't Ease Me In," which was produced when the band was still the Warlocks. The tracks were recorded by Gene Esterbough in a studio he owned at 737 Buena Vista West in San Francisco. Though the songs were both written in the late 1920s, Garcia was erroneously given writer's credit on the record. He sang lead vocals on both cuts, which were tunes he had performed with the jug band. Even on these early tunes Garcia's plaintive vocal style is evident. The band took advantage of their time in Esterbough's studio and laid down a number of other tracks for possible release. The group was considering putting out an album called *No Turn Left Unstoned*, but it never materialized.

The single got some airplay on local radio. That, and the notoriety they got for being the house band for the Acid Tests, spread their name throughout the Bay Area. They began performing on a regular basis, often appearing on the bills of Graham's Fillmore and Helms's Avalon.

It was at an Avalon concert on September 16 and 17, 1966,

that the symbol which has become synonymous with the Grateful Dead came into being. Stanley Mouse and Alton Kelley conceived of the skeleton-and-roses design for the concert poster, and the image soon became the band's logo. Mouse recalled, "[Kelley and I] were in a San Francisco library looking through all the old books on graphics, old artists. . . . One time we were looking through the stacks and we came across . . . *The Rubaiyat of Omar Khayyam,* and there was an illustration using a skeleton and roses. We had been looking for something to use for the Grateful Dead. Kelley and I looked at each other and said, 'There it is, the perfect picture.' And so we designed a poster around the picture. We knew when we did it that it was really hot because it felt right. It just fit so good with the name. The skeleton that symbolized death and the roses that symbolized rebirth and love. It just said Grateful Dead."

The Dead developed another distinguishing characteristic during the concerts of 1966, evolving into what Garcia described as a "dance band," playing stretched-out versions of songs. "We played long songs because people wanted to dance. That's what it was all about. We always had a tendency to play a little long anyway, even when we were back in the pizza parlors and a lot of stuff we did was just open-ended. We had a piece called 'Caution' that was really just a long breakdown. It went from up-tempo to ridiculous."

Bob Weir discussed the song, "How the 'Caution' jam developed is we were driving around listening to the radio, like we used to do a lot, and the song 'Mystic Eyes' by Them was on, and we were all saying, 'Check this out! We can do this!' So we got to the club where we were playing and we warmed up on it. We lifted the riff from 'Mystic Eyes' and extrapolated it into 'Caution,' and I think Pigpen just made up the words."

Another song that helped shape the Grateful Dead's sound was the instrumental "Cleo's Back" by Junior Walker and the All-Stars, which made it to number 43 on the Billboard Top Pop Chart in October 1965 and stayed on the charts for eight weeks. Junior Walker was part of the mid-1960s Motown stable of rhythm and blues acts, and his honking saxophone style had its roots in late 1940s and early 1950s rhythm and blues. Garcia explained the impact of the song: "['Cleo's Back'] was also real influential on the Grateful Dead—our whole style of playing. There was something about the way the instruments entered into it in a kind of free-for-all way, and there were little holes and these neat details in it—we studied that motherfucker! We might have even played it for a while, but that wasn't the point—it was the conversational approach, the way the band worked, that really influenced us."

The conversational style of playing became an essential part of the Grateful Dead's music as the band began to move more and more heavily into improvisation. As their music became less structured, the musicians had to really listen to each other in order to respond to the spur-of-the-moment changes that would occur in their improvisational jams. It was exciting to see the players interact as the band played an extended piece that went on an exploratory musical journey. Garcia, as lead guitarist, would often develop melodic themes in the middle of jams, taking the music in a new direction. This improvisational style of playing became the Dead's trademark over the next few years. It was an avant-garde approach to music more akin to jazz than rock 'n' roll. It was unusual for a rock band to take this approach, but Garcia and the others weren't inclined to stay with the safe, the tried-and-true. More than anything else—more than the symbols, more than the psychedelics, more than the caravans of supporters—this penchant for innovation was how Garcia and the Grateful Dead made their mark in the music world.

4

THE MUSICIAN
FOR THE
WOODSTOCK NATION

Since the Gold Rush in the middle 1800s, San Francisco had been welcoming disparate groups to its fair shores. People came to the city from all over the world in search of economic opportunity. As each group arrived, they were absorbed into the whirlwind of the city's life. In 1966, however, a new breed of emigrants, who were generally not interested in climbing the ladder of success, began to flood into San Francisco. The hippies had arrived.

The word *hippie* was coined by journalist Michael Fallon in an article about the denizens of Haight-Ashbury for the *San Francisco Examiner* in September 1965. Hippie philosophy embraced a few basic tenets: the use of mind-altering drugs to expand one's consciousness, with marijuana and LSD being the drugs of choice; the notion of "doing your own thing," which encouraged spontaneity and freedom from artificial social restraints—a sort of existential living from one moment to the next; a disregard for the trappings of capitalism, manifested in the formation of communes, where members lived cooperatively, sharing living space and daily expenses; and the notion of "the free trip," promulgated most practically by a group of people known as the Diggers, who worked in and around the San Francisco neighborhood of Haight-Ashbury.

In the early part of the twentieth century, Haight-Ashbury had been an upscale community known as Politicians' Row, and it was full of ornate Victorian mansions. However, by the 1950s the area had fallen into disfavor with the city's social elite, and also into general disrepair. In the early 1960s, an entire house, complete with leaded windows and ballroom, could be rented for a few hundred dollars a month. This made it attractive to college students, who could share a large house for a mere pittance compared to other areas in the city. In addition, since it was situated near Golden Gate Park, the neighborhood was close to the University of San Francisco and San Francisco State College. The same conditions—intellectual ferment and low rents—made the Haight attractive to other nonconformist groups. Beatniks, who had previously congregated in the North Beach section, started to migrate to Haight-Ashbury to get away from tourists, escalating rents, and police harassment. The Beat poets Michael McClure, Lawrence Ferlinghetti, and Gary Snyder, who lived in the Haight, had a natural affinity with the students, and this provided a solid basis for the 1960s bohemian community thus spawned—the hippies. But when the torch was passed from the Beats to the hippies, the semantics of alienation and nihilism were replaced with sex, drugs, and rock 'n' roll.

The rock 'n' roll part of this life-style was flowering in San Francisco in 1966, as dance concerts featuring local bands were held weekend after weekend at the Avalon, the Fillmore, and other venues. The Grateful Dead, Quicksilver Messenger Service, the Jefferson Airplane, and Big Brother and the Holding Company were evolving a style of music—the San Francisco sound—conducive to improvisation, to stretching the limits of the art form. Since San Francisco had a radical tradition in which eccentricity was accepted (for instance, noncommercial radio station KPFA had been on the air for more than a decade broadcasting commentary, poetry, literature, and music of all kinds in a free-wheeling manner), the environment encouraged experimentation and provided the possibility for a musical breakthrough.

In the meantime, the population of the Haight was exploding as word about the Acid Tests, the Trips Festival, and the dance concerts spread. By the middle of 1966, it was estimated that fifteen thousand hippies were living in Haight-Ashbury. Many of these young men and women were coming to the area with little except what they carried in old rucksacks, trusting that they would survive somehow. In the Haight they found a patron saint in the form of Emmett Grogan, the leader of the Diggers. This group set up the Free Store, which gave away secondhand clothing, and also had daily food giveaways in the Panhandle, a strip of park a few blocks north of Haight Street, for Haight-Ashbury residents.

Through the actions of the Diggers, the numerous communes, and other civic-minded people, a sense of community developed in Haight-Ashbury. Therefore, it was only natural that a local newspaper would emerge—the *San Francisco Oracle*, a psychedelic tabloid that made no secret of its editorial slant: promoting the virtues of LSD. The *Oracle* was financed by Ron and Jay Thelin, the owners of the Psychedelic Shop, a head shop on the corner of Haight and Ashbury streets that sold everything an acidhead might be interested in. Allen Cohen, the editor of the *Oracle*, wanted the paper's contents "to provide guidance and archetypes for the journey through the states of mind that the LSD experience had opened up." The paper's manifesto was, "We hold these experiences to be self-evident, that all is equal, that the creation endows us with certain inalienable rights, that among them are: the freedom of the body, the pursuit of joy, and the expansion of consciousness."

The Trips Festival and the weekly dance concerts had also caught the attention of a more worldly group of people—music executives, who sent scouts to San Francisco to recruit bands for their labels. Through Tom Donahue, the person who had recorded their Emergency Crew demo, the Grateful Dead met Joe Smith, an executive at Warner Brothers, who came to see the Dead perform at the Avalon one weekend in the summer of 1966 and was convinced that the music was the sound of the future. Smith decided he wanted to sign the band, but when Donahue escorted him backstage, the boys were less than hospitable. Firmly rooted in the antiestablishment distrust of big business, they feared being ripped off by the record companies. (Through the years, the group has had its share of problems with large record companies, both financially and artistically, so perhaps this distrust was well-considered.)

Although Smith sensed that the Dead's music was new and exciting, he really didn't have a clue to what it was all about, since his perspective was that of the square world of Top-40 popular music. He found it necessary to work through Donahue, who at least had the band's trust. During negotiations, Garcia, whom Smith recalled was "the most visible, but he refused to speak for the band," and the others made it clear that they would not compromise their artistic integrity just to get a record contract. They insisted on retaining control over their music, and Smith ultimately agreed to let the band have the final say on the content of their albums. Garcia explained their rock-ribbed stand: "We'd had all kinds of offers but we were never in a position to be able to control what we were doing. But because we held out, because we thought we were worth something, now we can do anything we want."

When the Warner lawyers had dotted the last i's on the voluminous contract, Smith brought it to San Francisco to be signed by the band. Even then, the straight Smith had to run a gauntlet, for the band insisted that he take some acid so that he could really appreciate what it was that they were doing with their music. Smith declined and managed to get the group to sign the deal. Included was a provision that Warner finance a series of free shows across the country when the band toured to promote their album. This fit in with the band's attitude toward playing, and it was a way that the band could give something tangible to their loyal fans.

* * * *

In September, the band got itself kicked out of their Camp Lagunitas retreat. It was then that most of the members moved into the house at 710 Ashbury Street. Rock Scully recounted how it came to pass: "Danny [Rifkin] was being the landlord at 710 Ashbury and I had a room upstairs, and we had to find a way to get everybody out of the house because we needed the whole house. Pig was so anxious to get back to San Francisco he said, 'Here's what we'll do: You and me come back to the house, even if we have to live in your room.' I said, 'Nah, why don't we just live in the kitchen?' Now Pigpen was so frightful-looking to regular people in those days. So me and Pig would just stay up late at night drinking in the kitchen of 710 Ashbury, and then one by one, the residents began to move out." Jerry, Bob, and Pigpen moved in, while Phil and Billy ended up getting a place nearby in Diamond Heights on Belvedere Street. Life for the Grateful Dead became a cooperative effort where food and money were shared by the band, which earned just enough for the members to get by and stay high.

The Dead played at the last official Acid Test on October 2, 1966, at San Francisco State, just a few days before LSD became illegal in California. This Acid Test was put on by Stewart Brand and was variously called The Awareness Festival or Whatever It Is. Ken Kesey, the original spirit behind the Acid Tests, had just returned from hiding out in Mexico for nine months. He was still wanted by the police, but planned to do a mystery broadcast on the campus radio station to the LSD trippers in the women's gym, where the Grateful Dead were playing. Mountain Girl, who had returned from Mexico with Kesey, resumed her budding relationship with Garcia. As she was one of the Pranksters, she and Jerry had gotten to know each other at the Acid Tests. David Nelson remembered, "When Garcia came back from the Portland Acid Test [January 1966] he was friendly with Mountain Girl, and before that he hardly knew her, and that's when I noticed a difference with Sarah."

The difference was that Garcia's relationship with Sarah had run its course. Jerry explained, "I suddenly realized that my little attempt at having a straight life and doing that was really a fiction and just wasn't going to work out." The two soon separated, with Sarah taking custody of their two-year-old daughter Heather.

Although the Garcias' life could hardly be characterized as "straight" in comparison to 1960s middle America, to Jerry what he had with Sarah was just that. Sarah had been wife and mother, while Jerry had been the breadwinner, despite the hippie trappings. Jerry was devoted to this situation, but his life and his aspirations had gone in a different direction. Mountain Girl was someone who was more in tune with where Garcia was heading.

With Sarah gone, Garcia's connection with Mountain Girl strengthened. Mountain Girl remembered, "[Kesey and I] had just come back from Mexico, and that's when I established a relationship with Jerry. I moved in with him at 710 Ashbury Street in San Francisco a few months later."

Mountain Girl, nee Carolyn Adams, was a well-educated woman from an upper-middle-class family in Poughkeepsie, New York. She was raised in the Unitarian Church, which gives its members the freedom to express their own individual belief. Carolyn apparently took this teaching to heart, and grew up to be bright, self-assured, and independent-minded. She moved from upstate New York to Palo Alto in 1963, and she was only eighteen when she hooked up with Kesey and the Pranksters the following year, courtesy of Neal Cassady, whom she had met at St. Michael's Alley. Cassady, who thought up her alias, convinced her to check out the scene at La Honda, so Carolyn jumped on her motorcycle and headed up to Kesey's place. She was a robust young woman, and her brash, out-front manner made her an immediate hit with the Pranksters. Self-confident and full of nerve, she jumped right into the psychedelic journey that became the Acid Tests. And she was just the kind of woman Garcia was attracted to—unconventional, game to try new experiences, and into getting high.

Staying high took on new dimensions after October 6, 1966, the day LSD became illegal in California. On that day the *Oracle* sponsored a free outdoor concert in the Panhandle called the Love Pageant Rally. The Dead, Big Brother and the Holding Company, and Wildflower performed for nearly a thousand hippies who were celebrating the expansion of consciousness that LSD brought about. The Dead played their new song, "Alice D. Millionaire," a thinly veiled reference to their benefactor, Owsley Stanley. (The day before, the *Los Angeles Times* had run a story headlined "The LSD Millionaire," detailing how Stanley had risen to be the King of Acid.)

The *San Francisco Chronicle* had reported Kesey's appear-

ance at the San Francisco State Acid Test and his announcement that he was planning an "LSD graduation ceremony" for
Halloween night. On October 20, Kesey, who had been playing
cat-and-mouse with the police, was arrested, and he told the
media that "taking acid is not the thing that's happening anymore"—but that he still planned to put on his Acid Test
Graduation. When asked what was going to replace acid, he
replied: "Leary's supposed to be coming out, and he's supposed
to know pieces of it. And Jerry Garcia with his music knows
pieces of it." When Kesey got out on bail, members of the
Haight community became suspicious of his motives and wondered whether he had been co-opted by the authorities.
Despite the controversy, the graduation went ahead as scheduled, with perhaps two hundred people in attendance, along
with newspaper reporters and television crews. The Dead had
another engagement, so Kesey enlisted the Anonymous Artists
of America, a group that featured Garcia's estranged wife
Sarah. The graduation had an actual commencement, and
diplomas were handed out to Acid Test veterans by Neal
Cassady, who made brief comments about each recipient.
Kesey made an address that surprised the authorities, who were
expecting a denunciation of drugs: "It [is] time to move on; this
doesn't mean to stop taking acid, but to do something besides
get stoned and go to rock 'n' roll dances."

At the beginning of November, Garcia was putting Kesey's
words into action, moving on into a new endeavor. His friend
Jorma Kaukonen of the Jefferson Airplane asked Garcia to help

his group produce their second album featuring the Airplane's new lead singer, Grace Slick, which they were recording in Los Angeles at RCA Records. As happened frequently to San Francisco bands in those early days of record industry awareness, the Airplane had been given a producer who didn't really know the sound they wanted to achieve. So Garcia went to Los Angeles, ostensibly to help with the musical arrangements. Instead, Garcia showed up at the RCA studio with Jorma on November 1 and essentially took charge of the recording of the album. Kaukonen recalled the effect that Garcia had:

> Rick Jarrard, the producer of the album, was a well-known L.A. producer, but we needed somebody that could really understand what we were doing, to help us pull together. This is where Jerry came in. Jerry could be credited with really being the producer in the real sense of the word, in that he was one of us and he knew what to do with the band. None of the rest of us knew what to do with dynamics, when to play, when not to play, how to leave holes, how not to overplay. I mean, you have to remember, that from my point of view, I was coming from being a folk guitarist to just starting to play electric guitar. I was probably shamelessly self-indulgent, probably would have played non-stop if somebody had not said, "Don't play here—lighten up, let the song breathe." I think that Jerry was a little ahead of me on electric guitar, and I learned a lot from him. So Jerry was really important in that in the real sense he really was the producer who arranged those songs, but because of the politics at the record company he gets credit as being the spiritual advisor.

Jerry's background as the band leader of a variety of different groups—folk, old-time, bluegrass, jug band, rock—gave him experience in a wide range of musical styles, and he drew on that knowledge when he worked with the Airplane in the studio. Not only did he help shape the sound of the album by giving the band critical advice about the dynamics of the songs and arrangement of the instruments, he also laid down guitar tracks on four of the songs. In addition, Garcia's ideas for the guitar instrumentation on "White Rabbit" and "Somebody to Love" gave the songs their distinctive psychedelic sound and their acid-rock sensibility. The album was named *Surrealistic Pillow* because Garcia felt it was "as surrealistic as a pillow," and the album reached number 3 on the charts in 1967, with "Somebody to Love" and "White Rabbit" becoming hit singles.

On December 31, Garcia and Kaukonen worked together again, and this time the public was invited. Bill Graham hosted a year-end gala, the "New Year's Bash" featuring the Jefferson Airplane, the Grateful Dead, and Quicksilver Messenger Service. The show was held at the Fillmore, and was sort of a capper for Graham's meteoric rise to major power in the San Francisco music scene. To celebrate his success, Graham put together the first of what would become annual elaborate New Year's Eve celebrations. At the approach of midnight he had his manager, Jim Haynie, make a grand entrance from the back of the auditorium dressed as the New Year's baby, with eight Fillmore employees carrying him in on a platform. (In later years, Graham would play the white-bearded Father Time.) When the baby got to the stage, Graham counted down the final seconds of 1966, and at the stroke of midnight the

Grateful Dead broke into the opening chords of "Midnight Hour." Thus began a tradition of New Year's Eve extravaganzas that Graham became famous for.

Free concerts were at the heart of the Haight-Ashbury soul. With the success of the Love Pageant Rally the preceding October spurring them on, the hippies planned another event, the Human Be-In. Held on January 14, 1967, at the Polo Fields in Golden Gate Park, the Be-In attracted an estimated twenty thousand people and was a celebration of the new spirit of consciousness that had imbued the Haight. The Diggers were present, distributing thousands of turkey sandwiches made from turkeys donated by Owsley, who had also contributed a batch of his latest brew, White Lightning, his strongest LSD yet.

The Be-In was billed as "a gathering of the tribes," bringing together the disparate elements of the antiestablishment community—the Berkeley political activists, the San Francisco spiritual community, and the hippies. It featured poets Allen Ginsberg, Gary Snyder, and Michael McClure; acid guru Timothy Leary with his "turn on, tune in, drop out" philosophy; and the music of the Grateful Dead, Quicksilver Messenger Service, and the Jefferson Airplane. The Grateful Dead's set was described by music critic Ralph Gleason in the *San Francisco Chronicle* as "remarkably exciting, causing people to rise up wherever they were and begin dancing."

Garcia sang the Dead's version of "Morning Dew," a tune written by folksinger Bonnie Dobson that addressed the possibility of nuclear annihilation. The crowd, primarily hippies who espoused a "make love, not war" philosophy and antiwar activists, could relate to the antinuclear theme of the song. When the Be-In was over the positive vibrations from the success of the event infused the hippies of the Haight with a feeling of exhilaration and inspiration and a sense that they were changing the world.

The free concert was an integral part of the musical philosophy of Garcia and the Dead, and they performed numerous such concerts in Golden Gate Park and the Panhandle for the people of San Francisco, becoming the city's community band. Most often the concerts were spontaneous gestures on their part. Totally ignoring the authorities and their codes, the band would play without permits. Getting flatbed trucks to use as a stage and a generator for power, they would set up and play until the cops shut them down. Afterward, sweep-ins were organized to clean up the grounds, with Garcia and the band joining in to keep the park clean. Jerry noted, "Our first free things were done sort of in conjunction with the Diggers, who were now working on giving free food to people down in the Panhandle. It seemed like a good idea to go down there and play for them one weekend. We got a truck and a generator with the help of the Diggers and Emmett and all those guys and we just went down there and played. . . . It was simple, and it was free in the sense that nobody had to do it, it was truly free. We were able to do that pretty comfortably for almost a year."

*   *   *   *

Several days after the Be-In, Garcia was headed to Los Angeles with the band to record their first album for Warner Brothers. The band chose Dave Hassinger as producer because he had engineered a couple of Rolling Stones albums that impressed them. The album, entitled *Grateful Dead*, was recorded in three days. There were two original songs on the album, "The Golden Road (to Unlimited Devotion)," credited to the fictitious McGannahan Skjellyfetti (a pseudonym the band used); and "Cream Puff War," which was attributed to Garcia. The remaining songs were covers of old blues, folk, or jug band tunes. The only extended cut on the album was "Viola Lee Blues," which was ten minutes long and more representative of the improvisational music the band was doing in concert.

The album cover, designed by Mouse Studios, consisted of a collage that Alton Kelley put together with cryptic lettering across the top by Stanley Mouse. Originally, the lettering formed a sentence from the Egyptian Book of the Dead that read: "In the land of the dark the ship of the sun is driven by the Grateful Dead," but the band wanted it changed. Garcia explained: "We didn't like it because we thought it was a tad pretentious. So we talked to Stanley and said could you do something that almost says something but doesn't quite. The result of that has been that all the places we've been where people have had that album, we've been able to hear their translations—fantastic ones, incredible ones!" The band is identified on the album cover in this way: SAN FRANCISCO'S GRATEFUL DEAD: Bob Weir, Pigpen, Bill the drummer, Jerry ("Captain Trips") Garcia, and Phil Lesh.

Although the songs were almost all standards that the band played in concert, the album had a different feel to it because the tempos of the songs themselves were accelerated. In fact, the band had been taking Mountain Girl's diet pills while they were in the studio. Mountain Girl had come down to Los Angeles with the band, staying with Garcia at the Tropicana Motel, and the boys got into her diet pills. Garcia described the experience, "At the time we had no real record consciousness. . . . We were completely naive about it. . . . So we went down there and what was it we had, Dexamyl? Some sort of diet-watcher's speed, and pot and stuff like that. So in three nights we played some hyperactive music."

Mountain Girl remembered, "Their producer was this typical L.A. guy, with jowls, heavy tan, long slicked-back hair, lots of Vitalis, white cardigan sweater with a gold wristwatch. They couldn't handle Dave Hassinger at all, but he was trying to be cool and they were giving him a hard time. He'd make suggestions and they would say stuff like, 'It'll ruin everything if we do it that way.' The album came out and it's my favorite album and will always be my favorite because that is the time Jerry and I got together and started living together."

Upon their return to San Francisco, Mountain Girl moved into 710 Ashbury and immediately began to give it her touch. The police had previously harassed the band about the living conditions there and were looking for any excuse to get them evicted. Rock Scully would get on Garcia and Pigpen to clean the place up: "I was pleading with them, cajoling them, threatening them with total doom—like your parents would—that if they didn't pick up their rooms we were going to be out on the street." Scully's harangues had about as much effect as if the band's parents had been doing the yelling. Only when Mountain Girl arrived did things begin to straighten up. She was determined to whip the place into shape, and she had the nerve to stand up to the others and get them moving on the project.

Mountain Girl and Garcia were very much into communal living. MG would prepare meals, and everyone would eat together. The house was jampacked all the time, and there would be great scenes on the front porch and steps. MG recalled, "Everybody from the street would come up and rap with us. . . . The sun would shine and we'd all sit out there on the steps and the fog would pour out. We'd talk and talk and smoke joints and have a good time." The other San Francisco bands—Quicksilver, Big Brother, Jefferson Airplane—would stop by at any time to hang out, play music, or talk, increasing the camaraderie amongst these musicians, the trading of influences that would show up in each band's work.

With the new order at 710 and the Dead's standing in the neighborhood, the house became a de facto community center, and was considered by many to be the spiritual center of what was happening in Haight-Ashbury. Garcia recalled, "Our place got to be a center of energy, and people were in there organizing stuff . . . trying to start various spiritual movements . . . trying to get various benefits on for various trips. . . . There would be a lot of motion, a lot of energy exchanged, and it was all real high in those days because at the time the Haight-Ashbury was a community . . . what the hippie scene was—it was just a very small neighborhood affair when we were all working for each other's benefit."

Jerry expanded on this idea in a 1967 interview at 710. When asked what the hippie movement was trying to accomplish, he replied, "We're thinking about a peaceful planet, we're not thinking about anything else. We're not thinking about any kind of power, we're not thinking about any of those kinds of struggles. We're not thinking about revolution or war or any of that. That's not what we want. Nobody wants to get hurt, nobody wants to hurt anybody. We all want to be able to live an uncluttered life, a simple life, a good life, and think about moving the whole human race ahead a step or a few steps."

The February 6, 1967, issue of *Newsweek* had an article on the hippies entitled "Dropouts with a Mission." It began, "They smile and call themselves a new race. . . . Psychedelic drugs are their instant passport to Nirvana. . . . Like the Beatniks of the '50s, they are in the long tradition of Bohemia: seeking a vision of the totally free life. They are, of course, the hippies." The article featured photos by Gene Anthony, one a color picture of Garcia in an Uncle Sam hat with the caption "Captain Trips," and the text described Garcia as "the leader of the Grateful Dead, who has earned the nickname 'Captain Trips' because of his interest in LSD excursions." Questioned as to whether the hippies wanted to change society, Garcia responded: "Our attitude is strictly laissez-faire," a statement to which Garcia has generally stayed true through the years.

*   *   *   *

Soon after *Grateful Dead* was released in March 1967, something happened in radio that helped ensure the band's place in music history. On April 7, radio station KMPX switched its format to become the very first FM rock station, ushering in a new era of free-form radio. The station played cuts from albums instead of Top-40 singles, did away with the three-minute maximum for songs that the AM stations had, and played sets of three or four songs in a row without interruption and without deejay chatter over the beginnings and endings. KMPX also became an open bulletin board for the hip community, announcing dances and benefits and news of the San Francisco bands. Word of this revolutionary radio format spread, and soon FM stations in New York, Boston, and other cities began broadcasting their own brand of free-form radio.

Tom Donahue, the person who helped the Dead land their record contract, had just taken over the eight-to-midnight slot on KMPX, and he helped the group launch their album by playing it on his show. But despite the airtime on KMPX and some of the other FM stations, *Grateful Dead* wasn't selling well nationally. Warner Brothers had attempted to market the band by running a "Pigpen Look-Alike Contest" and starting a fan club. To get some more exposure the band played New York for the first time, and word about the "community band" from San Francisco began to get out.

An even greater boost to the Dead's reputation came with their appearance at the Monterey Pop Festival in June. The festival was held on the Monterey County Fairgrounds, for years the site of the Monterey Jazz Festival. On the weekend of June 16-18, the fairground was home to rock 'n' roll before fifty thousand people. The festival organizers flew in one hundred thousand orchid blossoms from Hawaii and handed them out to everyone entering the fairgrounds on Friday. Owsley arrived with a special batch of LSD he called Monterey Purple, and he was distributing it freely to all takers backstage.

Reading the lineup of the festival is like reading a who's who of 1960s music. Some of the featured groups included Eric Burdon and the Animals, Simon and Garfunkel, Canned Heat, Big Brother and the Holding Company, Country Joe and the Fish, the Paul Butterfield Blues Band, Quicksilver Messenger Service, the Steve Miller Band, the Byrds, Laura Nyro, the Jefferson Airplane, Booker T and the MGs, Otis Redding, Ravi Shankar, the Buffalo Springfield, the Who, the Grateful Dead, the Jimi Hendrix Experience, and the Mamas and the Papas.

The three-day event attracted widespread media attention, made stars of Jimi Hendrix and Janis Joplin, and opened the nation's ears to groups who were on the verge of greatness. It also introduced the San Francisco sound to the world. The music of the Grateful Dead, the Jefferson Airplane, and Quicksilver Messenger Service represented the artistic vanguard of rock 'n' roll, and the bands' performances at Monterey gave them exposure to a wide audience.

When the Dead was due to play on Sunday, Phil Lesh encouraged the promoters to open up the gates and let in the people who did not have tickets. "This is the last concert, why not let them in anyway?" Even in a commercial venture, the free concert lived. A cheer went up as the crowd was let in, and Garcia led the band into "Viola Lee Blues." Despite this, thousands of music-lovers were shut out of the sold-out festival and arrangements were made to stage some free music at a nearby site, and some historic post-festival jam sessions occurred. Rock

Scully recalled, "I realized [Monterey] was going to be oversold, so consequently I helped arrange impromptu jam sessions at the free campground that we organized at Monterey College. . . . We set up a stage, and after the shows the various bands would put on jam sessions—Jimi Hendrix, Eric Burdon, Jerry Garcia, Phil Lesh, the Airplane. . . . It was Garcia, Phil, and individual musicians from various bands jamming together. At the time we hadn't met some of the musicians. We hadn't met Hendrix, and we didn't know the Who. We got to know them there. We all took acid together and played all night."

Chet Helms, who emceed part of the festival and also helped set up the free stage, observed, "Virtually everyone who played on the main stage played in some configuration on the free stage: members of the Dead, the Airplane, Quicksilver, Janis Joplin, and Hendrix. After the shows had ended, some of the musicians had a jam session. One jam involved Jimi Hendrix on guitar and David Freiberg on bass, and they played for several hours. We were totally out of our minds on acid and it was wonderful. . . . The last night of Monterey Pop everyone took a lot of Owsley acid. There were big gallon jars of Monterey Pop Festival Purple going around, and you could dip your hand in and take a fistful out and stick them in your pocket, and it was being passed out to the crowd and being taken by everyone."

Jorma Kaukonen remembered the jam session he was a part of: "There were all kinds of jams going on after the show. I recall it was one of the two times I got to play with Hendrix. There was Jimi, John Cippolina, myself, and some other musicians. The thing about jams like that is that some of them are probably more memorable in memory than they would be if the tapes existed, because we were just wailing and carrying on. But still in all, these were important interactions because of the dialogue. It's a great way to get to know people, and I'm sure these were all important moments for everybody there."

A persistent rumor—it remained only a rumor—circulated at Monterey that the Beatles were going to perform there. The rumor was probably fueled by a number of things. The souvenir festival program had a message from the Beatles— "Love to Monterey from Sgt. Pepper's Lonely Hearts Club Band." Sunday, June 18, the last day of the festival, was Paul McCartney's birthday. (He told the press that to celebrate, he had taken LSD and it had made him "a better, more honest, more tolerant member of society, brought closer to God." He said he wasn't advocating LSD, but if the leaders of the world took it even once, they would "banish war, poverty, and famine.") And earlier that month the Beatles had released their landmark album, *Sgt. Pepper's Lonely Hearts Club Band*, generally considered the most important LP in rock music history. It was the first record to publish lyrics on the cover and was the first "concept album" in rock music. It became a staple for FM underground radio. *Sgt. Pepper's Lonely Hearts Club Band* introduced millions of people to psychedelic music, and became the unofficial soundtrack for the Summer of Love.

The Monterey Pop Festival had been a hugely successful and peaceful event, and Monterey Police Chief Frank Marinello informed the press, "I feel the hippies are my friends, and I am asking one of them to take me to the Haight-Ashbury."

*   *   *   *

Although the summer solstice occurred on June 21 in 1967, the Summer of Love had begun months before when young people started to migrate to Haight-Ashbury in large numbers. The Human Be-In in January and the Monterey Pop Festival had focused a lot of attention on the San Francisco hippie scene, and it is estimated that in the first half of 1967 Haight-Ashbury's population of hippies grew by fifty thousand. The mainstream press continued to take the hippies seriously, and *Time* magazine's July 5, 1967 cover story was titled "The Hippies: Philosophy of a Subculture."

As increasing numbers of young people from across the country moved to Haight-Ashbury, the neighborhood atmosphere began to dissipate. With the spotlight of national attention focused on it, the Haight became a tourist attraction, and the Grateful Dead house at 710 Ashbury became a stop on the Gray Line bus tour.

The notoriety the Grateful Dead were receiving was certainly good for the band's career, but the downside was that they were perceived by the media as advocates of the hippie movement who were trying to change the world by spreading the message of peace, love, and flower power. Rock Scully explained, "Though at times we felt like the messenger, it was tough on the band because the Grateful Dead were just a band of musicians who didn't mean to be proponents of any movement. At best they were representative of San Francisco's music scene and never meant to be in the vanguard of any youth movement."

Garcia elaborated, "We're trying to make music in such a way that it doesn't have a message for anybody. We don't have anything to tell anybody. We don't want to change anybody.

We want people to have the chance to feel a little better. That's the absolute most we want to do with our music. The music that we make is an act of love, an act of joy . . . we're not telling people to go get stoned, or drop out." Though the Grateful Dead considered themselves hippies, they weren't leaders of the hippie movement. They wanted to be recognized as musicians, but they were being written up as pot-smoking, LSD-crazed hippies who happened to be musicians. In response to this misperception, Garcia stated, "We are trying to make things groovier for everybody so more people can feel better more often, to advance the trip, to get higher, however you want to say it—but we're musicians, and there's just no way to put the idea 'save the world' into music."

By the end of the summer, the optimistic view of the hippies expressed by Monterey Police Chief Marinello after the Monterey Pop Festival had worn thin. There were too many of these young kids on the streets, and too much of a drug scene for the nervous police and city officials. While tour operators included the Grateful Dead house as a landmark, and many in the hippie community considered it to be the spiritual center of Haight-Ashbury, the authorities decided to make an example of the Grateful Dead in an attempt to control the hippies. On October 2, San Francisco narcotics officers raided the house and arrested Weir, Pigpen, Rock Scully, Danny Rifkin, sound-man Bob Matthews, and some friends. (Garcia and Mountain Girl escaped arrest because they were away from the house at the time.) Two days later, the police again arrested Scully for "being the lessee of a house for the purpose of unlawfully selling, giving away, or using narcotics." At a press conference several days later Rifkin read a prepared statement protesting the bust and the onerous law making possession of marijuana a felony. The statement concluded, "all we wish is to be free Americans endowed with certain inalienable rights among which, somebody once said, are life, liberty, and the pursuit of happiness. Is this so frightening? The Grateful Dead are people engaged in constructive, creative effort in the musical field, and this house is where we work, as well as our residence. Because the police fear and misinterpret us, our effort is now interrupted as we deal with the consequences of a harassing arrest."

Although nothing ever came of the events, the authorities had sent a clear message to the hippies of Haight-Ashbury that their life-style was not going to be tolerated, even in this moderate city. The residents challenged the authorities in typical nonviolent fashion, announcing a Death of Hippie ceremony to be held on October 6, the one-year anniversary of California's prohibition of LSD. The ceremony reflected a feeling among many in the hip community that things had begun to sour for the movement with the influx of tens of thousands of people and all the media coverage that the hippies and the Haight were receiving. The Death of Hippie press release made an attempt to save the idealistic dream of the Haight from the nightmare of overcrowding, crime, and exploitation: "The media cast nets, creates bags for the identity-hungry to climb in. Your face on TV, your style immortalized without soul in the captions of the *Chronicle*." A Wake for Hippie was held at the All Saints Church, and a funeral procession that began at Buena Vista Hill marched down Haight Street with a cardboard coffin. It was the symbolic beginning of the end for a scene that had started out of a search for an alternative reality than what was offered by America in the early 1960s, but had begun to suffocate because of the attraction it held for the restless youth of America.

By March 1968 Haight-Ashbury was so crowded that the city decided to close portions of Haight Street to vehicles on weekends and make it into a pedestrian mall. On Sunday, March 3, the Grateful Dead decided to play a free concert on Haight Street without getting a permit. They piled all their equipment on to two flatbed trucks, parked them back to back across Haight Street in front of the Straight Theatre, and played to several thousand people who packed the street. It was an incredible experience for the community, but it was the culmination of the free era. Garcia remembered, "That was kinda like our swan song to Haight Street. To the whole scene. It was the very height of the most highly publicized, highly energized moment. . . . It was really a great day, but that was the end of it." The population of Haight-Ashbury had gotten too large for the community to support it. With the demise of the Haight-Ashbury scene, the musicians, the artists, and the hip merchants who made up the community began migrating north to Marin and Sonoma counties. Garcia explained, "When the big media flash came out—when the *Time* magazine guys came out and interviewed everybody and took photographs and made it news, the feedback from that killed the whole scene."

In the fall of 1967 the Grateful Dead went down to Los Angeles to begin recording their second album for Warner, *Anthem of the Sun*. Despite the unpleasant experience the band had with him earlier that year, Dave Hassinger was again their producer. The band took a different approach from the first album, deciding to spend the time to make it sound good. Thus, they stayed in Los Angeles for a few weeks laying down the basic tracks of songs. At the same time, though, managers Scully and Rifkin were anxious to promote the band, and booked another tour to the East Coast. Thus, December 1967 found them in New York City for several weeks, playing gigs at nights and recording at studios in their off time. Not surprisingly, friction again developed between the band and their producer, and halfway through recording, Hassinger quit the project.

Bidding a not-so-reluctant goodbye to their first professional producer, the band decided to produce the album themselves. Garcia hit upon the idea of using tapes of live shows in conjunction with the studio takes. He described the approach: "We weren't making a record in the normal sense; we were making a collage. We were trying to do something completely different, which didn't even have to do with a concept. It had to do with an approach that's more like electronic music or concrete music, where you are actually assembling bits and pieces toward an enhanced nonrealistic representation."

Anthem of the Sun was an attempt to re-create in the studio what the band was doing in concert. On stage, the band would often seque from one song to the next, which at that time was not a common format for albums. And because of the improvisational nature of the Dead's music, one live performance was always different from any other. The mixing of live tapes with studio tracks approached this feeling, producing an assembled version that was different from anything else.

The band recorded live performances in January, February, and March 1968 to get material for the album. Then Garcia, Lesh, and sound engineer Dan Healy spent two more months mixing the different performances to smooth the transitions and blend the edit. The result was a continuous suite of music featuring all original songs written by the Grateful Dead. Garcia was happy: "We mixed it for the hallucinations, and it worked great."

The bust in the fall of 1967 and the increasing deterioration of Haight-Ashbury finally drove the Grateful Dead out of their house at 710 Ashbury. Garcia was the first member of the band to go, fifteen or twenty miles out in Marin County where he and Mountain Girl got a place under the redwoods, up a canyon on Madrone Drive in Larkspur. Robert Hunter also moved into the house. This was the beginning of a serious Garcia-Hunter songwriting team, with Hunter providing the lyrics and Garcia composing the music.

Hunter recalled, "When we lived together in Larkspur, the way we'd write a song was I'd sit upstairs banging away at my three chords for days and days working something out. By the time I had it worked out, through the thin walls he'd heard everything I was doing. I'd come down and hand him this sheet of paper, and he'd say 'Oh, that's interesting,' and he'd play the whole arrangement of it right away, because he'd heard what I was doing and heard where it was going."

The collaboration resulted in a batch of new songs that formed the basis for the next Grateful Dead album,

Aoxomoxoa. All the words to the songs on that album were written by Hunter: "St. Stephen," "Dupree's Diamond Blues," "Rosemary," "Doin' That Rag," "Mountains of the Moon," "Chinacat Sunflower," "What's Become of the Baby," and "Cosmic Charlie." As the lyricist for the band Hunter became an essential member of the Grateful Dead, and his evocative poetry and story-telling formed the basis for the body of songs the band would record over the years.

Though Garcia liked the tunes on the album, he felt that the record was not very successful because "it was when Hunter and I were both being more or less obscure and there are lots of levels on the verbal plane in terms of the lyrics being very far out. Too far out, really, for most people." For example, Garcia described "What's Become of the Baby" as "madcap excursions into utter weirdness." At the time, Hunter was fascinated with the magical properties of words, and his poetry at times was difficult to set to music. *Aoxomoxoa* was their first concerted song-writing effort. Garcia explained, "I would just get words from him, and I would make an effort to set them as they were. I wasn't interested in interfering with them."

As Garcia was leading the Dead more heavily into improvisation, the group essentially split into two camps. Garcia and Lesh shared a common interest in experimentation, along the lines of modern jazz. Weir and Pigpen were more into music that was structured as songs, and they had a hard time with the direction the band was taking. Pigpen wasn't open to it, and Weir was still developing as a guitarist. Weir recalled, "I didn't have all that great a vocabulary as a guitarist at that point. And my role, then as ever, was a fairly difficult one: being in between the lead and the bass and intuiting where the hell they're going to go and being there. It took a while to work up a touch for that."

As the Grateful Dead's manager, Rock Scully was given the unhappy task of dealing with Weir and Pigpen. "Jerry kind of put it on me to [fire Pigpen and Weir]. It was a totally musical decision." To play the music that he had decided on, Garcia formed the group Mickey Hart and the Hartbeats in October 1968, using the name of the musician who had joined the Dead in the fall of 1967 as their second drummer.

Mickey Hart was a native New Yorker who had moved to California in the mid-1960s and was helping his father, Lenny, run his music store in San Carlos down on the Peninsula. Mickey's father had been a national- and world-champion rudimental drummer, and his mother had played drums as well. Naturally, Mickey became a champion percussionist himself.

The Hart Music Center at that time offered drum clinics at the store conducted by famous drummers. The biggest name involved with these clinics was Sonny Payne, who was Count Basie's drummer, and Mickey loved his style of playing. One night, Mickey was at the Fillmore for a Basie concert, and he met Bill Kreutzmann, another big fan of Payne's. The two young men struck up a friendship and began hanging out and drumming together. Kreutzmann asked Hart to sit in with the Grateful Dead during a gig at the Straight Theatre in Haight-Ashbury in September 1967; Hart accepted, and the music clicked.

Kreutzmann was more of a straight rhythm man, whereas

Hart was as much a percussionist as a drummer. Thus, the two complemented each other instead of distracting from each other and from the sound of the Dead. Although Garcia and Lesh definitely set the tone during the band's improvisational period, Hart's virtuosity and willingness to investigate odd time signatures well beyond the basic rock mold of threes and fours greatly aided the group's avant-garde sound.

Tom Constanten remembered that "Mickey Hart and the Hartbeats was a period of time when Garcia and Lesh were into a more extended improvisation trip, which was exactly what Weir and Pigpen were less into. Weir and Pigpen were more into songs, like song producers." Garcia, Lesh, Hart, and Kreutzmann performed a few shows in San Francisco, playing instrumental music with lots of improvisation and long jams. Blues guitarist Elvin Bishop and bass guitarist Jack Casady sat in with them at a couple of the shows to augment the ensemble. However, the grand experiment did not last, and the two factions joined again to re-create the Grateful Dead.

The Hartbeats was an interesting side trip for Garcia, but it wasn't enough by itself to hold his attention. Though the break with Pigpen and Weir could have been a serious split, Jerry found he missed the dynamics of playing with all the members of the Grateful Dead. It was a part of him he could not leave behind. However, the short break opened his eyes to the advantages of playing with other musicians when his schedule would allow it, and in 1969 he began doing more of that. This extracurricular performing allowed Garcia to scratch his musical itches in a way—he could play music he liked that the Dead didn't ordinarily do, and he could try out new instruments and new techniques. Garcia's love of rhythm and blues, bluegrass, and old-time music ultimately led him to form a number of different side groups over the ensuing years.

It was during the Grateful Dead's drift toward experimentation that Garcia and Lesh asked Phil's friend Tom Constanten to join the group as keyboardist. TC's first work with the Grateful Dead came in late 1967 when he helped out on a couple of tracks for *Anthem of the Sun*. Though TC was in the Air Force at the time, he managed to get away to join the band in Los Angeles during the *Anthem* sessions as well as the *Aoxomoxoa* sessions. TC summarized how he was asked to join the Grateful Dead: "It was basically an invitation from Jerry. He said, 'I think we can use you.'" Constanten's keyboards give *Aoxomoxoa* a distinctive sound, and Garcia thought his calliope-like organ playing on "Dupree's Diamond Blues" was perfect for the song. Though Constanten developed his own keyboard arrangements for the songs on the album, he readily admitted "everything was essentially subject to Jerry's approval." Constanten described Garcia as "one of the remarkable men of our times. So inventive, so assured, so alert, so amazingly aware in and out of musical contexts. He takes the responsibility personally, that the music should unfold interestingly." He elaborated, "He thinks of himself as a weaver of tapestries, and you provide the fabric."

Upon being discharged from the Air Force on November 22, 1968, TC started touring with the Dead. Constanten attempted to carve out a niche for his keyboard playing by trying "to wedge his organ runs in between Jerry's melodic leads and Weir's atonalist rhythm guitar, with its odd accents and emphasis on the offbeats." It was during Constanten's tenure in the band that the Grateful Dead evolved from a jamming blues-rock band into a septet capable of extraordinary improvisation. His background in avant-garde music was perfectly suited for the free-form music the band played during open-ended pieces like "Dark Star," which TC characterized as "exploratory ventures—possibly you could use the word *experimental* for that—it's not so much a set piece, that you know where you are in it and know where you're gonna go, as you're out on an ocean in a boat and you can choose your landmarks and response to things and move in certain directions as you wish—of course, always interacting."

Of the feedback passages that characterized the Dead's improvisational style of the time, Constanten likened them to "your mammoth bringing of a plane in for a landing at the end of a huge jam. A guitar solo would naturally lead into feedback because you're pushing it for its last ounce of explosive power."

Garcia related, "One time Pigpen and Phil and Weir and I went up to Los Trancos, in the hills up above Palo Alto, back when we were the Warlocks, playing divorcees' bars down the Peninsula. So we're up there on this hilltop, and this jet coming in for a landing comes right over our heads, and the sound that it made just absolutely split the universe—the vortex from its engines—and we're standing there and it was like somebody comes through and just wipes the slate clean! I mean that noise just took everything, it took all of history with it. The sound was absolutely cataclysmic, a huge sound. Right there for me was a moment in which everything—all sound, music, and everything else included—was born again. That was the moment when noise became a useful part of my musical vocabulary. I started working for a long time to get my guitar to sound like a jet engine."

There were times when the feedback passages at the end of a long jam were so powerful, listeners would swear it was thunder or the earth opening up. The effect on the audience was palpable, as the band roared into an incredible, ear-splitting barrage of sound. Depending on one's frame of mind it could wrench the senses or else be a cathartic, uplifting experience.

The recording of *Aoxomoxoa* turned into an eight-month project, with the band running up a $100,000 debt to Warner Brothers for the studio time they used, an amount that would be deducted from any royalties they earned from the album. It was another complex album, as *Anthem* had been, and it was recorded on sixteen tracks, which was state-of-the-art at the time. Garcia described it as "one of my pet records, 'cause it was the first stuff that I thought was starting to sound like how I wanted to hear songs sound." However, in order to extricate themselves from their debt to Warner Brothers, Jerry and the band decided to give the company a double live album at the same time. Warner Brothers went for the idea and the band started making sixteen-track tapes of their live shows at the Fillmore West and the Avalon during the early part of 1969. These tapes eventually became the album *Live Dead*, which captured the Grateful Dead at the height of their improvisational ability. It was a success financially as well as artistically, making enough money to pay the bills for *Aoxomoxoa*.

Though *Live Dead* was compiled from recordings of several nights, it was fundamentally one performance, and Garcia was pleased with the results. "We'd only recorded a few gigs to get that album. We were after a certain sequence to the music. In the sense of it being a serious, long composition, musically, and then a recording of it, it's our music at one of its really good moments."

There were a number of changes in the world of rock 'n' roll that were about to have a heavy impact on Garcia and the Dead. One was a local matter—the demise of the Family Dog concerts—the original source of the dance concerts that so excited Garcia. That summer, Chet Helms moved the Family Dog concerts to an old dance hall in the Playland amusement park, right across the street from the Pacific Ocean. The move was intended to cut expenses. His major competitor, Bill Graham, was winning the promotional duel of San Francisco because of his better business sense and some hard-nosed tactics. In an effort to block the Family Dog's access to bands, Graham drew up restrictive contracts barring groups from playing the Avalon for a year after they played the Fillmore. Though many of the out-of-town bands went along with this, most of the local musicians did not.

Shortly after the Family Dog on the Great Highway opened, the people who did the light shows at concerts went on strike for higher pay and equal billing with the bands. Anonymous letters were sent to Graham and Helms threatening pickets at the Fillmore West, Winterland, and the Family Dog if the demands weren't met.

On August 1, a picket line was thrown up outside a Grateful Dead concert at the Family Dog. (The Light Artists Guild figured that Helms would be easier to intimidate than the tougher Graham.) When Lesh and Weir showed up at the gig, tempers flared and a fight nearly broke out. Then Garcia arrived and managed to cool things down enough to get a dialogue going. Dennis McNally, the Dead's publicist, explained: "Jerry Garcia's grandmother, who raised him, was a co-founder of the Laundry Workers' Union of San Francisco. Jerry believes in labor. Jerry couldn't cross the picket line. When I asked him about it, his immediate response was, 'My grandmother.'" Garcia, Helms, and a contingent of picketers got into the Grateful Dead's equipment van to talk it out and determined that they all had more in common than they thought—everyone was in debt except Graham. Garcia mediated a decision to hold a meeting at the Family Dog the following Tuesday, and the picket signs came down.

Garcia declared, "The whole thing was stupid. What Jerry Abrams [of Jerry Abrams Headlights] hadn't figured out was that people didn't go to shows because of the light show. They went for the music. . . . I couldn't make any sense of it. But I felt I should take it seriously, since it was part of my community. I certainly would be involved in mediating it." Nothing was resolved at the Tuesday meeting, and it was the death knell for the light shows. Graham simply eliminated them from his concerts, and Helms would soon close the Family Dog for good because of his continuing financial problems.

*   *   *   *

Garcia and the other musicians had little time to mull what
was happening to the original patron of dance concerts in San
Francisco. Though the Summer of Love had ended in a crush
of humanity in 1968, the rock groups that were connected with
it had risen to national prominence. A couple of weeks after
the light show fiasco, the Grateful Dead, Jefferson Airplane,
and Janis Joplin found themselves on a farm in upstate New
York performing before the largest audience ever assembled for
a rock concert. The Woodstock Music and Arts Festival was
held August 15-17, and a crowd of nearly half a million people joined together for a joyous weekend of peace and love, and
rock 'n' roll played by dozens of the top bands representing the
entire spectrum of rock.

However, it wasn't the music that set Woodstock apart as
an historic event. With the whole world watching, it became
a communal experience that helped define a generation. Never
had a hippie gathering been so large or so successful. The community pulled together to keep the vibes peaceful. Wavy Gravy
and the Hog Farm commune were enlisted to help run security.
Asked by the press how he was going to control the immense
crowd, he replied, "Cream pies and seltzer bottles." At the Hog
Farm encampment a free kitchen was opened up that served
brown rice and bean soup. Sharing was the order of the day—
whether it was water, an apple, or a joint. The Pranksters drove
"the Bus" out from the West Coast and gave first aid to those in
need of medical attention.

Although Woodstock took on historic proportions, the
Grateful Dead's performance hardly matched the occasion.
The band's electrical equipment had not been grounded, and
the guitarists were getting shocked when they touched the

strings on their guitars. Garcia felt that their performance was "just plumb atrocious." He recalled, "We were on a metal stage and it was raining to boot and I was high and I saw blue balls of electricity bouncing across the stage and leaping onto my guitar when I touched the strings. No kidding—and all the intercom and CB radio, all that communication all came through the amplifiers, every bit of it. And there were helicopters buzzing by, drowning out everything. There was this hysterical rumor going round; guys yelling over the back of my amplifier, 'The stage is collapsing! The stage is collapsing!'"

Although the revelers out front of the stage probably didn't notice the difference in the band's sound, the professionals commiserated with the Dead. TC remembered, "I was sitting in a backstage tent after the set and someone came up to me and said, 'Great set!' Not five minutes later Paul Kantner walks up and says, 'Too bad you guys didn't have it tonight.'" When the *Woodstock* movie came out eighteen months later the Dead were nowhere to be found, although Garcia made a brief appearance in the makeshift backstage performers' pavilion, holding a joint and pointing it at the camera, stating, "Marijuana, exhibit A." It was altogether a disappointing venture for Garcia.

Although Garcia and company were not happy about their performance at Woodstock, the rest of the rock 'n' roll world had a sense that anything was possible in terms of large outdoor concerts. Soon, another large-scale concert was being planned, this time a free concert set for December in Golden Gate Park in the heart of San Francisco. The bill included the Rolling Stones, the Grateful Dead, the Jefferson Airplane, and Crosby, Stills, Nash, and Young. Unfortunately, the logistical mountains that the promoters of Woodstock had to climb were intensified for this date. The city of San Francisco had agreed to allow the concert as long as word about it was not made public until twenty-four hours before showtime. However, news of the concert inevitably leaked out, and city officials refused to allow the show to go on. At the last minute another venue was located—Altamont Speedway in the East Bay. Instead of the cool security of the Hog Farm, Sam Cutler, the Rolling Stones tour manager, had arranged for the Hell's Angels to provide security. Despite all the challenges, an estimated three hundred thousand people turned out for the event. Garcia reflected, "I think it was Emmett Grogan who wrote on the bulletin board up at Alembic, where we were rehearsing and a lot of the planning was going on, 'First Annual Charlie Manson Death Festival' before it happened. It was in the air that it was not a good time to do something. There were too many divisive elements. It was too weird. And that place—God, it was like hell."

Sadly, the vibes were not false. In the end, the scene turned ugly when the Hell's Angels, who were protecting the stage, started violently beating the encroaching crowd during the Rolling Stones's set. Things got out of hand, and a fan was stabbed to death.

The Grateful Dead were supposed to perform after the Rolling Stones, but after the knifing the band decided not to play, and refused to go on stage. They even scrubbed a scheduled appearance for Bill Graham later that night. TC remarked, "We were supposed to play at the Fillmore West that night, but we cancelled the show and instead went to Grison's Restaurant for a postmortem analysis of what happened."

The optimism and euphoria of Woodstock had dissipated with the tragedy at Altamont. It was amazing to Garcia how things could have changed so dramatically since the heyday of Haight-Ashbury, a little more than a year previously, when the band could spontaneously set up in the park without permits and play for a few hundred locals. Garcia realized that because audiences had grown so huge, his concept of doing free concerts was no longer workable. To Garcia a truly free concert meant spontaneity and a freedom to play or not if he wanted. That type of spontaneity was unrealistic now, for a large-scale free concert needed planning—all the logistics of the show had to be worked out well in advance to ensure that the musicians and audience would be satisfied and there would be no repeat of the Altamont debacle. The only freedom in such a situation was for the fans—the performers were locked in.

Altamont had brought the end of innocence to the rock 'n' roll world. "After Altamont I felt very depressed," said Garcia. "It started the focusing more and more on the idea of responsibility. I don't want to draw an audience into a situation where there's violence."

Thus, for Garcia, 1969 had brought new highs and lows, and the bad news seemed to carry over into the new year. The

Altamont mess had brought a bad spotlight on rock 'n' rollers, and authorities around the country were clamping down. On January 31, 1970, the police busted the Dead when they were in New Orleans to play at the Warehouse. When the band arrived in town, they were told that the New Orleans cops had busted the Jefferson Airplane a few weeks earlier, and the hotel detective had warned Garcia that the cops were going to bust the Dead, too. The band played the concert under this cloud, and sure enough, when the band got back from their gig at 3 AM, the police had already conducted their search and were waiting for them. They arrested everybody in the band except Pigpen and TC, handcuffed the suspects, and lined them up in front of the building for press photos. Nineteen people were booked for possession of marijuana, LSD, barbiturates, and amphetamines, and they spent eight hours in jail before being released on bail. All charges against the band were eventually dismissed.

Soon after the bust, TC left the band. With his departure, the band again shifted direction, this time back to a format of tighter songs with good vocal harmonies. The change was reflected on their next two albums, *Workingman's Dead* and *American Beauty*, which were released in 1970. The songs for these records were mostly written by Hunter, and the music went back to the blues, folk, and country traditions of the Dead's early days as a jug band. Although Garcia had led the band into its experimental period, he wholeheartedly endorsed this swing of the pendulum. As he said, "We were into a much more relaxed thing about that time. We weren't feeling like an experimental music group, but were feeling more like a good old band." The move away from experimental music gave him an opportunity to return to his musical roots.

Both albums emphasized the vocals and the songs, and Hunter and Garcia's technique of writing the songs began to evolve to match this. Instead of taking what Hunter gave him and making the music work around it, Garcia began to edit the lyrics to make them easier for him to sing. Jerry became more active in helping Hunter write the words; for example, he would frequently hum a melody to Hunter, who would then try to construct his words to fit the flow of the music. Garcia described his view of the songwriting process at this time: "Sometimes I'll start out with a set of chord changes that are just attractive to my ear. And then I'll hear a sketch of a melody over it . . . pretty soon there'll be more adjoining pieces to any one phrase, a melodic phrase, say. Then I hum it to myself for a long time and kind of play it on the guitar for everybody who's around, and then I'll get together with Hunter, and we'll go through what he's got. If he's got lyrics already written that he likes, I'll see if anything fits, or else we'll start working on something from scratch."

The song "Truckin'" is a good example of how Hunter's lyrics evolved as he started touring with the band and writing lyrics that were crafted to their life-style. Garcia explained, "The early stuff he wrote that we tried to set to music was stiff, because it wasn't really meant to be sung. [Hunter was a poet first, a lyricist second.] After he got further and further into it, his craft improved and then he started going out on the road with us, coming out to see what life was like, to be able to have more of that viewpoint in the music, for the words to be more Grateful Dead words. 'Truckin'" is the result of that sort of thing."

Garcia felt that *Workingman's Dead* and *American Beauty*

were commercially successful because they were singing records that emphasized vocals, in the style of Crosby, Stills, and Nash. In fact, Jerry readily credited those three artists for the improved harmonies. "That was really the result of hanging out with Crosby and those guys, just because they could sit down in any situation and pick up an acoustic guitar and it's instant music, these beautiful vocal harmonies. I used to think of myself as a guitar player, but hearing singing, and seeing it up close, has kinda made me want to sing."

Although Garcia's singing voice was never gilt-edged, the two albums represented a breakthrough for the Grateful Dead. The music on the albums appealed to a lot of people who weren't attracted to the avant-garde improvisational music the band had been playing. The tighter format of the acoustic-based country rock songs on *Workingman's Dead* and *American Beauty* was received well by the listening public, and these records sold better than any of the Dead's earlier efforts.

Since the stylistic shift was a throwback to Garcia's days as a folk and bluegrass musician, it was quite natural that he brought in two of his friends from that period—David Nelson and David Grisman—to play on the albums. Out of this association developed another musical direction for Garcia.

Garcia's love for bluegrass music was still strong, and he had bought a pedal steel guitar at a Denver music store while on tour. During the summer of 1969 Garcia had started jamming with John Dawson, a friend of Bob Weir's from the coffeehouse days in Palo Alto. Dawson had wanted to start a country rock band because he loved the sound of the pedal steel guitar. When Dawson found out that Garcia had a pedal steel, he asked Jerry if he could check it out. Dawson brought his guitar along to accompany the pedal steel, and he showed Garcia some of the tunes he had been writing. The two started playing together at Dawson's coffeehouse gig in Menlo Park.

Garcia recalled, "Dawson had this gig down the Peninsula playing coffeehouses. He was getting into writing songs, and he'd written five or six songs that I thought were pretty neat. . . . I thought, wow, this is the perfect chance for me to be able to get into pedal steel. . . . So I went down there and set up my pedal steel in the corner and slowly proceeded to try and learn how to play it. . . . Pretty soon it started to sound pretty good, and a couple of other friends who were around here sort of fell into the scene, and pretty soon we had a little band."

Thus, Garcia's adventurous musical mind was off again. The duo became a country-western honky-tonk band with the addition of Nelson on lead guitar, Lesh on bass, and Hart on drums. They called themselves the New Riders of the Purple Sage, and after gigging around for a while the New Riders started opening for the Grateful Dead. The shows were billed as "An Evening with the Grateful Dead and the New Riders of the Purple Sage," and consisted of three sets. Garcia would play the entire evening straight through from 8:30 PM until nearly 2 AM. The night would start with an acoustic Grateful Dead set with Garcia on acoustic guitar, followed by a New Riders set with Garcia on pedal steel, and then concluding with an electric Grateful Dead set with Garcia on electric guitar. It was a wonderful evening of Americana that featured a variety of songs covering the range of styles that Garcia had performed over the years—folk, old-time music, bluegrass, country, country-rock, rock 'n' roll, and acid rock.

Garcia summed up his fascination for performing, seemingly anywhere and anytime: "The main thing is that I play music because I love music, you know, and all my life I've loved music, and as I've gotten more and more into lookin' at the whole overall thing, that's where I am now, doin' that."

At the end of June 1970, Garcia was involved in a project that was great for the musicians as well as the audiences. The Grateful Dead and the New Riders rolled across Canada with a trainload of musicians as part of Festival Express, a rock 'n' roll tour that was the brainchild of Canadian Frank Duckworth. Duckworth explained the purpose of the tour: "The idea of the tour was to remind people of the romance of traveling by train in the old days when trains were still a vital form of communication, and to combine that with rock 'n' roll, which is the most vital form of communication today."

An entire train was chartered for the occasion, with "Festival Express" painted in ten-foot orange-and-black letters on the baggage car. The tour consisted of concerts in Toronto, Winnipeg, and Calgary, and also featured the Band, Janis Joplin, Delaney and Bonnie, Buddy Guy, Ian and Sylvia, Eric Anderson, Mountain, Tom Rush, Traffic, Sea Train, Ten Years After, Sha Na Na, Charlebois, James and the Good Brothers, and Cat.

Nearly all of the musicians traveled in twelve train cars for the trek through the scenic Canadian countryside from

Toronto to Winnipeg and Calgary. It was five days of nonstop partying, drinking, and jamming. The 140 musicians, crew, and friends had their own small sleeping compartments, and could congregate in the dining car, the bar car, or the lounge car, which was specially equipped for the musicians. David Nelson remembered, "There was a jam car that was set up with amplifiers and other gear. Between Toronto and Saskatchewan there was a lot of jamming. I remember as we pulled up to this one station people were staring because it was unusual to hear music coming from a train."

During the course of the five-day journey, all kinds of musical interactions took place. This was especially exciting for the performers, for it had been several years since they had had the time to get together informally in such a concentrated way. Since they had become national stars, their respective schedules no longer permitted this sort of action. On the first night aboard, Leslie West and Felix Pappalardi of Mountain got out guitars and start playing some Delta blues, with Garcia and Delaney Bramlett joining in. Another memorable part of the trip was when Joplin took out a guitar and began singing "Me and Bobby McGee," with Garcia adding lilting guitar licks behind her. The song was destined to become Joplin's biggest hit.

Joplin remarked about the trip to *Rolling Stone* writer David Dalton, who was along for the ride, "Whoooh! There's so much talent on this train. I knew it was going to be a party, man. I didn't take this gig for nothing else but that. I said, 'It sounds like a party, and I wanna be there. It's gonna be a Rocking Pneumonia and Boogie Woogie Flu' . . . Wow!" In their *Rolling Stone* chronicle of the trip, Dalton and cowriter Jonathan Cott described Janis as the "presiding spirit of the train . . . a Bacchanalian Little Red Riding Hood with her bag full of tequila and lemons."

On the last leg of the journey the supply of liquor was depleted. John Dawson recalled, "The train was about to run out of booze on the day after we left Winnipeg. . . . After a while there was no more CC left, no more tequila, and no more nothing. This was getting serious, so a bunch of self-appointed committee members went running around the place taking up a collection. . . . These people went up and down the length of the train asking for money, and they ended up with about four hundred bucks. . . . They jumped into a taxicab the second the train arrived in Saskatoon, and rode it several miles into town . . . and they ended up with this $400 booze run. Of course there was only going to be one more night on the train anyway, so we had to drink it all that night. . . . It was quite an interesting night with Janis Joplin and Jerry Garcia. It's the first and last time I ever saw Garcia high on liquor."

Garcia, Joplin, and Dawson spent some time that last night drinking and singing together, and at one point they led a chorus of voices into the Beatles' "I've Just Seen a Face." It seemed to go on forever, Bob Weir pondered. "If I could remember how it began, maybe we could [have found] an ending, or we could [have gone] on singing this all night." Janis Joplin and Rick Danko got into improvising on Leadbelly's song "No More Cane on the Brazos," singing one verse after another for about thirty minutes as each verse got funnier than the last. The night ended with drunken renditions of "Amazing Grace" and "Goodnight, Irene."

The next morning the effects of the nighttime bash were

apparent. Garcia quipped, "I promise never to drink again, your honor. How's my head? I need a lobotomy." David Nelson divulged, "The hangover was painful! But we played the show the next day." At the final stop of the tour in Calgary, in addition to the regular schedule of acts, there was a jam session with Garcia, Delaney and Bonnie, Ian and Sylvia, and Rick Danko. Garcia, ever the consummate musician, wouldn't pass up the opportunity to jam despite the apparent success of Janis Joplin's claim the night before that she "got the Dead drunk."

Festival Express was best summed up by Bob Shuster, an aide to Janis Joplin's manager, Albert Grossman: "Woodstock was a feast for the audience; the train was a feast for the performers."

While 1970 saw the Grateful Dead gain popularity with the commercial success of *Workingman's Dead* and *American Beauty*, it was a tough year for the band and Garcia personally. The band had always had a difficult time handling the business end of things, and managing their money was a constant problem. It seemed that no matter what income there might be, the Dead was always on the verge of going broke. Garcia observed, "Our managers were Rock Scully and Danny Rifkin, who were really our friends, and they were a couple of heads, old-time organizers from the early Family Dog days, and they agreed to sort of manage us . . . but really they weren't too experienced at it and we weren't very experienced at it and so what we really managed to do in that whole world was get ourselves incredibly in debt, just amazingly in debt, in just about two years."

It was at this point that Mickey Hart's father, Lenny Hart, began to manage the Grateful Dead in an attempt to straighten them out financially. But this relationship landed on the rocks. Much to the band's chagrin, during the recording of *Workingman's Dead* they discovered that Lenny had been embezzling large amounts of money, taking nearly $150,000 from the band. The ripoff not only hurt the Dead financially, but was a devastating blow to Mickey, who had to deal with the pain of his father's betrayal.

Garcia reflected on that period: "Being busted in New Orleans was hanging over our heads; we were in the middle of a management hassle." To make matters worse, on September 8, during the recording of *American Beauty*, Garcia's mother was involved in a tragic accident. While she was driving, she lost control of her car. In the ensuing wreck, she suffered multiple traumatic injuries. She was brought to San Francisco General Hospital where she had been a nurse for the past twenty years. Although she lingered for three weeks, her injuries were ultimately fatal, and she died on September 29.

The tragedy gave Jerry the opportunity to renew his relationship with his older brother Clifford, who had become a Marine. The two had not spoken for years, but they shared the vigil by their mother's bed.

Garcia mused, "It was raining down hard on us while that record was going on." He discussed Ruth Garcia's feelings about him: "She always respected what I did and liked the fact that I was a musician, and liked the music, too. She never judged me outwardly, even though she didn't approve of my involvement with drugs." It must have made her proud that her youngest son had become a bandleader just like his dad.

5

TAKING CARE
OF BUSINESS

he death of Garcia's mother Ruth was followed by the death in October 1970 of Janis Joplin. Over the next few years, both the Jefferson Airplane and Quicksilver Messenger Service broke up. Garcia was left as the one most recognizable musical icon of the counterculture to many young Americans who wanted to be part of the Woodstock Nation. This was a particularly charged position, since music and psychedelics were such a large part of the lifestyle for those who were coming of age in the 1970s. For his part, Jerry had no intention of assuming that role—being a model or a symbol for other people was never his life's mission. Whenever he was asked about being a leader of the counterculture, he always sounded the same themes: "I mean, with us and politics, man, generally none of us are political thinkers or into political trips or activist or any of that kind of bullshit."

"The thing about us, I guess, is that we're not really layin' any-thing on anybody." As he had maintained throughout his career, Garcia was simply into being a musician. "As far as my responsibility, I'm anxious not to mislead anybody, because really, what I do is play music."

Though the music of the Grateful Dead could be consid-ered the soundtrack for the Woodstock Nation, to Garcia the music was always more important than the public's perception of his involvement in the counterculture. Jerry never endorsed the media's portrayal of him as a cultural symbol, nor did he pretend to be anybody's guru. He viewed himself as a musician who demonstrated his commitment to his craft by his prolific involvement in musical projects of all sorts. His fascination for a broad range of music enabled him to develop a career not only as a member of the Grateful Dead but as a solo artist, ses-sion player, and bandleader.

After ending the Mickey Hart and the Hartbeats experi-ment in 1968 and healing the split in the Grateful Dead, Garcia began to perform with groups other than the Dead whenever there was a break in the band's tour schedule. He didn't have to have any set engagements, either—one of his joys was simply putting together an impromptu group, finding a willing watering hole, and filling the space with music. He explained, "I'm a total junkie when it comes to playing. I just have to play. And when we're off the road I get itchy, and a bar's just like the perfect opportunity to get loose and play all night." This was something he would not ordinarily be able to do with all the other members of the Dead, because the audi-ence would have too many expectations for that sort of session. Also, playing with other people gave Garcia a chance to

refresh himself—by jamming with new partners he could sat-
isfy his urge to play while also keeping his chops up on the guitar. Though Mountain Girl described Jerry as obsessive about
his playing, and talked about him practicing sometimes six or
seven hours each day to get to where he wanted to be musically, he clearly preferred playing with other musicians in front of
an audience. "Rather than sit home and practice—scales and
stuff—which I do when I'm together enough to do it—I go out
and play because playing music is more enjoyable to me than
sitting home and playing scales."

An ideal opportunity to play outside the band was provided by
the Matrix, a nightclub that Marty Balin of the Jefferson
Airplane had opened in 1965 on Fillmore Street in the Marina
District of San Francisco. The club featured Monday night jam
sessions in a relaxed atmosphere. The audience accepted the
jams for what they were—outstanding musicians testing themselves with new ideas and new forms—and wasn't put out if the
sound wasn't perfect. In 1969 Garcia began playing guitar there
with jazz keyboardist Howard Wales, bassist John Kahn, and
drummer Bill Vitt. Kahn remembered, "We played Monday
nights there for a while, and for the longest time, hardly anybody would show up. We'd get ten people and split ten dollars
four ways at the end of the night."

The music they played was mainly jazz-infused instrumentals inspired by Wales, who led the band with his improvisations on organ. Garcia remarked, "We'd plug in and play with
Howard and spend all night muttering to each other, 'What

key are we in?' Howard was so incredible, and we were just hanging on for dear life. . . . Playing with Howard did more for my ears than anybody I ever played with, because he was so extended and so different." Despite Garcia's offhand opinion of his playing with Wales, the collaboration lasted for a couple of years and was good enough to result in the release in 1971 of the instrumental album *Hooteroll* on Douglas Records.

Wales eventually dropped out of the Matrix jam sessions, and Garcia invited keyboardist Merl Saunders to sit in. Saunders grew up in San Francisco and had been a musician virtually his whole life. He'd had his first trio at the age of fifteen and played his first national gig in the early 1960s with the Billy Williams Band. Merl had a fondness for gospel, rhythm and blues, and jazz, and during the early 1960s while he was living in New York he became well known in jazz circles, playing with the likes of Miles Davis, Sonny Stitt, and James Moody.

Saunders moved back to the Bay Area in the mid-1960s and in 1965 signed with Berkeley's Fantasy Records. He quickly earned the reputation as *the* keyboard artist around town and began doing everything from recording sessions to soundtracks. Saunders related how he hooked up with Garcia: "I was doing these sessions at Columbia Records on Fulton Street in San Francisco. I met Garcia in the studio and we did some session work together. The producer heard the sound we had together, and he started booking studio work for Jerry and me to back up different artists. We had a chemistry together. Then Jerry said, 'Hey, man, I'm playing at the Matrix. Would you come down and sit in with me; we don't have a keyboard player.' So I went down there, and that's where it all started. We began jamming there. It was Jerry and I and a drummer named Bill Vitt, and then John Kahn came down and joined us."

Garcia and Saunders began playing mostly free-form jazz and avant-garde instrumentals, but soon the music evolved into a more standard rhythm-and-blues-based sound. Saunders observed, "We started doing standard songs because I loved standards. Jerry was very interested in those songs and how to play them. As a matter of fact, one of the classic songs was 'My Funny Valentine,' which we recorded. Jerry loved standard songs. He liked the challenge." Garcia stated, "When I started playing with Merl, I went to a more organ-trio style. . . . I played big, fat chords and did a lot of that walking-style chord shifting on the blues numbers and things that Merl is so good at. My style is much more conventional, in a way, with him, and it's very satisfying for me to play and hear myself as a conventional player. It's a kind of playing that I don't do in the Grateful Dead."

With Saunders on board, what began as a loose jamming group that played for fun began getting tight and became the Garcia and Saunders Band, which started gigging around the Bay Area and then the East Coast. Garcia credited Saunders's influence on his guitar playing: "Merl taught me structure. He filled me in on all those years of things I didn't do. I'd never played standards. I'd never played in dance bands. I never had any approach to the world of regular, straight music. He knows all the standards, and he taught me how bebop works."

* * * *

Garcia's studio work at that time included playing on Paul Kantner's solo album *Blows Against the Empire* and David Crosby's solo effort *If I Could Only Remember My Name*. Coincidentally, both were recorded in November 1970 at Wally Heider's studio on Hyde Street in San Francisco, and both Kantner and Crosby invited many Bay Area musicians to participate. Thus, the two discs featured a virtual who's who of the San Francisco sound, including members of the Grateful Dead, Jefferson Airplane, and Quicksilver Messenger Service, and others.

The idea of a core of Bay Area musicians working on each other's projects was an outgrowth of the community spirit and camaraderie that developed in the Haight-Ashbury days, and the idea dated back to Garcia's involvement with the Jefferson Airplane's *Surrealistic Pillow* in late 1966, which was the first of a growing series of what could be called cross pollinated projects. Jorma Kaukonen explained how these talented musicians made the idea work, despite all the opportunities for bumping heads and bruising egos: "We were part of the same scene, and we were friends who respected each other as musicians. We weren't competitive, so we could play together and make it work as a band."

This loose ensemble of San Francisco musicians became known unofficially as the Planet Earth Rock 'n' Roll Orchestra. Tom Constanten recalled, "I was at Phil Lesh's house in Fairfax in 1971 when he coined the phrase. Phil was talking about an all-inclusive band where everyone would fit in: 'I'm in favor of a planet earth rock 'n' roll orchestra where different musicians can play on each other's albums.'" During the next couple of years this "orchestra" helped out on Kantner and Slick's

Sunfighter; Mickey Hart's *Rolling Thunder*; and Kantner, Slick, and Freiberg's *Baron Von Tollbooth and the Chrome Nun*.

Garcia also discussed this intermingling of the bands: "The reason that there isn't one huge band that we all are, which in fact there is—because we all play together in various combinations—so there is a huge band, but we are all expressing different parts of it for the sake of being different from each other, to express a little individuation in the universe. . . . I expect all the groups to continually be unfolding and playing in different manifestations and everybody creating new stuff."

One of these manifestations—Garcia, Lesh, Hart, Kreutzmann, and Crosby—played at the Matrix in December 1970. Although Garcia was used to playing lead guitar, in this combination he was playing behind another star. That didn't matter to him. "We had a little band called David and the Dorks," Garcia mentioned. "He was the star, and it was his trip that we were doing. It was right around the time he was in the Bay Area a lot. . . . We did maybe two or three shows. . . . They weren't announced or anything; we just went in there on a Monday night and had a lot of fun, and the sound was cool. In fact, that was the core of the band that played on David's album."

Another reason for Jerry to spend time away from the Grateful Dead was that he could work out his own personal musical dreams that the other members of the band might have stunted. The culmination of this was his first solo album, *Garcia*, which he began recording in 1971. He played all the instru-

ments on the album except the drums, which Kreutzmann handled, and he did all the singing on the album, too. (He and
Hunter had written the songs.) Garcia divulged his motivation
for doing the album: "I'm doing it to be completely self-indul-
gent musically. I'm just going on a trip. I have a curiosity to see
what I can do, and I've a desire to get into sixteen-track and
go on trips that are too weird for me to want to put anybody
else I know through. And also to pay for this house!"

The house he was referring to was the new home he had
acquired above Stinson Beach, an hour north of San Francisco
in Marin County, which he shared with Mountain Girl, their
daughter, Annabelle (born in 1970), and Sunshine, Mountain
Girl and Ken Kesey's four-year-old daughter. Garcia had borrowed the $10,000 he used for the down payment on the house
from Warner Brothers as an advance against his solo album.
The house was on a bluff overlooking the ocean, and its privacy was guarded by eucalyptus trees, tall hedges, and large rose-
bushes. On the front lawn, which had flowers on all sides,
Garcia could read books, sketch and paint, practice guitar, listen to music, or just relax and watch the colors of the day
change over the Pacific. As she had been at 710 Ashbury,
Mountain Girl was the one who was concerned with running
the house. She also had her hands full taking care of her two
young daughters, but she managed to find the time to cook for
the family, work in the garden, and sew Big Jer a custom-made
shirt or two.

Amazingly, Jerry Garcia—who epitomized to many the
Beatnik-hippie counterculture—was in a way living a middle
class, straight suburban life. Absent from Stinson Beach were
the days-long parties with hundreds of people, as had occurred

at the Chateau almost a decade before. Garcia was quite far out of San Francisco, and though small groups came out to jam, talk, and get high, there was no urgency to re-create the party atmosphere of the earlier years. In addition, the people who had been at those parties were going their own ways: the musicians had become famous and were touring, the philosophers of the movement were involved with other matters. When Garcia was touring with the Grateful Dead, his life-style continued to be that of a rock 'n' roll musician, and he was on the road a lot during this period. (In 1969 and 1970 the band played almost three hundred concerts across the country.) But when he was home, he could almost be a traveling salesman stopping in for a weekend with his wife and kids.

Almost, but not quite. Jerry was still Jerry—long hair and a beard, and apt to be wearing just a t-shirt and jeans for any occasion. Getting high still contributed a great deal to his creative energies. Although he had reached the ripe old age of twenty-nine, he remained unconventional in his thinking, never settling for the tried-and-true when new avenues were left unexplored. And he was still ready to shake up the establishment for a cause he felt was righteous.

In February 1971 Mickey Hart left the Dead in an attempt to come to terms with his father's embezzlement of the band's money the previous fall. With his departure, the group simplified the arrangements of many of their songs, and recorded a live album in March and April that captured the honed-down sound of the quintet. Unfortunately, the group's dealings with Warner Brothers were becoming hairy, and Garcia came up with the idea of naming the album *Skullfuck* to reflect their strained relationship. The artwork the band submitted for the record showed a skull with "Skullfuck" written on a scroll across it. Naturally, Warner was not thrilled.

Joe Smith, the Warner executive who had signed the band, called a meeting with the Dead in Los Angeles at the Continental Hyatt. A total of fifty-five band, crew, and family members showed up to confront the record company executives about the title. After a lengthy debate, Garcia said he would settle for fifteen thousand in sales if the album could go out with the *Skullfuck* title. Smith pointed out that not only would it be hard to get the record into stores (he had already checked with many of the major retail outlets), but also that no radio station would want to touch an album with that title. He then told them that if sales were dismal, the Dead would again be in debt to Warner to the tune of $100,000. Faced with these practicalities, the band had to relent, and the album was retitled *Grateful Dead*.

Out of this crisis came a hit record, and *Grateful Dead* became the group's first gold album. The band celebrated their success with a dinner party at the Coachman restaurant in San Francisco. The good wine flowed as the group hammed it up at a predinner photo session, with smiles on everybody's faces as they received their gold discs. Garcia was happy with the album. "It's us, man. It's the prototype Grateful Dead. Basic unit. Each of those tracks is the total picture, a good example of what the Grateful Dead really is, musically."

*   *   *   *

Although Garcia and the Dead had been through many changes since their days as the Warlocks—shifts in musical styles, personnel coming and going—a change on the elemental level was on the horizon for them. Pigpen, who was only in his mid-twenties, became seriously ill. Although he had never indulged in drugs as Garcia did, he found his inspiration in alcohol. His years of heavy drinking caught up with him, and he was hospitalized because of cirrhosis of the liver and a generally weakened condition brought on by his romance with the bottle. His situation was so serious that Garcia and other band members each gave a pint of blood to help him regain his health. Needing time to recuperate, Pigpen took a hiatus from performing in September 1971, not getting back on stage until December.

The loss of Pigpen was a major shock, as his voice and blues riffs had been a major part of the band's sound. To replace him, Garcia found keyboard player Keith Godchaux and his wife, singer Donna Godchaux. Keith, who had begun playing piano at age five, was playing in jazz trios, performing cocktail standards at bar gigs around the Bay Area. He had also developed an interest in blues, and spent hours listening to blues and big band jazz records. He wasn't interested in rock 'n' roll until he met Donna, who had been a studio singer backing up Elvis Presley, Sam Cooke, Aretha Franklin, and others before moving to California in 1970. "She was well aware of the roots of rock 'n' roll, and she gave me the flash," Godchaux noted.

After Keith and Donna got married, Godchaux began practicing rock 'n' roll piano at home. In September 1971 they went to see Garcia performing at the Keystone in Berkeley and introduced themselves. Donna recounted it: "At the break

Garcia walked by going backstage, so I grabbed him and said, 'Jerry, my husband and I have something very important to talk about.' And he said, 'Sure.' So Garcia told us to come backstage, but we were both too scared, so we didn't. A few minutes later, Garcia came up and sat next to Keith, and I said, 'Honey, I think Garcia's hinting that he wants to talk to you. He's sitting right next to you.' He looked over at Jerry and looked back at me and dropped his head on the table and said, 'You're going to have to talk to my wife. I can't talk right now.' He was just too shy. So I said, 'Well, Keith's your piano player, so I want your home telephone number so I can call you up and come to the next Grateful Dead practice.' And he believed me! He gave me his number."

Godchaux passed the audition and was put on the Grateful Dead's payroll, joining in time for the start of the fall tour in October 1971. A few months later Donna was also collecting Dead paychecks as a vocalist. The first recorded tracks to include the Godchauxs were on Bob Weir's solo album, *Ace*, which was released in 1972. The album was mixed by Garcia and was for all intents and purposes a Grateful Dead album, since the band played on almost all the cuts. Weir sang lead vocal on each song, all of which he had either written by himself or co-written with Robert Hunter and John Barlow. Barlow had been a friend of Weir's since they went to prep school together in the early 1960s, and the two had become a formidable songwriting team.

When Pigpen felt well enough to return to performing, the band operated with two keyboardists. Pigpen remained healthy enough to travel to Europe with the band in the spring of 1972. An entourage of forty-three people went along for the fun, as the Grateful Dead sprang for a European vacation for their staff, crew, and family. The band toured Europe for nearly two months, traveling in a pair of buses referred to as the "Bozo Bus" and the "Bolo Bus." "The Bozo Bus was for people who wanted to be tripping out and raving all the time," Robert Hunter said. "The Bolo Bus was people who preferred to sink totally into their neuroses, or just sleep."

The band played more than twenty concerts, recording the shows on sixteen-track equipment for another live album. Garcia explained, "We had a lot of people we wanted to take to Europe . . . so we needed to record an album there to pay for the bills." And that's what they did—*Europe '72* was released as a triple album and made enough money to pay for the trip. However, the tour proved to be Pigpen's swan song, as it was the last time he sang with the Grateful Dead in concert. Less than a year later, he was dead due to his chronic liver problems.

The final loss of Pigpen marked the end of an era for the band. When the Warlocks first got together, Pigpen was the star because he was the best singer in the group and knew how to work an audience. Though it was Jerry's band, Pigpen stood out because he was the only one who could carry the show. Jon McIntire, a longtime business associate of the group, remarked, "There was a time when Jerry and I were in Tommy's Joynt [a San Francisco restaurant] and these kids came over, and they didn't say, 'Are you Jerry Garcia?' They said, 'Are you with the Grateful Dead?' That's how it was back then. Pigpen was the one everyone knew, because for a while he was the one who could really sing and play. It was later that it became 'Jerry Garcia and the Grateful Dead.'" Garcia observed, "Pigpen's decline represented some kind of imminent change. He was more of a showman, more out there than the rest of us. We don't have that anymore. I tend to think of the Grateful Dead's existence in terms of the Pigpen-as-center period and then the more self-sufficient, growing-out time that came when we got used to playing without him. It's not a question of better or worse—it's just different. Getting Keith, we became a different band."

After Garcia returned from Europe, he picked up with the Garcia and Saunders Band again. Garcia's joy for playing music with his friends was apparent as the band performed for a packed house on June 30 for the last night of Freddy Herrera's Keystone Korner in North Beach. After the Garcia and Saunders Band had played a lengthy opening set, Paul Butterfield came out on stage for the last forty minutes of the second set. Butterfield played his trademark harmonica licks while Garcia ripped it up on guitar. The band was clearly having a good time. "It's so much fun," Saunders said after the show. "Every time it's different—it just depends on how we're feeling."

Playing with Saunders meant so much to Garcia that he even flew back from New York in the middle of a Grateful Dead tour to play a benefit concert with him at the Berkeley Community Theatre on September 22. Saunders recalled, "Garcia was on tour back East. I asked him, 'Jerry, do you want to play the Farmworkers Relief Fund Benefit?' He responded, 'Yeah, but I'm in New York, have a limo waiting at the airport for me.' I then told him the time and he flew in. The limo picked him up and brought him to the gig, and when it was over he flew back to New York. Both of us got plaques for doing the benefit."

Beyond the personnel changes that were occurring at the end of 1972, the band's record label was about to change. With the release of *Europe '72* late that year, the Grateful Dead were nearing the end of their commitment to Warner Brothers and were considering other options. Columbia Records had made them an offer, but the group was of a mind to form their own record company. Garcia had grown weary of the constant record-company hassles. "Our contract with Warners lapsed last December," said Garcia at the time, "but we still owe them a disc since we agreed to do one more album in exchange for their putting out the three-record set of Europe. . . . None of us are terribly enthusiastic about the possibility of another Warners album. We've sort of used up Warner Brothers. Or vice versa."

The idea to form their own company was the brainchild of Ron Rakow, who had conceived of an independent production and distribution system controlled by the band. Rakow had been introduced to the Dead in 1967 by a mutual friend, and Garcia and he had developed an immediate rapport. Rakow started working with the band, and was involved with running the Carousel Ballroom in San Francisco in 1968. This was an abortive attempt by the Grateful Dead and other San Francisco bands to promote their own concerts, independent of Bill Graham and Chet Helms.

Despite the failure of the Carousel, Garcia had confidence

in Rakow's business acumen. He had studied economics and worked on Wall Street before dropping out of the straight business world and moving to San Francisco. Rakow had been researching the distribution systems of the major labels, and spent time at the Securities and Exchange Commission photocopying the big record companies' financial statements. He compiled a ninety-three-page report called the "So What Papers" to convince the band to put together their own record company. Rakow remembered, "I presented the papers to the band on July 4, 1972. I was surprised they didn't okay it right away, so I went on the road as part of the equipment crew to work off my frustration. It was finally approved on April 19 [1973], but of course in changed form."

The original plan had called for a distribution system that bypassed record stores and sold discs through mail order, head shops, and Grateful Dead Good-Humor-type trucks. Business manager David Parker nixed that idea, however, and stuck with record stores. Garcia, a big advocate of Rakow's plan, helped Ron prepare the presentation that he made to the entire band. Discussing the proposal in the spring of 1973, Garcia stated, "I really like the idea of starting our own record company. It's the most exciting option to me just in terms of 'What are we gonna do now that we're enjoying amazing success?' The nice thing would be not to sell out at this point and instead come up with something far out and different, which would be sort of traditional with us."

In April 1973 Grateful Dead Records was set up, co-owned by all the voting members of the organization, with Rakow as president and general manager. A second label, Round Records, owned fifty-fifty by Garcia and Rakow, was set up to handle solo projects that members of the band might want to produce. Rakow financed the start-up by selling the foreign manufacturing and distribution rights for $300,000 to Atlantic Records, and he got the First National Bank of Boston to underwrite the eighteen independent record distributors who were going to dispense the Grateful Dead's records throughout the country. Determined to make the albums out of the highest quality vinyl, the band sought out pressing plants that met their stringent requirements for state-of-the-art records.

Part of the band's confidence in starting their own label was rooted in the Dead Freaks Unite campaign initiated by Garcia on the inside of *Grateful Dead*, which had the following notice:

> DEAD FREAKS UNITE Who are you? Where are you? How are you? Send us your name and address and we'll keep you informed.

The response was overwhelming, and the band quickly built up a list of twenty-five thousand names. With this direct-mail list and a newsletter to communicate information, the band had an effective link with their fans, by now known as Dead Heads. Eileen Law was made Dead Head liaison. Eileen grew up in northern California and met the Dead because she was a fan who went to many of their concerts in the 1960s. "If you went to all the concerts, you just inevitably met the band," she said. "And if you fit in, you became part of it."

Law began sending out newsletters telling the fans about tour dates, solo projects, and any other information that might be of interest. Due to financial constraints, however, the quality and frequency of the newsletter was erratic. "We can't afford to do what *Dead Heads* was supposed to have done," Garcia admitted in an early dispatch, "but what we can do is let everybody know we got their letter. The way it could have worked out, for example, if we really had it super together, if we had a lot of money, was to organize rough lists of the members of the Grateful Dead weirdness scene or whatever, and have them get together in their town and put on some trips or something, to provide a communication system of some loose sort. But we're limited economically because the Dead Head trip doesn't have any income, and the Grateful Dead doesn't make all that much money."

What Garcia was trying through Grateful Dead Records and the *Dead Heads* was really an extension of the communal spirit he had been a part of in Haight-Ashbury. Even though the hippie movement was dispersed and the country was turning to other issues, here were Garcia and the band trying to take their message to their legions through their own channels, bypassing the straight world of record companies and media as they had done in the heyday of the Haight. Garcia understood that not all young Americans could come together in one place and live in peace and harmony—that had been tried during the Summer of Love, and the attempt had suffocated. But what they could do was take the spirit that created the wonderful scene of 1967 back to their hometowns and create their own Haight-Ashburys. And the fact that such a movement would occur on a largely underground, unofficial basis fit in perfectly with Garcia's philosophy of steering away from the mainstream and the authorities.

* * * *

Although the startup of Grateful Dead Records took a lot of his time, Jerry was still working out with other musicians. One such project that was interesting to Dead Heads too was Garcia's involvement with the bluegrass band Old and In the Way, which debuted at the Lion's Share in San Anselmo, California, on March 1, 1973. Garcia broke out the banjo for the first time in many years to perform with mandolin player David Grisman, guitarist Peter Rowan, and bassist John Kahn. This was a trip back to another of Garcia's musical roots, which he hadn't explored with the Dead or anyone else in years. "God, it's been eight years since I've played banjo," Garcia declared in early 1973. "We all used to be heavily into blue-grass, so we got together a little over a month ago, started play-ing, and then decided, 'Shit, why don't we play a few bars and see what happens?'. . . We're thinking about finding a fiddle player and then doing some of the bluegrass festivals this sum-mer. It's a whole different world from the rock 'n' roll scene—really mellow and nice. People bring their families and kids and grandmas and dogs and lunch. And they're all aficionados who really get off behind the licks. That'd be a lot of fun."

Old and In the Way did add a fiddle player—Richard Green and occasionally Nashville's legendary Vassar Clements—but they didn't play any bluegrass festivals. Instead, they performed approximately twenty-five gigs during 1973. The recording of a show at the Boarding House in San Francisco was later released as the album *Old and In the Way*. The live recording captured the band on an especially inspired night, which was fortuitous since the group was together for less than a year.

After Old and In the Way broke up, Garcia was not finished with bluegrass. He formed another group with Grisman called the Great American String Band, which was together for a few months. It featured Garcia on banjo and vocals, Grisman on mandolin and vocals, Taj Mahal on bass and vocals, David Nictern on acoustic guitar and vocals, and Richard Green on fiddle.

Despite his work with the Dead, various bluegrass groups, the new record venture, and his solo projects, Garcia was not completely scratching his itch to play. He continued performing with Merl Saunders as often as his schedule would allow. These engagements not only enabled Garcia to expand his repertoire into rhythm and blues standards, but also enabled his fans to see him in a more intimate setting than the Grateful Dead's mushrooming popularity would permit. In 1972 and 1973, the Garcia and Saunders Band did three albums for Fantasy Records—*Heavy Turbulence*, *Fire Up*, and *Live at Keystone*. Garcia's lead vocal work on these albums reflected his expanding repertoire as he sang a number of covers, including "The Night They Drove Old Dixie Down," "After Midnight," "Positively 4th Street," "The Harder They Come," "It Takes a Lot To Laugh, It Takes a Train To Cry," "It's No Use," and "That's All Right, Mama." Saunders observed, "When I went into these projects Fantasy questioned why we were doing so many Motown songs and Dylan songs. I said, 'Because people like it.' We were playing Motown songs after they had died. We started playing them instrumentally and doing the vocals our particular way, and they were a hit. Jerry was very unique in picking songs. He was very soulful and could capture a song and bring feeling to it. He also got me singing. We'd come off a tour and he'd say, 'Man, you gotta help me out singing.' I didn't think I could sing, but I figured if Jerry could sing, I could sing. He'd say, 'You hear how bad I can sound; you don't sound any worse than I do.' I said, 'I guess I don't.' We used to laugh about it, but that's how I started singing."

In case all this activity and popularity was going to Jerry's head (it really wasn't), the authorities stepped in once more to try to knock him down a peg. During the Dead's 1973 tour of the East Coast, Garcia was busted. After a gig in Baltimore, Maryland, he was driving a rented Chevrolet with Hunter to the band's next show in Springfield, Massachusetts, when he got stopped by a New Jersey state trooper for speeding on the New Jersey Turnpike. Garcia had no driver's license on his person, and when the officer searched the car's trunk he found a suitcase containing marijuana, cocaine, and LSD. Garcia spent several hours in jail before getting bailed out. The New Jersey judge was sympathetic—Jerry received a year's probation with counseling as a condition of his sentence. However, Garcia's attitude toward society's official opinion of drugs remained cavalier: "Where does it say in the Scriptures you can't get high or raise your consciousness?"

As the Grateful Dead's audience continued to grow with the success of the albums *Workingman's Dead*, *American Beauty*, *Grateful Dead*, and *Europe '72*, they began playing ever-larger venues, with sports arena and stadium shows becoming more common. Consequently, the band's technicians began developing a new sound system that could provide good, clear sound in the farthest reaches of even the largest concert venue. The system was introduced at Kezar Stadium in San Francisco on May 26, 1973, and was expanded and improved until it developed into what the techies called the "wall of sound." Weighing 25 tons, with 641 speakers and a combined power output of 26,400 watts, it delivered the clearest sound and widest frequency range of any sound system being used at that time and set a standard of excellence for years to come. The sound system was the product of the collective effort of a group of hi-fi technicians who were part of Alembic, a company started by Owsley Stanley in 1969.

Alembic began informally as a Dead family endeavor and developed into an independent business with a workshop and recording studio. Owsley brought in electronic wizard Ron Wickersham, guitar-maker Rick Turner, and Grateful Dead sound technicians Dan Healy, Bob Matthews, and Betty Cantor. Guitars, amplifiers, speakers, and other electronic equipment were reworked and refined to enhance their performance and sound quality. Garcia used to go into the electronic shop to tear his guitar down and rebuild it. He reminisced, "That was fun. We got a lot of shit done there. That's where we smashed the shit out of Weir's Acoustic amplifier. We executed it, jumped up and down on it."

After Alembic started designing their own products, they got a retail shop on Ninth Avenue in San Francisco. It was at that location in late 1972 that Garcia met Doug Irwin, who was working as an apprentice for Rick Turner. Irwin had built his own guitar, which was on display in the front of the store.

Irwin recalled, "I was in the back of the shop one day and one of the guys came back and said that Jerry Garcia was in the shop and wanted to buy my guitar. I thought that it was a joke, so I ignored him and kept on working. About twenty minutes later he came back again and said that Jerry was out front and he really wanted to buy the guitar. I still didn't believe him, so he dragged me out front—and sure enough it was Jerry Garcia, and he bought the guitar." Garcia liked the feel and configuration of the neck on Irwin's guitar, because it allowed him to play all the way down the fretboard without constricting his hand. This gave Garcia the ability to play two full octaves, because the neck was accessible at the point where it joined the body, which was very unusual. Irwin has been custom-designing guitars for Garcia ever since.

At the end of July 1973 the Grateful Dead played at the largest rock 'n' roll concert of all time. Dubbed "Summer Jam" by the promoters, it featured the Grateful Dead, the Allman Brothers, and the Band. An estimated 600,000 people showed up for the concert, which was scheduled for July 28 outdoors at the Grand Prix Racecourse in Watkins Glen, New York. The concert was put on by promoters Shelley Finkel and Jim Koplik, who brought in Bill Graham for support. The day before the show tens of thousands of fans showed up at the site to get a good spot at the outdoor show. Since there were so many people already there, Graham convinced the bands to do a sound check that afternoon. As a result, those who showed up early got to see a mini-concert, with the Band performing one song, the Allman Brothers playing for an hour, and the Grateful Dead doing a set of ten songs. As usual, the Dead got caught up in just playing, and wouldn't leave the stage. Graham said, "The Dead played for an hour and a half. By seven o'clock that night, the kids had seen a great, great show."

On the day of the actual show the Grateful Dead played a matinee in the afternoon, followed by the Band and then the Allman Brothers. After the Grateful Dead's performance a jam with members of all three bands came together with the musicians doing "Not Fade Away," "Mountain Jam," and "Johnny B. Goode." Phil Lesh described the Watkins Glen show: "We put a tremendous amount of planning into that gig. We practically had to do it ourselves, despite the promoters. The biggest hassle was convincing the Band to come out and play— 'Hey, man, it's just down the road a piece. Come on out and play. What can you lose?' They played great!"

In a bit of irony, Jim Koplik was thrown off the stage by road crew member Steve Parish. Parish had joined the crew in the early 1970s; at six feet, four inches, he was well suited for the rigors of being a "quippie." He later became (and still remains) Garcia's right-hand man. Parish summarized: "He kept telling me he was the promoter, and we didn't know him; nobody knew him, and he was bothering us. Me and [another crew member] just looked at each other and gave him the heave-ho. He landed in grass, you know."

With the release of the album *History of the Grateful Dead, Vol. 1 (Bear's Choice)* in July 1973, the band satisfied their commitment to Warner Brothers. They immediately began taping their first album on their own label and completed it by September. The sessions at the Record Plant in Sausalito went smoothly as the band recorded some new songs they had been performing in concert. True to their word, the band kept their fans informed:

Dear Fellow Dead Head,

There are two reasons for writing to you now; first, to give you the earliest specific information on our new record distribution program; secondly, to ask you to join us as part of our eyes, ears, and feet on the ground to keep the scene straight locally.

We've decided to produce, manufacture, and distribute our records ourselves. The band today finished the recording of an all-new studio album (been a long time) called *Wake of the Flood*. The album will be made from the highest quality vinyl available, which has the best technical properties. In addition, it will be heavier (weigh more, that is) than most albums available in this country. It will be handled locally through independent record distributors and should be available everywhere.

This adventure is a jumping-off point to get us in a position of greater contact with our people, to put us more in command of our own ship, and for unspoken potentials for the "far out."

If you're interested in getting involved, drop us a line here. In any case, you'll enjoy the record—it's dynamite!

GRATEFUL DEAD RECORDS   September 4, 1973

Wake of the Flood bore the catalog number "GD-01." It came out in October 1973 and sold more than four hundred thousand copies, despite numerous counterfeit copies that were sold on the East Coast.

In early 1974 Garcia went back into the studio to begin work on his second solo album, which was produced by his friend John Kahn. Garcia was again stretching his musical limits, and asked Kahn to produce the record because he wanted to try something different. Kahn helped Jerry pick out a collection of cover tunes. Kahn commented, "I would present him with a bunch of ideas, and he'd take the ones he liked and work on those. It was mainly stuff that he wouldn't ordinarily have thought of, and I think that was part of the challenge for him— to try something that was really new to him." Garcia ran through some thirty songs during the sessions, and Kahn was impressed with his attitude. "I admired Jerry for being game for that stuff. A lot of performers wouldn't do something like that—stuff they're not familiar with—risking possible embarrassment or making mistakes." It was one thing to do this sort of playing in a small club with an indulgent audience, and strictly another thing to do it when a considerable amount of money and time were on the line.

Unlike his first solo effort, Garcia brought in studio musicians to fill out the sound—keyboardist Michael Omartian, drummer Ron Tutt, percussionist Bobbye Hall, and backup vocalists Clydie King, Merry Clayton, and Maria Muldaur. Though the record was titled *Garcia*, just like his first solo album, it became known as *Compliments of Garcia* because of the promotional sticker that said "Compliments of" on the cover.

Grateful Dead Records was active in early 1974. Besides *Compliments of Garcia* and Hunter's solo album *Tales of the Great Rum Runners*, the first two releases on the Round Records subsidiary, the company was producing *Grateful Dead from the Mars Hotel*. A promotional package for Dead Heads was sent out in May. It included a letter announcing the completion of *Mars Hotel*, miniature facsimiles of the covers for *Mars Hotel* and the two solo albums, as well as a record called *Sampler for Dead Heads* that had two cuts from *Compliments* and three from *Rum Runners*.

The release of *Mars Hotel* showed that the new record company, although founded in the tradition of community that the band espoused, was serious about making money and protecting its product. To try to preempt the counterfeiting threat remembered from the experience with their first production, *Wake of the Flood*, the cover designers had the word *authentic* stamped on the front. The venture was less than a year old, yet negative business considerations were already creeping in that would lead to its demise.

By the fall of 1974 the band was chafing under the expense of maintaining the "wall of sound," which had caused their operating budget to balloon to $100,000 a month. Rock Scully disclosed, "It was horribly expensive. We had four tractor trailers and our own stage to accommodate it. In fact we had two stages. While one stage was being put up, the other stage was being taken down. As a tour progressed the stages would leapfrog from one venue to the next so that it would be ready when the equipment arrived. . . . We had more than twenty guys to help set it up and break it down. When we would get home from this monster road tour we would have hardly any money left."

Essentially, the band was locked into using the "wall" when touring. The number of people who wanted to see them had grown so fantastically that the band was playing larger venues. And the band insisted that their fans be given the best possible sound for their money. The only way to reconcile their financial difficulties and their creative needs was to take some time off. Garcia explained, "We were all pretty depressed. If we were going to do it, we felt it should be fun; it should be the things we liked about it originally and the things that we still wanted to have as part of the experience. It had turned into a thing that was out of our control, and nobody was really doing it because they liked it. We were doing it because we had to."

The band played one last set of shows at Winterland in October 1974, which was filmed for possible use in a feature-length Grateful Dead movie. As far as anyone knew, the band members included, this was the Grateful Dead's farewell engagement. On the final night of the run, Mickey Hart sat in with the band, figuring if this was going to be the last night forever, he didn't want to miss out.

* * * *

Garcia missed touring with the Dead, but he didn't miss the financial and business gremlins that were plaguing the band. After the Grateful Dead stopped performing in 1974, he played regularly with the Garcia and Saunders Band, which he and Saunders renamed the Legion of Mary. The Legion featured Garcia on lead guitar and vocals, Saunders on keyboards and vocals, John Kahn on bass, Martin Fierro on tenor saxophone, and Paul Humphrey on drums. Saunders laughingly recounted their first trip to Southern California after the Grateful Dead retired: "We came off the plane in San Diego, and this porter is looking at us very strangely as we got into the limo. He said, 'Oh, my God, what kind of band is this? You've got a hippie [Garcia], a black guy [Saunders], a white guy [Kahn], an Indian [Fierro], and a Super Fly [Humphrey, who dressed in sharp flashy colors].' We got a good laugh at that!" The limo took the band up to the Golden Bear in Huntington Beach where they played a mixture of rock, rhythm and blues, and jazz to a sold-out house.

Legion of Mary performed steadily, doing nearly one hundred shows in California and on the East Coast from October 1974 through June 1975. Merl Saunders recalled, "The band toured heavily. We would go out and tour the East Coast, mainly New York, Boston, Philly, and D.C. We were playing to about two thousand people. In New York we packed them in."

While in New York in April 1975, the group had an experience they would cherish forever. Saunders described the scene: "I will never forget when we played the Bottom Line in the spring of 1975. We did three shows in three days, and the place was jampacked. We were playing and the audience was just freaking out, and all of a sudden we hear all the noise stop. We hear an 'oooh,' and we see a flash go by into the dressing room. We look at each other because we didn't know who went in there. When we went into the dressing room John Lennon was sitting there. We were shocked. He came to thank us for doing his number, 'Imagine,' on my album *Heavy Turbulence*. I had done the first cover version of his song. Lennon wrote 'Imagine' in 1971 and the record had just come out that September. I was at Fantasy Records that fall with Garcia, Tom Fogerty, John Kahn, and Bill Vitt to record my album. This guy at the studio had a promotional copy of the record. I listened to 'Imagine' and thought it was gorgeous, so I wanted to do an instrumental cover version of it. This was before 'Imagine' became a hit. I let Jerry hear the song and he said, 'It's a neat song, let's do it.'"

The music of John Lennon meant a lot to Garcia not only because Lennon's songs helped change rock 'n' roll and fuel the counterculture, but because the Beatles had inspired Jerry to play rock 'n' roll back in his jug band days. Garcia would go on to cover a number of songs Lennon had sung with the Beatles, including "Dear Prudence," "Revolution," and "Lucy in the Sky with Diamonds"—one 1960s legend paying tribute to another.

Though Saunders and Garcia were good friends and the Legion of Mary was filling theaters across the country, in the summer of 1975 the two musicians decided to go their own way. Jerry experienced another split that year—with Mountain Girl.

Garcia, a self-described "music junkie" whose life was controlled by music, was never much of a traditional family man. He became an absentee husband and father because he was constantly performing or on the road with one of his bands. Mountain Girl, who as one of the Pranksters had been an integral part of the social milieu in the 1960s, had a sense of frustration about life with Jerry. She expressed her feelings in a typically up-front way in a 1971 interview: "I don't play with the band. There's nothing for me to do. I don't go for the freak-out dancing trip. They don't let me rave over the microphones very much. So I get really bored. Immediately, in fact. Frustrated, 'cause there's nothing for me to do, so I usually stay home." As an intelligent, independent person, she had no use for what she saw as an empty life on the road. She also had a well-grounded life of her own, not only with her daughters (including her and Jerry's second daughter, Theresa, born in 1974), but with her own friends and interests. Playing the good camp follower was not for her.

With Mountain Girl at home, Garcia had a number of encounters with interesting women who were captivated by his creative genius. One such woman was Deborah Koons, an attractive woman in her twenties, whom Garcia met in the early 1970s when he was in her hometown of Cincinnati during one of his tours. Koons was from a prominent, well-to-do family, and had attended prep school and the University of North Carolina. She was a bright, cheerful, intellectual person who wanted to make a career in filmmaking. Koons moved to the Bay Area in the mid-1970s, and her relationship with Jerry lasted a few years.

In 1975, Mountain Girl and Garcia decided to separate.

The split was hard, but both made the best of it. "She had a different life," Garcia explained. "It was painful, but it's more honest this way. We're all very close." The connection between Jerry and Mountain Girl ran deep, and their friendship didn't end. Their paths would cross many times in the years ahead.

6

A DECADE OF CHANGE

he Grateful Dead did not tour in 1975. Although this was a great disappointment to their fans, it was a boon to Garcia and the others. Since the decision to stop doing major live performances had been based on business considerations this time, rather than on musical grounds (as with the short Mickey Hart and the Hartbeats interlude), Jerry still had a strong desire to play with his mates. The band got together to work on the album *Blues for Allah*, which was recorded in Bob Weir's studio at his home in Mill Valley. Instead of trying to mix recording time with concert dates, the band was able to tape the album in a relaxed manner, spending five months in the process. "I think that's the first record we've made in years where we really had fun," said Garcia. "We laughed a lot and got good and crazy. We had an opportunity to get weirder than we normally get to getting."

An example of this weirdness was Mickey Hart going out and getting a cardboard box full of five hundred crickets, the sound of which the band attempted to record by sticking microphones inside the box. This particular episode started out with the solid purpose of re-creating the sounds of the desert—the dry, brittle sound of sand being blown across the landscape. It was an inspired idea that worked well, but by the time they were through the crickets had escaped and were all over Weir's studio.

Garcia viewed the record as an experiment, but not in the sense that the music had swung back to the avant-garde. Instead, he was talking about the group's preparation for the recording: "We all went on the trip of 'Well, we're gonna make a record, and we're gonna go into the studio with no preconceptions, and with no material.' . . . It was a chance to let us hang out together and let ideas evolve from absolute coldness, from absolutely nothing."

The majority of Garcia's third solo LP, *Reflections*, was also recorded at Weir's studio in 1975. The members of the Dead played on it, and half the album is essentially a Grateful Dead record. Garcia advised: "A lot of the energy from that record is really a continuation of the *Blues for Allah* groove that we got into. We sort of continued the same energy because we were having a lot of fun doing it."

To help celebrate the release of *Blues for Allah*, the Dead performed live on August 13 at the Great American Music Hall. This concert, which served as the record-release party too, was for family members, friends, and music-industry people, and admission was by invitation only. It was held at the Music Hall because of Garcia's fondness for the venue, built on his experience playing there with the Garcia and Saunders Band. Contrary to its name, the room had a seating capacity of just 425, and those who were lucky enough to squeeze in saw the band play in a club-like setting for the first time since the 1960s.

The arrangements for the event had been made by Ron Rakow, who had help from Al Teller, president of United Artists Records. This collaboration signified an important change in the band's business dealings. By the time *Blues for Allah* was ready for release, Grateful Dead Records was struggling financially, and a deal had been cut with United Artists to manufacture and distribute the Dead's records. The agreement also included solo albums that would otherwise be produced by Round Records, which was also in need of financial assistance.

The break in touring had enabled the Grateful Dead to extricate themselves from the $100,000-a-month overhead they had incurred from carting around the "wall of sound," paying a crew of forty people to maintain it, and meeting the payroll for their entire organization. It also helped them realize that they couldn't be businessmen and musicians at the same time. Their first love was playing music, not making money. During the break, the "wall" was dismantled and the organization was pared down, and the band pushed their briefcases to one side and got back to the business of making music.

*   *   *   *

As usual, studio work was not enough for music-junkie Garcia. The Grateful Dead weren't touring and he had split from Merl Saunders, so he naturally formed another group—the Jerry Garcia Band. Next to the Dead, this has been Garcia's longest-lived ensemble, and the group still tours today. The original members of the band included John Kahn on bass, Nicky Hopkins on piano, and Ron Tutt on drums. Although over the years musicians have come and gone, the group's formula has remained basically the same—it's a good-time band in which Garcia sings mostly cover tunes and gets the chance to work out on lead guitar. Garcia and the original members quickly established the style of all the future configurations of the band, moving away from the jazzy, funky-soul sound of the Garcia and Saunders Band and the Legion of Mary to a mixed repertoire of rhythm and blues, rock 'n' roll, and some Hunter-Garcia originals.

Hopkins left the band at the end of 1975, and soon after the new year, Keith and Donna Godchaux began performing with the group. (The previous summer, Garcia had helped out with *their* other group, the Keith and Donna Band, sitting in at several Bay Area gigs.) Garcia felt that the repertoire of his band suited Keith's melodic piano playing and Donna's vocal style, and the husband-and-wife team developed a rapport with others in the Jerry Garcia Band that lasted for several years.

John Kahn recalled, "Keith lived over on Paradise Drive [in Corte Madera], and we used to play over there all the time. He had a room downstairs that was set up so we could just go in and play. . . . I lived in Mill Valley and Jerry lived in Stinson Beach, so it was real easy for us to get together. Anyway, we had this scene where we'd get together just about every night and play. We'd go through everything. We had Dylan songbooks and we'd do stuff like play everything from *Blonde on Blonde*. Then we'd do all sorts of Beatle songs. It was great. Most of it never even got past that room." Garcia was getting his kicks with these fellows, playing for the pure enjoyment of it in someone's basement.

With the Grateful Dead still on hiatus, the Jerry Garcia Band toured heavily, performing extended versions of old Motown hits like "How Sweet It Is" and "I Second That Emotion," tunes from Garcia's solo albums, and an occasional Grateful Dead song. Playing with this group was like sitting in a favorite old easy chair for Garcia. He claimed, "I haven't been as happy with any little performing group since Old and In the Way in terms of feeling this is really harmonious; this is what I want to hear."

But this was not all Jerry wanted to hear, for in June 1976 Garcia brought the Grateful Dead out of retirement and the group started touring again. Mickey Hart, who had played with the band only once in over five years (at the "farewell concert" back in October 1974), came back too. With his reintroduction, new arrangements of old songs were worked out and fresh material was added.

In contrast to his own band, Garcia could appreciate the musical diversity of the Grateful Dead. This was key for Garcia, who liked the challenge of playing with the Dead: "One of the things that makes the Grateful Dead interesting is that it's incredibly dissonant. Everybody in the band is so different—we couldn't be more different. So I can almost expect that when I put forward an idea, what everyone will play will be incredibly different from what I had imagined."

About this time, the Dead closed down Grateful Dead Records for good, coming full circle to working with the record industry again. They also parted company with Ron Rakow, who had been involved in the production of *Steal Your Face*, the double live album culled from the recordings of the "retirement shows" at Winterland in 1974. The LP was a major disappointment for the band and their fans. It was mixed by Phil Lesh and Owsley Stanley at Burbank Studios in Burbank, and Lesh convinced the others that the best way to go was not to include any tunes that had already appeared on any other live album. Lesh grumbled, "We owed United Artists the product, and I relied on Rakow's word. He said we had 'good material.' Look, Rakow wouldn't know good material if it came up and pissed on his shoe. . . . That album would never have been released if we hadn't needed the money for the film."

Garcia discussed the album: "None of us liked it. I'm sure even Phil and Owsley didn't like it that much. . . . I think part of it was that we were not working, and we didn't have anything else to deliver." The general pessimism about the work was even reflected in the name, which was chosen by Lesh because he felt it best conveyed his sentiment about it.

Rakow left the band after the master tapes for *Steal Your Face* were delivered to United Artists. In an interview in *BAM Magazine*, the band claimed that he also walked off with a

$275,000 check which was money United Artists owed them for *Steal Your Face*. Rakow responded in the same article in *BAM*. He didn't deny that he left the band abruptly with a large amount of money, but he said that the check resulted from separate negotiations that were going on at the same time as the tapes were delivered. Thus, the band's independence from the record industry ended ignominiously with a bad album and a big hole in its budget.

Having fulfilled their agreement with United Artists, the Grateful Dead started looking for a new label. After shopping around they decided to sign with Arista Records. Garcia thought that Clive Davis, the head of Arista, signed the Grateful Dead because "he likes to be associated with elements of integrity," and the band came to Arista with a sense of optimism. Garcia reflected, "When we started working with Arista, we did it thinking 'What the fuck—it'll be nice to be involved with a record company and not have to be doing the marketing ourselves, not have to do distribution.' So, fundamentally, we were into the space of 'Let's just make music, and let's go as far into it as we can.'"

That attitude carried over into the actual production of the music, and the band brought in an outside producer to help with their next album, *Terrapin Station*. Although it had been ten years since they had used an outsider—Dave Hassinger was up to this point the first and only professional they had tried—the band was ready for input from someone with a new insight. Perhaps this was a reaction to the experience with *Steal Your Face*. Garcia explained, "We wanted some fresh ears, and that's part of the reason the idea of a producer didn't seem outrageous to us. We're very conscious of how easy it is to get into your own trip so much that you have no objectivity at all."

The band decided to bring in Keith Olsen, who had produced *Fleetwood Mac*, that group's breakthrough album, which had made its way to the top of the charts and gone gold. The band was hoping to put out an album with broader appeal than any of their prior records. For his part, Olsen wanted to get material that would play well on the radio but would retain the trademark Grateful Dead sound. He also wanted Garcia's vocals to stand out. He commented, "Garcia has amazing color in his voice if you place it just right, bridging the gap between Donna and Bob. He has a George Harrison quality to his voice that makes an incredible blend if you voice the parts correctly."

As it turned out, the collaboration worked out in a strange way. The band began recording *Terrapin Station* in January 1977 at Sound City Studios in Van Nuys, California. The songs comprising "Terrapin Station" were based on a series of verses written by Hunter that were some of his finest lyrics. The suite ended up being one entire side of the album, and became a unique piece of work for the band when the decision was made to orchestrate it. Olsen composed the fifty-six-page score with Paul Buckmaster, who had worked with some of the biggest names in rock, including the Rolling Stones and Elton John. The Martyn Ford Orchestra was used for the orchestration, and almost a hundred musicians and singers were involved. The use of horns, strings, and choral singers was a radical departure from what the Grateful Dead were used to doing.

While the majority of the album was recorded at Sound City, additional overdubs were done at Automated Sound Studios in New York, and the orchestration for "Terrapin Station" was recorded at Abbey Road Studios in London. Garcia said that it was a real boon to work with Olsen: "He has a really excellent ear, and he's worked really well with us. . . . The performances are really amazing, much better than we're able to flog out of ourselves when we're in there producing ourselves."

Terrapin Station was released on July 27, 1977, and was unlike anything else the Grateful Dead had put out. Garcia felt that "it actually sounds like a record. People won't believe it's us." The goal to appeal to a wider audience was met, as the disc went gold a few months after its release and several of the cuts on the album got good airplay. However, critics, including a number of Dead Heads, contended that the album, especially the "Terrapin Station" side, was badly overproduced. Many fans disparagingly referred to the album as "disco-Dead" because of the blatantly commercial mix of "Dancin' in the Streets," the old Motown hit.

Though the heavily produced album was unusual for the band, it was nothing more than an attempt to try something different in the studio. Garcia's response to questions about being accused of selling out was, "Fuck 'em if they can't take a joke." Of course, the album was not a joke, but his attitude was appropriate. *Terrapin Station* didn't signal any substantive change in the Grateful Dead's music. As Garcia always maintained, the best way to judge where the band was going was by listening to their live performances rather than their efforts on vinyl.

That live experience was what the Grateful Dead was all about. Garcia had spent his career trying to give that experience to listeners, and his attempts had taken him into new genres, new venues, and now, new media. On June 1, 1977, *The Grateful Dead Movie* premiered at the Ziegfeld Theatre in New York.

Several earlier attempts had been made to film the Grateful Dead, with mixed results. In 1967, a one-hour news special called *The Hippie Temptation* was made by CBS, with Harry Reasoner taking a trip to Haight-Ashbury during the peak of the Summer of Love. The show included a five-minute visit to 710 Ashbury Street for a short interview with Garcia, Lesh, Weir, Scully, and Rifkin. The program ended with a brief clip of the Grateful Dead playing "Dancin' in the Streets" on a flatbed truck in Golden Gate Park. The special was not strictly a news piece, as Reasoner's condescending comments about the bankrupt state of hippie culture gave the show an obnoxious slant.

One worthwhile film made in 1967 was called *Grateful Dead*. The seven-and-a-half-minute short was made by avant-garde filmmaker Robert Nelson, who had met Lesh when they were both involved with the San Francisco Mime Troupe.

Nelson, who had received a grant from the Belgium Film Archive, thought the Grateful Dead would make an interesting subject for an experimental movie he wanted to produce, utilizing a montage of close-ups and wide-angle shots, color and black-and-white images, slow- and fast-motion sequences, in-focus and out-of-focus pictures, and single and double exposures to re-create the psychedelic experience. To make up the body of the movie, Nelson used concert footage plus candid shots of the band at the heliport in Sausalito and canoeing on the Russian River in Rio Nido. The visuals worked well with the pieces of Grateful Dead music used for the soundtrack.

Nelson retained the rights to the film, but never did anything commercially with it. Some years later he sold the movie to the band. Nelson recounted, "I was in financial trouble and I needed money, so I decided to sell the rights to the movie. I called Garcia up and asked him if he wanted to buy my film. I didn't really know what it was worth or how much to ask for it, so I just came up with the figure of $11,000. Garcia said, 'No problem, man.' At that point I didn't know whether I asked too much or too little for the film. When the check came in the mail a few weeks later I discovered Jerry had sent me $15,000. Now that's what I call class!" Garcia's high-minded attitude toward money could be traced to the cooperative living experience he had in the 1960s, when he lived with friends and they helped each other survive by sharing what they had.

In February 1970, PBS made a notable documentary called *A Night at the Family Dog*, which featured the Grateful Dead, Jefferson Airplane, and Santana in concert at the Family Dog on the Great Highway in San Francisco. The program showed several songs by each group, then a jam featuring members of all three including Jerry Garcia, Bob Weir, Jorma Kaukonen, Jack Casady, Paul Kantner, and Carlos Santana. Jorma recalled the jam at the end of the evening: "That night was one of the good ones where the jam really came together. We played as a band and gave each other the space to play. It was real lucky they got it on film." A *Night at the Family Dog* aired on public television throughout the country later that year.

Another documentary, *Sunshine Daydream*, didn't fare as well. The ninety-minute movie was the brainchild of Phil DeGuere, a young filmmaker in Palo Alto who was a fan of the Grateful Dead and who, together with his friends John Norris and Sam Field, decided to make a film about the band. DeGuere happened to run into Garcia in February 1972 at a San Francisco club before a Garcia and Saunders show, and he proposed the movie idea to him. With Jerry's encouragement, the trio got the go-ahead to film the Grateful Dead at an outdoor concert in Veneta, Oregon, on August 27, 1972. The concert was a benefit for the Springfield Creamery, which was owned by Ken Kesey's brother, Chuck.

Sunshine Daydream was more than a concert film, however; it documented hippie culture in its heyday. A total of twenty-five thousand people came together for the biggest Grateful Dead/Prankster reunion since the 1960s. When clothing became optional due to the oppressive 103-degree temperature, the cameras caught the smiling faces of the vast assemblage dancing in the sun. The opening scenes showed clips of the stage being constructed, and the film also included Merry Prankster footage of the Acid Tests and Neal Cassady at the wheel of the Bus. Although the movie was a great exhibition of hippiedom at its peak, Grateful Dead band members were less than enthusiastic about its release because the heat had made their guitars go out of tune. They had little to worry about, for *Sunshine Daydream* was shelved before it was distributed on a national level.

The Grateful Dead Movie became Garcia's project because film-making was something he had always wanted to get into. In the early 1960s he had spent a considerable amount of time working on film soundtracks at the Stanford University Communications Department when he was with his first wife, Sarah, and he had enjoyed the experience. And since his second artistic love was drawing and painting, he had a strong interest in the visual aspect of art.

Garcia was aware of all of the video pieces about or featuring the band that had gone before. He wanted to avoid the problems of the worst of them, and he did want *The Grateful Dead Movie* to get into wide circulation. He spent two and a half years working on the picture, which he edited from the "retirement shows" at the Winterland in 1974. The five concerts were filmed by nine crews, who shot 150 hours worth of film. Garcia admitted, "Filming five nights was a gamble. The possibility was that we would ideally have a good night in the five . . . so let's go for broke. But the only way we'll get it is if everybody shoots all the time."

Working with Grateful Dead soundman Dan Healy, Garcia took the film to Burbank Studios to mix the soundtrack and carefully labored to sync the footage with the music. He also edited the film down to the final length of 131 minutes. Garcia was not oblivious to the pitfalls of moviemaking, and he described the process he went through as "two years of incredible doubt." He spent countless hours working on the movie, editing the film and perfecting the soundtrack so that it would meet the approval of bandmates and fans alike. He revealed, "Every time I thought about something, my mind would come back to the film and I'd get depressed. It's boiled down to two hours and ten minutes now, but it sure took a lot of energy."

The film opened with an extraordinary animation sequence by Gary Gutierrez that conveyed the feeling of the psychedelic experience, then segued into nostalgic stills of the 1960s, concert footage of the band and audience, and interviews with band members, crew, and Dead Heads. Garcia felt that the film was "a good movie example of the Grateful Dead experience. It's a translation of that idea, both coming from what it's like for me—in my head, as abstract ideas, nonspecific images—and what it's like for anybody." *The Grateful Dead Movie* was the definitive take on the music of the Grateful Dead and the spirit of their fans.

After the release of *The Grateful Dead Movie* Garcia turned his attention to recording an album with the Jerry Garcia Band. The tracks on the record were laid down at the Grateful Dead's newly acquired studio on Front Street in San Rafael, which became known as Le Club Front. The band recorded all-new material, much of it recently penned by Robert Hunter, who worked in the studio alongside the musicians. Unlike Jerry's prior solo efforts, this was more of a band project, with John

Kahn and Donna Godchaux contributing some songs. Additionally, Garcia brought in Merl Saunders to play organ parts; Steve Schuster to add flute, clarinet, and saxophone; Brian and Candy Godchaux to play violins; and vocalist Maria Muldaur to sing some backup vocals. Muldaur was a former member of the Jim Kweskin Jug Band whose 1974 solo debut album, *Maria Muldaur*, contained the pop hit "Midnight at the Oasis."

Jerry thought the album, entitled *Cats Under the Stars*, "had everything—chops, production, songs." Though Garcia was disappointed when the LP did not sell as well as he had hoped, *Cats Under the Stars* represented the best of what the Godchaux version of the Garcia Band had to offer. In addition, the songs penned for the album provided new material for the band to play in concert and gave their live performances new vitality. For instance, "Rubin and Cherise" and "Cats Under the Stars" were livelier than many of the slow ballads that Garcia liked to perform with his band.

During the rest of 1977 and into 1978, Garcia was spending his time on the road with his band or the Grateful Dead, recording albums, and working on various other projects. One of these projects was special, involving a long-standing dream of Garcia's. The dream was fulfilled in September 1978 when the Grateful Dead gave three concerts at the base of the pyramids in Egypt. The venture cost the band $500,000, which was "all the money we have in the world for the next two years," Jerry said at the time. "This is kind of like giving ourselves a present or taking a vacation. Frankly, we're amazed we're getting to do this. If we had asked to play the Washington Monument, we know damn well what they'd say." The concerts were arranged through the Egyptian Ministry of Culture, which granted permission for the Grateful Dead to perform at the foot of the Great Pyramid, specially floodlit for the occasion. All proceeds from the three concerts went to the Egyptian Department of Antiquities, which maintains the monuments of Egypt's past, and the Faith and Hope Society, an organization that helps the handicapped.

Because the expense of transporting all their own equipment from San Francisco was prohibitive, the band arranged to have the Who's sound system shipped to Egypt from England, and they also hired the Manor Mobile Recording Unit to record the three shows for a possible album. "It doesn't matter if we play horrible, if everything breaks up—all the things that can go wrong, from an aesthetic point of view to a technological point of view, all those things would be okay here," said Garcia. "This place has really freed me from something that I am normally quite concerned with, which is just professional competence; if I'm touchy about anything, that's it. But this experience is greater than the elements of performance in a normal sense."

A charter of Dead family and Dead Heads took a package flight from San Francisco for $999 apiece to be part of the experience. Among those who went to Egypt were Ken Kesey, Mountain Girl, George Walker, Owsley Stanley, Bill Graham,

David Freiberg, Nicki Scully, and Bill Walton. The band and entourage stayed at the Mena House, a stately old Egyptian hotel overlooking the pyramids.

Despite the fact that the Grateful Dead were famous in the West, most Egyptians had never heard of them. However, as Garcia claimed, "We would've played [Egypt] whether there was an audience or not. But the reality of it, as it's unfolded, is that the audience has become as much a part of the show as Egypt, the Pyramids—as the idea! If you were to think of this whole thing as a piece of concept art, rather than as a performance, they are full participants." The concerts were held on Thursday, Friday, and Saturday, September 14-16, and by the final night there were several thousand locals dancing to the music. To add some local flavor, the band performed with Hamza El-Din, a popular Nubian singer who played the oud, a guitar-like Egyptian instrument. Each night Hamza performed with a group of Nubian musicians, and as the Nubian music progressed, various members of the Grateful Dead would join in, and the music would gradually segue into a Dead set.

On the final night, the band performed during an eclipse of the full moon, and the music went on until after 3 AM. At the conclusion of the concert, Bill Graham hosted a lavish party at a nightclub in Sahara City, a small town in the desert that was an hour away by horseback. Graham arranged for horses and camels to be delivered beside the stage at the end of the concert, and when the show was over the Grateful Dead and family mounted up and rode off into the desert.

Egypt made a lasting impression on Garcia. "That was a wonderful adventure and an old fantasy of ours, to play the Great Pyramid. It totally blew my mind. For me, it was one of those before-and-after experiences—I mean, there's my life before Egypt and my life after Egypt. It expanded certain levels. The Great Pyramid itself is such a wonder, it completely burns out your concepts of things like size and the realm of possibility."

The Egyptian concerts were supposed to be followed by a tour of Europe, but the concerts were cancelled so that the Grateful Dead could complete work on their next LP, *Shakedown Street*. The band returned to California to finish mixing and overdubbing the album, which they had been recording at Le Club Front. *Shakedown Street*'s release was slated for November to coincide with a national tour, so pressure was on. "It's the first time we have ever coordinated a tour with the release of a record," Garcia observed. "We really have to deliver it by deadline." The band asked Lowell George of Little Feat to produce the album because they thought he would work well with them due to their common blues background. Though *Shakedown Street* received mixed reviews, the disc did contain two great originals: Hunter-Garcia's "Shakedown Street" and Hunter-Hart's "Fire on the Mountain."

To kick off their tour and publicize the release of the album, the Grateful Dead appeared on *Saturday Night Live* on November 11, 1978. They performed "I Need a Miracle" and "Good Lovin'" from the new album and also played "Casey Jones." Unfortunately, the band was not able to capitalize on the release of the album and the national TV exposure. The East Coast tour was cut short when Garcia developed a throat condition too severe to ignore. Jerry had been fighting recurring throat problems for some time, a condition exacerbated by the three packs of unfiltered Camels he smoked every day and by his chronic use of central nervous system stimulants.

One artistic relationship that resulted from the abortive tour was the rapport with several of the cast members and writers of *Saturday Night Live* that developed. John Belushi and Dan Aykroyd had formed a band called the Blues Brothers, which put on an outrageous show featuring the kind of Chicago blues that Garcia loved so much. Bill Graham brought the Grateful Dead and the Blues Brothers together on December 31, 1978, along with the New Riders of the Purple Sage. The occasion was the final concert at Winterland. This final show was an all-night party that started with a screening of the movie *Animal House*, followed by the expert juggling act of the Flying Karamozov Brothers and then a set by the New Riders of the Purple Sage. After an introduction that warned, "By the year 2006 the music known today as the blues will exist only in the classical section of your local library," the Blues Brothers energized the crowd with an upbeat and tight set. At midnight, thousands of balloons came down from the ceiling while Graham, dressed as Father Time, flew down to the stage from the rear balcony perched atop a huge facsimile of a joint. It was a legendary show with the Grateful Dead playing at the stroke of midnight, bringing in the New Year with three sets that ended at dawn. The show was a throwback to 1970 when the band frequently played three sets. At dawn when the music was over, Bill Graham provided a catered breakfast for the entire audience and bid adieu to Winterland.

It was a wonderful tribute to an era that was over—a time in which Bill Graham and the bands he promoted became famous in the relatively restricted confines of the Fillmore West, the Fillmore East, and Winterland, now all closed. Rock 'n' roll had moved beyond these venues, into bigger quarters.

After saying goodbye to their performing roots, the Grateful Dead also bid adieu to Keith and Donna Godchaux, who were asked to leave the band in February 1979 after seven years with the group. "Essentially," said Phil Lesh, "it was: 'Don't you guys feel you could profit from being on your own, doing what it is you do best, 'cause you're not doing it with us?'" The band was once again stretching out in new directions. Keith played acoustic piano almost exclusively, and the band wanted more and different keyboard sounds. And Donna's penchant for singing off-key during live performances with the Grateful Dead had become irritating.

Garcia recalled, "Donna was great in the studio—she's got good ears—and she was able to sing in my band okay. . . . But with the Grateful Dead, she never really learned to hear herself on stage—or she was never positioned appropriately, or we never had a monitoring system that allowed her to hear herself clearly; I don't know. She had a hard time singing in key on stage." In July 1980, approximately a year and a half after the Godchauxs left the band, Keith died tragically in an auto accident.

Brent Mydland was nominated to replace Keith and Donna. When the Grateful Dead had a meeting to discuss a replacement for the Godchauxs, Garcia suggested Mydland. Brent had been the keyboard player in Weir's band, and Jerry had noticed him when the Garcia Band toured with Weir's band for a few shows in October 1978. Mydland described being asked to join the Grateful Dead: "Sometime in February 1979, Bob [Weir] gave me a call and asked me if I was interested. I don't think they tried anyone else out, but they did want to hear me. I went to their studio and played with them, and apparently they liked the way I played."

Mydland was born in Munich, Germany, where his father was serving as an Army chaplain. His family moved to Antioch in the Bay Area in 1953 when he was a small child. Brent began taking piano lessons as a youngster and had classical training for seven or eight years; but when he was in high school, as happens so frequently, he started performing in rock bands. After graduating from high school Mydland gigged in clubs, then moved to Los Angeles, where he was the keyboard player for Batdorf and Rodney before forming his own band, Silver, with John Batdorf. The band released the album *Silver* on Arista Records in 1976. John Mauceri, the drummer for Batdorf and Rodney, introduced Mydland to Bob Weir in 1978.

On April 22, 1979, Mydland debuted with the Grateful Dead at Spartan Stadium in San Jose. The band's set that day was a surprise to the new keyboardist. "Before my first gig with the band, I asked what tunes we were going to play, but no one would tell me. When we got on stage, I realized that nobody knew what we were going to play." Mydland rose to the occa-

Jerreeee. (BARON WOLMAN)

The Grateful Dead, Laguna Street, 1969. (HERB GREENE/MICHAEL OCHS ARCHIVES)

Jerry looms above the camera at the Christian Science Monitor in 1972. (MICHAEL DOBO/MICHAEL OCHS ARCHIVES)

The Dead, Jefferson Airplane, Quicksilver Messenger Service, Janis Joplin & Big Brother and the Holding Company, and the Charlatans pour out of the door in front of 710 Ashbury Street in 1967. (GENE ANTHONY)

An all-star cast performs for the Cambodian refugee benefit at the Oakland County Coliseum, January 13, 1980. Left to right: John Cipollina, Carlos Santana, Jerry Garcia, Mickey Hart, Bill Kreutzmann, Joan Baez, Paul Kantner and Bob Weir. (GREG GAAR)

Phil Lesh impressed Garcia with his perfect pitch. The Greek Theater, 1981. (RON DELANY)

"A meeting of 60s legends," Bob Dylan tours with the Dead, July, 1987. (RON DELANY)

Jerry Garcia and David Grisman in the late 80s. (JON SIEVERT/MICHAEL OCHS ARCHIVES)

Nothing left to do but Smile, Smile, Smile! 1987. (RON DELANY)

Donna Godchaux with Jerry, 1977.
(RICHARD MCCAFFREY/MICHAEL OCHS ARCHIVES)

"Marijuana Exhibit A," 1975.
(GREG GAAR)

Garcia Acoustic Band, 1988. (RON DELANY)

The Jerry Garcia Band, 1989. (RON DELANY)

*Merl Saunders and Jerry Garcia—
Blues from the Rainforest, 1989.*
(COURTESY OF MERL SAUNDERS)

Garcia, 1987.   (JAY BLAKESBERG)

As lyricist for both The Grateful Dead and The Jerry Garcia Band, Robert Hunter's evocative poetry and storytelling formed the basis for many of the songs Garcia performs and has recorded over the years, 1991. (JAY BLAKESBERG)

"Garcia on Broadway," NYC, 1987. Left to right: Kenny Kosek, fiddle; Sandy Rothman, banjo; John Kahn, acoustic bass; David Nelson, guitar; Jerry Garcia, guitar. (JAY BLAKESBERG)

Jerry and Manasha Matheson relaxing with their daughter Keelin at Disneyland in 1990. (TIM MOSENFELDER)

Closeup of Jerry's "Rosebud" guitar with J. Garcia engraved on the fretboard, October, 1991. (BRIAN GOLD)

Garcia joins the MTV generation; on location for the "Throwing Stones" music video shoot at an abandoned school in Oakland, CA, November, 1987. (JAY BLAKESBERG)

Jerry and his daughters Theresa and Annabelle vacationing in Hawaii, 1988. (UNKNOWN)

Garcia, 1987. "Most of us who play music for a living consider it an honor and privilege and exceptional good luck. We'd do it for nothin'." (RON DELANY)

Members of The Grateful Dead (Jerry Garcia, Bob Weir, and Mickey Hart) pose with a tropical rain forest mural at the United Nations where they announced an effort to save rain forests with a benefit concert at Madison Square Garden. September, 1988. (BETTMANN ARCHIVE)

Vince Welnick, Bob Weir and Jerry Garcia sing the National Anthem at the San Francisco Giants season opener, April, 1993. (JAY BLAKESBERG)

Rockin' at The Greek Theater, May 15, 1983.   (GREG GAAR)

Garcia at Frost, 1980.
(RON DELANY)

Deborah Koons tied the knot with Jerry Garcia on St. Valentine's Day, 1994.
(DEBRA TROY)

Jerry Garcia, November, 1992.   (MARK SELIGER/OUTLINE)

sion. His versatility on piano, organ, and synthesizer added color to the arrangement of the songs, and his harmonies gave the group a good vocal blend.

Brent injected new life into the Grateful Dead, and Garcia was pleased. He enthused, "What we wanted was keyboards to provide color and sustain and some of those qualities that guitars don't provide, and Brent [is] real good at that. He's been adding a lot of texture and color, and also he's a fine singer—probably the best of all of us—so our trio singing is really nice now."

The Godchauxs also left the Jerry Garcia Band in February 1979, and Garcia decided to go in a different direction for a while. Rather than audition a new keyboard player to keep the Garcia Band going, Garcia and John Kahn got back together with Merl Saunders to form Reconstruction, which played primarily black music—funk, jazz, soul, blues, and reggae. Though Garcia was the main attraction for the audiences who went to see Reconstruction, which performed mostly in the Bay Area, his role was different than in the Jerry Garcia Band. He shared vocals and solo time with the other members of the group, and he played few songs from the Garcia Band repertoire.

But Garcia's desire to have his own band as a creative out-let was strong; consequently, Reconstruction was together for only eight months when he felt the need to reconvene the Jerry Garcia Band. In October 1979 the Garcia Band, with John Kahn on bass, Ozzie Allers on keyboards, and Johnny de Fonseca on drums, began performing the repertoire Jerry had been doing with Keith and Donna. Garcia also brought some new material to the band list, introducing "Deal" and "Dear Prudence," songs that became Garcia Band standards. Jerry took his band on an East Coast tour in February 1980 and shared the stage with Robert Hunter, who opened a majority of the shows and also sang with the band on several occasions. It was the first time the two old friends had performed together on stage since the mid-1960s.

Garcia had come a long way since Hunter and he first performed as a duo for five bucks apiece in Palo Alto in the early 1960s. In his nearly twenty years of performing, Jerry had maintained the integrity of his own musical vision and helped shape the contemporary musical scene. Garcia's accomplishments were recognized when he was selected Bay Area Musician of the Year in March 1980, through a readers' poll in *BAM*, the Bay Area Music Magazine.

Despite the recognition Garcia had received, and the Grateful Dead's continued popularity, the group had never had a hit single. While the band had placed a few singles on the charts over the years—"Truckin'," "Uncle John's Band," and "Good Lovin'"—none were bona fide hits. In an attempt to achieve this goal, the Dead made a second appearance on *Saturday Night Live*, in April 1980, to coincide with the release of *Go to Heaven*. The album was produced by Gary Lyons, who had commercial success producing records for Aerosmith and Foreigner.

The band performed two cuts from *Go to Heaven*—

"Alabama Getaway" and "Saint of Circumstance"—on *Saturday Night Live*, and because of the national exposure, "Alabama Getaway" started getting significant airplay on album-oriented rock stations throughout the country, and was even played on a number of AM stations. Delighted with the airplay "Alabama Getaway" was getting and with the prospect of a hit record, Garcia laughingly declared, "That's incredible—we were sure our very first record was going to be a hit." (Coincidentally, the band had re-recorded "Don't Ease Me In" from their first 45 for *Go to Heaven*.) Despite the attention "Alabama Getaway" received, sales didn't take off, and Garcia had another near-miss. However, the album did make the Top 20 and gained the band legions of new fans.

It had been fifteen years since Garcia had put the electric band together—he had had no idea the band would have such staying power: "I wasn't thinking about time. I was hoping it would do something like what it's done. It went way past all my expectations—I mean, I've been over the hill of amazement for so long now. It continues to blow my mind."

The band celebrated its official fifteenth anniversary with two concerts on June 7-8, 1980, at the University of Colorado at Boulder. During their stay in Boulder, the group held court at the Holiday Inn and partied with family members, journalists, and any Dead Head savvy enough to find them. Jerry hung out in the hospitality room and occasionally sat in the small hotel lobby rapping with friends and fans alike. Asked to explain the Grateful Dead's appeal, Garcia replied, "They might like us in the same spirit that people like drugs. I think we're like a drug in that sense—people turn each other on to us. And there's that personal contact involved with every Dead Head. There are very few Dead Heads who are Dead Heads in complete isolation."

To further commemorate the Grateful Dead's fifteen years together, Garcia and Weir decided to break out the acoustic guitars and incorporate acoustic sets into a run of twenty-five shows that began September 25, 1980 and concluded Halloween night. It was the first time the band had performed acoustically since 1970. They played fifteen shows at the Warfield Theatre in San Francisco, followed by two shows at the Saenger Arts Center in New Orleans and eight shows at Radio City Music Hall in New York. Resurrected were some of the old folk, country, and blues songs from the jug band era and those performed during the acoustic sets of 1970, as well as first-time acoustic versions of some Grateful Dead standards. After each acoustic set, the band played two electric sets. The shows were recorded, and the band planned to release a live album of material from the shows.

There were other special twists for these shows. In San Francisco, the band collaborated with Al Franken and Tom Davis of *Saturday Night Live* at the shows at the Warfield to perfect gags to be used for a closed-circuit simulcast on Halloween night at Radio City Music Hall. The band worked with the comedians developing skits around Grateful Dead folklore. One bit was a takeoff on "Jerry's kids," with various Dead Heads appearing as Garcia's poster kids for a mock telethon fundraiser. Another skit showed Jerry and Phil in a backstage dressing room prior to a show, when a couple of fans barge in and proceed to make pests of themselves by interrupting and asking if anyone has any drugs. One of the interlopers picks up Garcia's guitar and accidentally drops it on the floor. The look of shock on Garcia's face is priceless, Steve Parish is about to go nuclear, and the scene cuts to black.

Bill Graham, who was producing the Warfield run, also went out of his way to make the anniversary series memorable. He assembled a collection of Grateful Dead memorabilia and displayed it in the lobby of the theater, along with a slide show and speakers that relayed the live music from the stage into the lobby during the show. On the final night, Graham brought enough champagne for the entire audience—some 2,200 people—and during the last set he managed to have it discreetly served to them. After the band went offstage at the end of the last set, Graham set a table on the stage, with a tablecloth, a bucket of champagne, and enough glasses for the group. When the band came back out for the encore, they found the champagne sitting there. For a moment or two they didn't know what to do, but then Garcia and the others raised their glasses to the crowd and began toasting *them*. Just then, the house lights went on, and the audience toasted the band right back. Nicki Scully recalled the night lovingly: "That was one of Bill Graham's gems. It was his way of saying thank you to the band and he did it in such a tasteful way."

The gratitude was mutual, she noted: "Rock also thought of a wonderful gesture and decided that he wanted to give something back to all the people that were involved in the production. We were living with Jerry at the time [in San Rafael], and he found a sketchbook of Jerry's cartoons. Rock picked out several of the best of these cartoons and, with Jerry's permission, had them copied and made enough copies to give out. Jerry even signed them." And in another act of good will, the Grateful Dead and Graham donated the proceeds from the final concert at the Warfield to charity. The show earned $27,500, which was distributed to at least eight different charities.

Although the fifteenth anniversary had come and gone, the band continued to thrive from it well into 1981. *Reckoning*, a double album of acoustic tunes derived from the fifteenth-anniversary shows, was released on April 1. Superbly recorded by Dan Healy and Betty Cantor-Jackson, the disc featured a wonderful collection of folk, country, and blues tunes, as well as some Grateful Dead originals. The band also released *Dead Set*, a companion double album of electric songs from the same set of shows, in August. The project had originally been planned as one two-record set, but once again the band had to make the constraints of vinyl fit the way they played. Garcia thought the dual release made sense: "We really ended up with so much good material that it was a struggle. The idea of just one acoustic and one electric record was sort of pathetic, since our electric tunes are seldom less than eight minutes long. And that meant our nice fat electric album would have two songs on a side. It was kind of silly."

Finally, the Grateful Dead released two videos involving the Radio City Music Hall shows. The videos featured a selection of acoustic and electric songs, plus the Franken and Davis comedy skits. Surprisingly, it was with the videos that the Dead caught their only flak for the anniversary shows, and it was from an unexpected source—Radio City Music Hall itself. That venerable institution, along with Rockefeller Center, filed a $1.2-million suit in New York Federal Court alleging that the band was seeking to damage the reputation of Radio City Music Hall. The lawsuit complained that the Grateful Dead intended to smear the image of Radio City by distributing a promotional poster that showed "macabre skeletons" leaning against the outside of the hall and by including in a video of the Halloween concert "assertions that illicit drugs were available at the music hall." (The Halloween show had been videocast to twenty-five other theaters and included references to illegal drugs.) The lawsuit was dropped when the band withdrew the poster from distribution and edited the video to delete the offending material. A spokesman for the band remarked, "The Radio City people were apparently totally unfamiliar with Grateful Dead symbology." With the legal problems behind them, the Grateful Dead sold one video of the performance to Showtime Cable and produced another version, which was marketed as a commercial video.

While working on the anniversary materials, Jerry did not ignore his solo band. At the beginning of 1981, he once again decided to reconfigure the Jerry Garcia Band, bringing in organist Melvin Seals, pianist Jimmy Warren, and drummer Daoud Shaw. Like longtime bassist John Kahn, Seals was a most significant addition to the band. He was suggested to Garcia by Kahn, who had met Melvin through Maria Muldaur. A Bay Area native, Seals had spent much of his life involved with the music of the black Baptist Church. Though he had played in rock bands, including the Elvin Bishop Group, his roots were firmly in gospel music, and he found inspiration in the music of the church. The gospel influence that Seals brought to the Garcia Band was very much to Garcia's liking;

although not sharing Seals's religious beliefs, Jerry shared his enjoyment of the rhythms and patterns of the music. John Kahn explained the dynamics: "[Melvin] brings a heavy-duty gospel element to the band, and everything that goes along with that—which doesn't mean just playing in a gospel style and knowing gospel songs. In gospel music the role of everything is much more strictly defined. Music is a background to the singing, and you lay out during the singing, maybe swell up in between vocal lines."

Part of the allure of the bands Garcia plays in comes from Jerry being the type of musician who loves to take chances. Rather than rely on a prearranged set list or formula, he loves to play open-ended songs where he can improvise freely, or seque into another song if the mood strikes him or if another band member takes the lead. This element of surprise is what keeps the music interesting for Garcia and the fans, and is the reason why so many fans go to see as many concerts as they can. Each new show gives the audience the opportunity to hear songs that might never be played again in the same way.

This aspect of Garcia's playing led devoted fans to begin making bootleg tapes of his shows, to preserve each performance for future listening enjoyment. People had been taping his concerts since the 1960s, but as the years went by the tapers had become more assertive. Some started bringing almost professional quality equipment to concerts, wanting to get the best sound that they could on tape. However, this put them into direct conflict with the mass of fans, who were there just to enjoy the show, and who wanted to dance and sing to the music without being told to be quiet or to get out of the way.

As with other aspects of the band's existence, this matter had become a serious problem because the band had become so popular. Although dealing with this would never have crossed anyone's mind in the early days, the band now had to take responsibility for the actions of their fans. The response could have been draconian—banning tapers from concerts. However, true to the communal spirit that they imbibed in Haight-Ashbury, the band accommodated all comers by setting aside an official "taping section" at each of their concerts beginning in October 1984. This allowed tapers to have their own area to set up their recording equipment without inconveniencing anyone.

Conventional wisdom in the music industry was that the taping of live concerts hurt record sales, but convention never counted for much with Garcia. He recognized that this theory didn't necessarily apply to Dead concerts. First, since each concert was unique, the Dead didn't have a static product that they needed to control. Second, taping and trading tapes was an integral part of the Grateful Dead scene, and probably complemented record sales. Jerry felt that when he was done with the music, the audience could have it. He proclaimed, "If somebody can find a use for music after it's been performed, fine with me. I used to be a bluegrass music freak, and I spent a lot of time taping bands. I loved being able to do it, and I loved having the tapes afterwards and being able to trade them around. I think that's healthy stuff." In this way Garcia was able to give something back to the loyal fans who devotedly attended his shows and supported his music.

*   *   *   *

From the early days in Haight-Ashbury, Jerry had always been
interested in giving something back to the community,
whether in the form of free concerts in the park or benefits for
organizations he considered worthwhile. As the band became
more successful, requests for assistance began to pour into the
Grateful Dead office. The decisions over which causes to support became more and more difficult—from a financial stand-
point as well as time-wise, the band couldn't possibly do benefits for all the worthy causes they were asked to help. Once
again, the band could choose between positive and negative
solutions. Instead of turning Scrooge-like and rejecting people
out of hand, Garcia proposed setting up a foundation to help
coordinate and administer funds raised by the band, and in
1984 a nonprofit charitable organization, the Rex Foundation,
was set up as an entity that could make contributions to various
worthwhile causes. The foundation was named to honor Rex
Jackson, a road crew member who died in an automobile accident in 1976. Though the foundation is not affiliated with the
band in a legal sense, various members of the Grateful Dead
family help run it and are also involved in deciding how to
allocate contributions. The board of directors has included
Jerry Garcia, Bob Weir, Mickey Hart, John Barlow, Carolyn
Garcia, Bill Graham, Bill Walton, Bernie Bildman, Larry
Shurtliff, and Hal Kant.

The aims of the foundation include supporting environmental, social, and cultural endeavors in order to secure a
healthy environment, assist those in need, and ensure the cul-

tural survival of indigenous peoples around the world. Additionally, a $10,000 award in memory of music journalist Ralph J. Gleason was set up in 1986 to honor individuals and groups making an outstanding contribution to culture.

Each year since the foundation's inception the Grateful Dead has played a set of Rex benefit shows, then distributed the proceeds to different causes. The band has helped hundreds of recipients in this way. Interviewed in 1985, Bill Graham remarked, "All these years, very quietly, the Dead have probably done more benefits for more varied causes than anyone. Whether it was voter registration, or a nursery school, a recreation center in Mill Valley, or when kids were getting busted in the Haight in the late 1960s and the Dead helped raise money for HALO, the Haight-Ashbury Legal Organization—nobody has done more than the Dead."

Garcia was in need of legal representation himself when he again got busted for drugs. On January 18, 1985, he was arrested in Golden Gate Park for freebasing cocaine in the front seat of his parked BMW. Officer Mark Gamble had noticed that the car's registration had expired, and when he approached the car he saw Jerry drop a piece of foil between the seats and also noticed a strong burning smell. Gamble asked Garcia to get out of the car and then saw an open briefcase on the passenger seat. The briefcase had twenty-three bindles in it, several of which contained cocaine and heroin.

Garcia had been taking drugs since the early 1960s, and had been using cocaine and heroin for a number of years. What had started out as an effort to reach a new consciousness had turned into a simple addiction. Jerry's use of hard drugs had begun to affect his health and his music. He had put on considerable weight, and his stage performances were becoming so erratic that his fans were beginning to recognize his problem.

The group had been through this once before, when Pigpen slid out of the band in 1971 because of his drinking and soon thereafter died from the consequences of alcoholism. Shortly before Jerry was busted in the park, the other members of the Grateful Dead put it to him squarely—he was killing himself. They even gave him an ultimatum that could have effectively ended the band—Garcia had to choose between the drugs and the Grateful Dead.

Garcia told the others that he would seek help, and the bust a few days later simply hurried him along in this direction. Jerry was arraigned on drug possession charges, and the court allowed him to participate in a Marin County drug diversion program that included treatment, education, and counseling. Garcia also agreed to perform a benefit concert for the Haight-Ashbury Free Food Program. He said to the press, "I want to return something to the community. I'm from [San Francisco], and the town has always been good to me."

The treatment program helped Garcia get free of his habit, and afterward, Garcia pondered his drug usage: "There was something I needed or thought I needed from drugs. . . . But after a while, it was just the drugs running me, and that's an intolerable situation. . . . Luckily, my friends pulled me out. Without them, I don't think I ever would have had the strength to do it myself."

*   *   *   *

Soon after Jerry completed the drug diversion program, the Grateful Dead celebrated their two decades together with a set of shows at the Greek Theatre in Berkeley in June 1985. The media gave the anniversary a big play, but the band seemed somewhat blase about it, in contrast to their fifteenth anniversary. Before the first show at the Greek, the band held a press conference to field questions. A table with microphones was set up backstage, and a contingent of local and national television and newspaper reporters diligently recorded every word for electronic and print enshrinement. But as Bob Weir said, "It's no big deal. We're not sure when the date was anyway."

The band was pressed to pick an exact anniversary, but the best they could do was to settle on the month—June 1965—when Phil Lesh moved to Palo Alto to join the Warlocks. "I showed him how to tune the bass and where to place his fingers for the scales," recounted Garcia, "and two weeks later he played the first gig." At the anniversary show itself, the crowd was in a festive mood, and a huge banner was held up in the audience proclaiming "Happy 20th Boys!" Garcia's portly stature had inspired a new slogan among the fans: "It's not over until the fat man rocks."

Despite Jerry's arrest and the time he lost in drug rehabilitation, 1985 turned out to be a banner year for the Grateful Dead. The band played seventy-one concerts and sold out all but six shows, with ticket sales in excess of $11.5 million. They were now one of the most popular acts in the country.

"The years are starting to pay off," remarked Garcia. "It's

like the Budapest String Quartet or the Duke Ellington Orchestra, which had the same horn section for more than twenty years. It matters." In the world of rock music the Grateful Dead never succumbed to trends or formulas, but maintained the integrity of their unique improvisational style. "It's the only way I know how to play," said Garcia. "Everyone in the band is that way. I never heard anyone repeat a thing in a song two nights in a row. I've been playing with [Weir] for twenty years, and I couldn't predict what he's going to do. Same with Phil. They all continue to surprise me."

Garcia's drug addiction was under control, the Grateful Dead were more popular than ever, and life looked like Easy Street. But nothing was to come easy for Garcia. On July 10, 1986, Jerry fell ill and lapsed into a diabetic coma a few days after the conclusion of the summer tour. Garcia had been feeling tired during the tour, but didn't know why. "I felt better after cleaning up, oddly enough, until that tour. And then I didn't realize it, but I was dehydrated and tired. That was all I felt, really. I didn't feel any pain; I didn't feel sick—I just felt tired. Then when we got back from that tour, I was just really tired. One day, I couldn't move anymore, so I sat down. A week later, I woke up in the hospital, and I didn't know what had happened."

Jerry was at his home in San Rafael when he passed out. His housekeeper found him slumped in the bathroom, unconscious. An ambulance was called and he was rushed to Marin General Hospital. The coma lasted three days, and during that time Garcia came very close to death. Doctors reported that the diabetic attack had been brought on by Garcia's weight problem, an abscessed tooth that had lowered his body's resistance, and exhaustion and dehydration resulting from the band's gigs on July 6 and 7 at RFK Stadium in Washington, D.C., where the temperature was close to one hundred degrees. David Nelson, who was traveling with the band at the time, recalled, "It was a very, very hot day. Garcia was getting real overweight at the time. He had kicked drugs and wasn't strung out. I got into the van he was in, which took us back to the hotel. The first thing, he says, 'I'm so dry, anybody got anything to drink? I'm dyin', man. My throat is like stuck together.' We get to the hotel and get some water, and everything seemed okay. We fly home and then I get the message that Jerry is in serious fuckin' trouble, in a crisis."

Merl Saunders also told how he found out about Garcia's condition. "I was out of the country when he collapsed. I was in the Caribbean laying on the beach one day and I started to feel ill, so I put a wet towel over my head. After about an hour I felt better and I took it off. The next day I went to New York and a couple of days later I ran into Paul Shaffer at a club in the Village. Shaffer walked up to me and asked me how Jerry was doing. I said, 'Jerry who?' He told me that my friend Jerry Garcia was in the hospital and he was in a coma. I flew back to San Francisco the next day and I immediately went to the hospital. They wouldn't tell me where he was, but somehow I knew. I went right to the floor and to his room and found him lying there. I asked him what had happened. He told me that he was passing out on the bathroom floor at his house and he put a wet towel on himself. I told him about the day that I put a towel on myself, and it turned out it was the same day. I asked him what time it happened, and it was the same time! He didn't believe me, so I had to show him pictures that my wife, Marina, took of me lying on the beach. I was telling the story to him and we both had tears running down our faces."

When word of the situation reached his legions of fans, a massive outpouring of love and healing energy was sent his way. The Grateful Dead hotline received sixty-five thousand calls from fans concerned about his health. The hospital was inundated with gifts. Knowing Garcia's penchant for black and red T-shirts, one fan sent him a set of matching black and red hospital gowns. Another sent him a comic book for diabetics. Garcia recalled, "I am not a believer in the invisible, but I got such an incredible outpouring. The mail I got in the hospital was so soulful. Every conceivable kind of healing vibe was just pouring into that place. I mean, the doctors did what they could do to keep me alive, but as far as knowing what was wrong with me and knowing how to fix it—it's not something medicine knows how to do. I really feel that the fans put life into me." When Garcia woke up from the coma, he found himself full of tubes and IVs in a roomful of people including Mountain Girl, members of the Grateful Dead, and Robert Hunter. Looking up at their blurry, worried faces, he tried to remember how to talk. His first words, "I'm not Beethoven," broke up the room. He hadn't lost his sense of humor.

Although his sense of humor was intact, the doctors were not positive that he would ever return to being the musician he was. Specifically, there was doubt that he would regain the muscular coordination needed to play guitar. But a very important element in any rehabilitation was present in Garcia—the desire to make it back. "When I was in the hospital all I could think was 'God, just give me the chance to go back to being productive and playing music and doing the stuff I love to do. Shit, man, I'm ready.' And one of the first things I did—once I started to be able to make coherent sentences—was to get a guitar in there to see if I could play. But when I started playing, I thought, 'Oh, man, this is going to take a long time and a lot of patience.'"

Jerry had the desire to come back, but it was those around him, especially Mountain Girl, who supplied the time and patience at the start. Upon her arrival at the hospital soon after Jerry was admitted, Mountain Girl made sure everything possible was done to facilitate Jerry's recovery. Believing that Jerry deserved the chance to be what he was, she denied the doctors permission to do a tracheotomy on Jerry while he was comatose because she feared it would ruin his singing voice.

David Nelson remembered the help that Mountain Girl organized: "When he started to come out of it, the psychological team at the hospital told Mountain Girl that what helps is something that will trigger the old familiarity from years before this happened. I was one of the first ones Mountain Girl called right away because I have all these tapes of old stuff. She said, 'If you want them back, put your name on the tapes, because I've got other people bringing tapes down, and he's gonna have a pile of them.'"

* * * *

Garcia was discharged from Marin General Hospital on August 1 and was able to celebrate his birthday at home with his family. According to a statement released by his doctors and the Grateful Dead management, Garcia had been receiving dialysis treatments in the hospital, but those were discontinued as his recovery strengthened. Marveling at his miraculously rapid return to good health, Garcia's doctors gave him a regimen of exercise and diet rather than a prescription for insulin. Upon his discharge, Garcia said, "I really want to thank all the well-wishers for the cards and letters and healing vibes. I felt them. I wouldn't be out of the hospital this soon if it weren't for the thoughts, healing help, and all the stuff people sent."

David Nelson described going to see Garcia at his home for the first time after his release from the hospital, "We sat there and talked and talked and cracked up about stuff. We tripped out about what it was like being in a fuckin' coma. I asked him if he could remember anything. 'Yes,' he said, 'God, it was horrible. It was like a fuckin' nightmare, man, it was just horrible. I had this image of bugs. I pictured cockroaches running real fast, with teams of them in single file carrying stuff. And then, as I expanded from that and took a look at it, it was my blood vessels and the cockroaches were my blood cells. They were going up and down with this mechanical kind of repetition.'"

Jerry initially had some motor problems, but his recovery went well with the help of his good friend Saunders. Garcia began spending afternoons with Merl trying to regain his musical chops. Saunders remembered, "He was worried that he couldn't play the guitar because he couldn't hold it. I told him, 'Don't worry about it.' I started walking with him every day from the house out to the road and back to the house. It was about twenty-five yards. We started practicing five minutes a day. . . . It was very weird at first because he literally didn't know how to play anymore. It scared me to death. It was quite an experience to see him completely unable to play guitar and barely able to walk. . . . It was rough going at first, but everything builds on everything else, so once we really got going, things came back to him and he actually progressed very quickly. . . . It came back in little blocks, because we could never practice more than ten minutes at first because he would get tired. We would stop and go for a walk and then come back and play again. We'd do that eight or nine hours a day, and it started coming back. We went over the fundamentals. We went back to basics with standard songs again."

As a measure of how devoted Jerry's friends were to him, Saunders worked with Garcia like this for about three months until Jerry got his chops back. Garcia recalled, "Merl was very encouraging. He would run me through these tunes that had sophisticated harmonic changes, so I had to think. It was like learning music again, in a way."

During his recuperation Garcia went up to Oregon with Mountain Girl, Annabelle, and Theresa for some rest and relaxation. She was living with the kids on a farm about five miles from Ken Kesey's place and had been working for a nearby publishing company. Almost since they had met at the Acid Tests, they had had a powerful bond that remained unbroken over time and distance and despite whatever disagreements drove them apart. Mountain Girl, ever needing to make her own way in life, had moved around quite a bit after separating from Garcia in 1975. She lived on the East Coast for a while, and eventually settled in Oregon in the early 1980s. Seemingly to cinch their relationship, the two independent lovers had gotten married at the end of 1981, although even this didn't change their approach to each other. As Annabelle noted, "We all really love each other, but we're not really a family unit."

After Garcia's near-death, Mountain Girl decided to come back to the Bay Area with the girls to help Jerry during his recovery. She monitored his progress, making sure he followed doctors' orders. Garcia spent August and September relaxing with his wife and children, getting his strength back and working on his music. During his spare time he listened to his collection of records—Billie Holiday, Charlie Parker, Los Lobos, and his favorite composer, Charles Ives. He also devoted some time to his other passion in life—painting and sketching.

After getting his chops back, Garcia began rehearsing with the Jerry Garcia Band, and by the end of September he was feeling fit enough to step on stage and perform again. Dates were set for the Garcia Band at various venues around the Bay Area for October, November, and December. On October 4 at the Stone nightclub in San Francisco, Garcia returned the cheers of the fans gathered on the street with a salute as he made his way into the club for his first public performance since his collapse. The atmosphere inside the club was electric, and as Garcia took the stage with bandmates Kahn, Seals, David Kemper, Jackie LaBranch, and Gloria Jones, the capacity crowd showered him with adoration. His singing and guitar playing showed none of the stage fright he was experiencing, and the crowd celebrated every note. It was indeed "The Triumphant Return of Jerry Garcia!" as the tickets to the show proclaimed.

Garcia discussed his comeback: "It was a long time since I'd played, so naturally I felt nervous. But the Stone's really a familiar environment to me; that's one of the reasons I wanted to play there rather than someplace else. Even there, the pressure's on."

The music that Garcia played with his band now took on a decidedly gospel edge, even beyond the influence of Melvin Seals. (The 1991 live album *Jerry Garcia Band* captured the intensified gospel sound of the group.) Seals discussed this: "I think there's a more spiritual focus to what we're doing. Any time you come close to death it makes you think about things differently, and it does something to you inside."

Gloria Jones noted, "We've always had a little taste of it, but [Jerry] put more in after he was sick—maybe it hits a little closer to home for him now. He likes the tone of gospel music and tries to bring it in whenever he can."

7

MILLION SELLERS
AND AN ICE CREAM
CALLED GARCIA

G arcia's return to performing was not only a relief to his fans, but it was also a boon to the many people whose livelihoods depended on his continued good health. Because of Jerry's illness, the Grateful Dead organization had suffered a major financial setback, losing millions of dollars in income when shows had to be cancelled. Ticket sales was the organization's main source of revenue, and so a number of people had to be laid off during this hiatus. This was a different situation than when the Dead stopped touring in 1975 and 1976, for the layoffs at that time were intended to streamline the band's operation. When Jerry was hospitalized, the staff was already pared down, and so necessary functions had to be cut back. Therefore, the prayers of thanks were truly heartfelt when the Grateful Dead family got together for their private Thanksgiving party in San Anselmo with their leader,

Captain Trips, still at the helm. Everyone was in good spirits, and when Garcia played banjo on some old bluegrass tunes with David Nelson and Sandy Rothman, it was a real joy.

Nelson looked back: "We had Thanksgiving at the Log Cabin in San Anselmo. It was a Grateful Dead thing, and everybody from grannies to little sprouts was there. It was just a warm family thing, you know. Sandy and I brought our acoustic instruments. Sandy and I were thinking, 'Let's not push him; if he doesn't remember, we'll just go on to the next song.' To our amazement, Garcia remembered most of the words of the old songs. We did 'Little Glass of Wine,' which is a long ballad with lots of verses, and he was reminding me of the words!"

Garcia returned to the stage with the Grateful Dead on December 15, 1986, at the Oakland Coliseum. The sold-out crowd cheered with delight when the band opened with a rousing rendition of "Touch of Grey," and when Jerry sang the words of the chorus—"I will get by, I will survive"—it was time to get the handkerchiefs out. Garcia remarked, "There wasn't a dry eye in the house. It was great to be able to play again. And the Grateful Dead is like nothing else. You never know whether you can do it or not; you can't rehearse for it. Only doing it makes you able to do it. . . . When I was in the hospital, the thing I found myself thinking most was, 'Boy, when I get out of here, I'm going to play as much as I possibly can.'"

With Jerry anxious to perform, the Grateful Dead played a full schedule of eighty-five shows in 1987. The highlight of the year was when the Grateful Dead backed Bob Dylan for six shows in July. Rumors of the collaboration had been circulating ever since Dylan had jammed with the Dead at a couple of shows in July 1986, prior to Garcia's collapse. Jerry had long been a fan of Dylan's music, and he had covered Dylan's songs with both the Grateful Dead and the Jerry Garcia Band.

The project started unfolding early in 1987 when Dylan went to the Dead's studio and rehearsed with the band for a couple of days to see if it would work. Dick Latvala, the Grateful Dead tape archivist, recalled, "I was in the studio working when Dylan showed up, and it looked to me like they were having a good time rehearsing. About a month later Dylan phoned Jerry and said, 'It's a go; let's do it.' That resulted in a twenty-one-day rehearsal schedule in May. The Dead and Dylan ran over a lot of songs, some of which didn't get played on the tour."

The six Dylan-Dead concerts were taped so that the historic union of the 1960s legends could be preserved for music-lovers. "It was our idea to record it," said Garcia. "We thought, 'Who knows if this is ever going to happen again?' And even if the tapes just sit in the vaults, some musicologist of the future may enjoy himself going through them."

The music was not relegated to obscurity, for a couple of years later *Dylan & the Dead*, a live LP, was released thanks to Garcia's persistence. Jerry and John Cutler, who had recorded all the gigs in a mobile studio, produced the disc at Le Club Front, with Dylan being consulted on the song selection and mixing. Garcia recounted an ironic experience working with Dylan on the album: "We went over to [Dylan's] house in Malibu. He takes us into this room that's kinda baronial—

y'know, big fireplace and wooden paneling and steep roof. And there's this big table and about four or five chairs around it—no other furniture. And on the table is about a $39 ghetto blaster and he's got the cassette and he sticks it in there and he says, 'Don't you think the voice is mixed a little loud in that one?' So we just sat around and listened to it on this little funky thing. . . ." Jerry later elaborated on his relationship with Dylan: "When you're collaborating with Dylan and he says, 'Hey, I think that my voice is too out front,' what am I going to do? Punch him? I'll say 'okay' against my own instincts."

This sounds strange coming from the independent-minded Garcia, but this wasn't a case of Jerry kowtowing to a bigger rock 'n' roll name. Garcia trusted his own judgment for the work that he did in the studio. However, Jerry was a fan of Dylan's music and appreciated the man's genius. He recognized that in a collaboration such as the one he was crafting with Dylan, sometimes his judgment would rule, and sometimes Dylan's would.

The Grateful Dead released *In the Dark*, their first studio album in seven years, on July 6, 1987 to coincide with the start of their tour with Dylan. The long break between studio discs was not just by chance. From 1977 to 1980, the band had put out three consecutive studio albums using outside producers—*Terrapin Station*, *Shakedown Street*, and *Go to Heaven*—that were designed for commercial airplay. And though Garcia and the band maintained that the albums were top-quality efforts on their part, they were dissatisfied with the goings-on that surrounded the making of commercial music. "All that pressure to make commercial records more or less drew a backlash from us. I wouldn't say we were disheartened during that time so much as we just lost interest," mused Bob Weir.

After *Go to Heaven* was released in 1980, the band still owed Arista two albums of new material, but they were reluctant to go back into the studio. Arista compromised, accepting the two live albums, *Reckoning* and *Dead Set*, and then asking for only one more studio album to fulfill the contract. But the band even had trouble meeting this deal. In 1984 they had gone to Berkeley's Fantasy Studios to record, but after two weeks they gave up. "Everything was kind of lackadaisical," admitted Brent Mydland. "We had the tunes, but there was no real drive to go in and record."

Arista was still looking for that last record, though, so finally the band hit on a novel approach to studio work that would be inspirational to them. In 1985, they had shot some footage of the band playing without an audience at the Marin County Veterans Auditorium for a possible video, and the band liked the almost-live feeling they managed. So they decided to do the same thing for this album. In January 1987, they hauled their instruments and recording equipment over to the auditorium, set up the same way they would if they were performing live, and recorded the basic tracks. Garcia related, "Marin Vets turns out to be an incredibly nice room to record in. There's something about the formal atmosphere in there that makes us work. When we set up at Front Street to work, a lot of times we just sort of dissolve into hanging out. Going in [the auditorium] without an audience and playing just to ourselves was in the nature of an experiment, to see if there's some kind of a situation that isn't performing live where we can get off."

After the basics were laid down, the band spent most of February and March recording and mixing the tracks at their studio on Front Street, where all of the vocals and the sound effects were added on. Garcia co-produced the album with John Cutler, with Jerry the ultimate decision-maker. This was not an easy task, as Garcia had to keep his roles as musician and producer separate. "The days when I had to do vocals for the record, I wouldn't actually evaluate my vocals till another day, because being a performer and being a pair of ears—which is how a producer functions—are two different kinds of energy, and I'm not good at doing both at the same time." Although the production was under a tight deadline to make the release date, and he spent many long days at the console board mixing the sound, Jerry was happy. "I think the band has never played better on an album, ever. I don't think we've ever had better singing, either." The band had been performing most of the songs on *In the Dark* in concert since the early 1980s, and the album managed to capture some of the energy of a live performance.

The critics' reactions to the album confirmed Garcia's opinion—the Grateful Dead had produced their best-sounding album in many years. The buying public also agreed, giving the band their first bona-fide hits: the single "Touch of Grey" and the album both went to the top of the charts.

*   *   *   *

To capitalize on the increasing popularity of music videos, and to take advantage of *In the Dark*'s success, the band released three MTV song videos—"Touch of Grey," "Hell in a Bucket," and "Throwing Stones"—the first of a number of such videos that the band and its members have done to promote their music. In addition, a fifty-five-minute Grateful Dead video, *So Far*, which was co-directed by Garcia and Len Dell'Amico, was released in October 1987. *So Far* featured the music and video the band recorded without an audience at the Marin County Veterans Auditorium in 1985, plus a segment from the 1985 New Year's Eve telecast. Accompanying this were thousands of visual images and computer-generated animation that were seamlessly incorporated into the video. Garcia and Dell'Amico reviewed a massive amount of archival footage in a series of conceptual jam sessions trying to find the best combination of visual images to match the music. Garcia remembered, "We did a lot of brainstorming, . . . a sort of a free-associative thing that took place over several months, just collecting lists and lists."

The music in *So Far* was structured like the second set of a Grateful Dead concert: "Uncle John's Band" opens the video with multipanel images of classic Americana; next is "Playing in the Band" overlaid with archival footage of chorus girls, dancers, musicians, and marching bands. "Lady with a Fan" (from *Terrapin Station*) follows with computer-generated images of a chessboard stretching to the horizon, with tarot cards and chess pieces gliding across it; the ensuing "Space" jam has cosmic imagery with planets, lunar surfaces, shooting stars, and exploding astral bodies. The "Rhythm Devils" segment starts with images of Stonehenge, pyramids, and primitive man in the desert, then jumps to modern industrial society with skyscrapers, billowing smokestacks, clogged freeways, and throngs of harried office workers rushing through the city. "Throwing Stones" offers images of war and destruction and then a multicultural collage of religious icons that ends with a white dove flying out of a stained-glass window; and finally, "Not Fade Away" showcases the band performing to a sold-out Oakland Coliseum audience.

The format of *So Far* gave new perspective to the experience of a Grateful Dead concert. True to his desire to expand the consciousness of his audience, Garcia chose visual images that added another dimension to the music. The video and musical images combined to give a special insight into Garcia's personal view of the meaning of the Grateful Dead's music. He also made certain political statements through the video that were consistent with the band's beliefs—condemning war and the degradation of the environment, while at the same time expressing a sense of optimism about the future.

The movie also gave a close-up look at Garcia and the others as they performed on stage. Considering the kinds of shows that some rock legends put on, it is a tribute to the Grateful Dead's ability that so many come to see them for their music, not for their act. There is Weir on rhythm guitar—tall, thin, and intense, stepping forward and back to emphasize his notes, his face and wide eyes showing his emotion as he belts out a song. And there is the bespectacled Lesh on bass, also tall and thin, his head bobbing to the beat. Then there is Brent Mydland, poised over the keyboards, longish hair swaying. In the back are the two drummers—Hart and Kreutzmann—sitting or standing, bodies in motion across their drum sets.

And finally, there is Garcia on lead guitar, standing firm. Unless he is singing, he scarcely moves a muscle, except for his right fingers plucking the strings and his left hand moving on the frets. Occasionally, he stops playing a beat to push his glasses up on his nose. But then he settles back into his stance, head down, looking at the strings, brow furrowed as he listens intently for the nuances of the others, seldom moving from his spot. When the music is hot, he might look up slightly, like a teacher peering over his glasses at a young student. Then you might see a small grin on his face, as if he were thinking, "There is no life better than this!"

In addition to his work with the Grateful Dead, Garcia also performed forty-four shows with the Jerry Garcia Band in 1987. Combined with the dates for the Grateful Dead tours, this meant that Garcia was on the road somewhere for almost one-third of the year. Jerry added acoustic sets to the Garcia Band show for the fall tour, which included a run of eighteen shows at the Lunt-Fontanne Theatre on Broadway in New York, three shows at the Warfield Theatre in San Francisco, and three shows at the Wiltern Theatre in Los Angeles.

David Nelson described how the acoustic part of the show came together: "Garcia and Kahn were scheduled to play at this benefit [the Artists Rights Today Benefit on March 18, 1987] for the San Francisco artists that was put on by Bill Graham. Garcia said, 'Hey, Nelson, why don't you and Sandy come and play? Why don't we do some of that old stuff like we did at the Thanksgiving party? It'll be cool. We'll do anything we want to do; we'll do those old songs.' After we played at the benefit Bill Graham bursts into the room [backstage]: 'Jerry, everybody, I can see the roots of the music. This is important. I love it that you guys play this. I've got to do something with it. I'm serious; I really think a lot of it, and I've got to do something with this.' Nobody else says anything, so Garcia goes, 'Take us to Broadway, Bill.' And Graham goes, 'Broadway,' and he leaves the room going, 'Broadway—can't you just see that?' Everybody thought it was too good to be true, but Bill pulled it off."

Suddenly, from this one flash of inspiration, Garcia was playing the Great White Way. "Garcia on Broadway," read the ads, "Acoustic . . . Bluegrass . . . Electric." Graham, who produced the shows, remarked, "One month prior [Garcia was] playing five sold-out shows at Madison Square Garden [with the Grateful Dead]—that's 100,000 people. For the lead guitarist of that same group to play eighteen shows at a 1,400-seat theater, obviously there's a desire to do this, not a need to do this. Since the very first day I met him, he has not changed his seemingly unquenchable desire to just play. And this is an opportunity to show the spectrum of the rainbow."

The music that the Jerry Garcia acoustic band played was a throwback to the folk music scene of the early 1960s when Garcia, Nelson, and Rothman performed around the Bay Area. Garcia returned to one of his first musical loves—bluegrass—to construct a facsimile of one of his earliest bands, the Black Mountain Boys, which had performed more than twenty years earlier. The repertoire consisted of songs Jerry had performed in the 1960s, as well as bluegrass, country and western, down-home blues, and spiritual numbers, with Garcia, Nelson, and

Rothman sharing lead vocals and harmonies. Some of the shows were taped on a two-track stereo DAT machine, and the music was used for the album *Almost Acoustic,* which was released the following year.

Garcia also recruited Nelson and Rothman to help him cut a short radio advertisement for Levi's 501 jeans when the San Francisco-based company offered him the opportunity to make a thirty-second spot. The commercial, Garcia's first, was part of an ad campaign that included commercials by other musicians, among them Leon Redbone and Robert Cray. Jerry played acoustic guitar and sang, "A good pair of Levi's are bound to set me free" and "Levi's 501 jeans shrink to fit only me."

Garcia also agreed to license the use of the name "Cherry Garcia" to Ben & Jerry's Ice Cream for one of its flavors. The agreement included royalty payments to Garcia and the Rex Foundation. The company ran a print ad claiming that the ice cream was the first one named after a musical legend.

The fact that Garcia was featured in two advertisements touting commercial products shows how far he—and the country—had come. Twenty years before, at the height of the Haight-Ashbury days, Jerry was viewed by most mainstream Americans as one of the leaders of the counterculture, and thus as a definite threat to American society. Through his career, he had been arrested for drugs and lambasted for his life-style, and he never tried to promote himself. He was simply a guy who played music as best he knew how, and if people wanted to listen to him, more power to them. Now, during the Reagan years—a time of perhaps the most blatant comsumerism the country had ever seen—Jerry Garcia was an ice cream flavor.

But it wasn't Jerry who had changed—it was society. The young people of the mid-1960s who had looked to Jerry as a symbol of the hippie life-style were now in their forties. For the most part they were no longer hippies, but were account executives, parents, and pillars of their communities. However, the Dead's music was still with those people, either as a nostalgic memory or as the key that unlocked the idealism and spirit of that time. And Jerry, through no intention of his own, had evolved for this generation into a symbol of the 1960s. Like it or not, he was an effective marketing tool.

While 1987 was a year of unparalleled public success for Jerry, his private life was once more going through upheaval. He and Mountain Girl once more turned away from each other when one of Jerry's extramarital relationships resulted in the birth of his fourth daughter, Keelin Noel Garcia, who was born on December 20, 1987. Keelin's mother, Manasha Matheson, was a young, star-struck fan of Garcia's who had gone to great lengths to meet him. After succeeding in her quest to be part of Jerry's life, Manasha became pregnant. Garcia's relationship with Manasha, who became his companion, was too much for Mountain Girl, and their marriage ended in divorce.

The birth of Keelin put Garcia once again in the role of family man, and he enjoyed being the involved parent he couldn't be with his other daughters. "At this [point] in my life I wasn't exactly expecting it, but [now] I have a little more time to actually be a father. My other daughters have all been very good to me, insofar as they've never blamed me for my absentee parenting. . . . I never did get to spend a lot of time with them. So, this one I'm getting to spend more time with, and that's pretty satisfying."

Garcia was also satisfied with the results of the Eleventh Bay Area Music Awards, held at the San Francisco Civic Auditorium on March 12, 1988, where he won awards for Musician of the Year and Best Guitarist. With the million-selling album *In the Dark* and the hit single "Touch of Grey," the Grateful Dead were the most successful Bay Area band during 1987, and it was no surprise that they also won Bammies for Best Album (*In the Dark*), Best Drummer/Percussionist (Hart and Kreutzmann), and Best Bassist (Lesh).

Accepting his award for Best Guitarist, Garcia thanked the Dead Heads for their support and dedicated the award to them, and upon receiving the Bay Area Musician of the Year award he declared, "Most of us who play music for a living consider it an honor and privilege and exceptional good luck. We'd do it for nothin'."

8

I WILL SURVIVE

Due to the Grateful Dead's immense success in 1987, the scene outside of shows across the country grew dramatically as legions of new Dead Heads got on the bus and started going to concerts. Often, the number of people outside a hall far exceeded the seating capacity of the facility, which caused serious problems at the concert site and in surrounding neighborhoods. Some fans would camp out in their vans for a two- or three-day run of shows, resulting in impromptu Dead Head villages popping up around concert areas. Whereas this phenomenon was accepted in a way in the late 1960s and early 1970s as part of the hippie scene, and was apt to be looked upon as an interesting sideshow as much as a logistical problem, in the late 1980s other people had less patience with it.

Part of the problem could be attributed to the vending

scene that had developed, in which Dead Heads would travel across the country from show to show, selling their wares of tie-dyes, artwork, jewelry, and other handcrafted items at the informal shopping bazaars that sprang up outside the shows. There would often be hundreds of vendors hawking their goods in the parking lot, displaying items on blankets, on racks, or in their hands as they walked through the crowd. With so much of the space around the auditorium taken by these vendors and others, many of whom were not actually going to see the concert, traffic became unmanageable as cars full of concertgoers lined up for miles attempting to park. Frustrated fans would end up parking illegally along the side of the roads leading to the facility or in nearby residential neighborhoods. Police and city officials received complaints from local citizens about the congestion, noise, and litter that the onslaught of Dead Heads brought to the community. As a result, a number of concert facilities across the country—for example, Irvine Meadows Amphitheatre and the Henry J. Kaiser Convention Center—began to ban the Grateful Dead from doing shows at their venues.

While the band initially did not oppose the vendor scene, the problems it was causing were too significant to ignore. Once again the Dead were faced with a responsibility they could never have imagined when they were just a San Francisco band, and the group had no choice but to forbid vending at many places. Security guards were given instructions to keep the parking lots and surrounding areas free of vendors.

*   *   *   *

The whole idea of responsibility took on a new meaning for Garcia and the others in the band when they decided to get out front on the environmental issue of the earth's vanishing rainforests. Although Garcia had spent years telling people that he wasn't a leader for any movement, the importance of this issue for him outweighed his career-long philosophy. The band held a press conference at the United Nations in New York on September 13, 1988, to announce that they were joining the fight to preserve the world's tropical rainforests. Standing next to a specially designed rainforest painting by Robert Rauschenberg, Garcia charged, "They're wiping out the rainforests at the rate of fifty million acres a year. That's the equivalent of England, Wales, and Scotland every year. In sixty years, they'll be gone. As a citizen of Earth, I object."

To back up their words, the band added a ninth concert to their Madison Square Garden run—a special benefit concert for the activist groups Rainforest Action Network, Cultural Survival, and Greenpeace. The concert, which featured the Grateful Dead, Bruce Hornsby and the Range, Mick Taylor, Suzanne Vega, Daryl Hall and John Oates, Jack Casady, Baba Olatunji, and Michael Hinton, raised $600,000. The profits were used to increase public awareness and concern in the United States about rainforests and to aid projects supporting the efforts of indigenous tribes and rainforest activists in developing countries. The effects of the band's involvement with the issue went beyond the money. According to Dr. Noel Brown, head of the United Nations Environmental Program, the Grateful Dead's involvement had brought more press attention to the issue than he had seen in the preceding ten years.

Garcia made clear at the press conference that the benefit

concert was just the start of the band's involvement to preserve the rainforests. "We don't want to gloss over the complexity of the issue," Garcia said. "But we're fully aware that a multitude of political, social, and ecological factors affect the fate of rainforests. There's no one magic bullet that's the solution. It's going to take a lot of people—here in America, in Japan, in Western Europe—working to change things at the consumer level, with official government policies, and corporate and international banking policies that finance rainforest destruction."

In 1989 Garcia, Weir, and Hart took the case to Congress when they gave testimony about the plight of the rainforests at the Congressional Human Rights Caucus, which was trying to decide what to do about the destruction by the timber and meat industries of the rainforests around the world. During this session, Garcia mentioned why the group was taking such an active stance on the issue: "We're really just citizens who have a constituency," he said, referring to the legions of Dead Heads. "They are people who listen to us."

Garcia's regard for the survival of the rainforests brought him back together with his good friend Merl Saunders. It had been nearly ten years since Garcia and Saunders had played together in a band, and fifteen years since their last album together. Saunders was working on the production of the album *Blues from the Rainforest*, having been inspired to record music that captured the spirit of the rainforests. He hoped such music would overcome language barriers to be heard by people around the world. He began recording in March 1989, and he asked Jerry to add guitar parts to some of the songs.

Saunders wanted Garcia to be creatively involved with *Blues from the Rainforest* because of Jerry's concerns about the environment. "This project is another way of calling attention to the rainforests as a whole biological entity," said Garcia. "Everybody has their own process of discovery, but I believe that this record might help some people experience the ethos of the rainforest." Merl felt that Jerry's guitar playing could express exactly what he was trying to communicate on the album. Saunders explained, "Garcia understands my music, anything I might do. I just sit down and talk to him and he can come up with the right part." Garcia agreed: "Merl and I worked together a lot, so there [is] that sense of musical understanding."

Garcia also got creatively involved with the production of the Grateful Dead's next studio album, *Built to Last*, which was released on October 31, 1989. The band had initially wanted to record the LP in the same manner as *In the Dark*, laying down the basic tracks at the Marin County Veterans Auditorium, but the live energy that had characterized the previous album did not materialize for this one. After preliminary taping at the auditorium, they decided to scrap the idea and take another approach.

Instead of recording the standard bass and drum basics, the group spent time figuring out what the right tempo for each tune was going to be, then set the basic rhythm of the tune on a drum machine. Once the band had a sense of how the song would hang together, each member worked on the number individually and added his own track to the tune. The result was that the music was never heard in its entirety until it was mixed, at which time all the pieces were put together by Garcia and John Cutler.

Another new feature on this album was Garcia's use of computerized sound. Although this technology was barely out of its infancy, Jerry was already exploring its possibilities. He added his MIDI (musical instrument digital interface) guitar to several tracks on the album. The use of MIDI technology gave Garcia the ability to talk to a computer and call up the actual sound of other instruments with all their parameters, such as attack, velocity, and sustain. Garcia had begun experimenting with a MIDI guitar in concerts, and he was effectively reaching voices of other instruments such as flute, saxophone, and trumpet.

Built to Last was viewed as Brent Mydland's coming out with the band, since he sang four songs on the album that he had written with John Barlow: "Just a Little Light," "Blow Away," "We Can Run," and "I Will Take You Home." As the newest member of the Grateful Dead, it had taken Brent years to step out of the background and take a more assertive role. With his songs on *Built to Last* and the larger role he was playing in concerts, Mydland became a force in the group's brand of rock 'n' roll. Thus, it was a serious setback for the band when Brent died from an accidental overdose of a cocaine-and-morphine speedball on July 26, 1990. He was found in the bedroom of his home in Lafayette, California, by friends who had become concerned when they couldn't reach him. The autopsy revealed a recent puncture mark on his left arm that was consistent with an intravenous injection.

Brent had been fighting a drug problem for more than a year and had been rushed to the hospital when he almost overdosed the prior December. Garcia pondered Brent's death: "Brent was not a real happy person. . . . Brent had this thing that he was never able to shake, which was that thing of being the new guy. And he wasn't the new guy—he was with us for ten years! . . . It was heartbreaking when Brent died, because it seemed like such a waste. . . . He couldn't see what was good about what he was doing, and he couldn't see himself fitting in. And no amount of effort on our part could make him more comfortable."

With Brent gone, the band put the word out that they were looking for a new keyboard player, and Garcia began informally jamming with some prospects while other band members auditioned tapes. Bruce Hornsby, a friend and longtime fan, volunteered to perform with the group as a temporary replacement.

Hornsby and his band, the Range, had opened several shows for the Grateful Dead, and he had sat in with them at a number of gigs in 1988 and 1989. Hornsby was a star in his own right. His debut album, *The Way It Is*, sold two million copies and produced three Top-20 singles. It also won him the 1987 Grammy Award for Best New Artist.

Hornsby explained how he got involved with the Grateful Dead: "My older brother, Bobby, who used to play in bands with me for years, was a Dead Head. He was a diehard—a true dyed-in-the-wool Dead Head who used to collect the tapes and all that. . . . [He] put together this band called the Octane Kids where they did virtually all Dead songs, a few Allman Brothers, and a couple of Band—basically the Watkins Glen repertoire. I got really into the piano by then so they asked me to come play with them. That made me a Dead fan. . . . My connection with the Grateful Dead comes from the fact that the Dead asked [the Range] to open shows for them. We only had nine [original] songs so we did a few songs by other people, and one of them was a Dead song, 'I Know You Rider.' I guess they got hold of a tape, and they really liked the music. The [Range] opened a couple of shows for them in the spring of 1987, and it just kind of went on from there."

While Hornsby was helping out, the Grateful Dead continued to look for a person who could play synthesizers and sing high harmonies. Several keyboardists were auditioned, including Tim Gorman, Pete Sears, and Vince Welnick. Welnick, a former member of the Tubes and more recently Todd Rundgren's band, got the job and began rehearsing with the Dead before their fall tour in September. Welnick was a native of Phoenix, Arizona, who had classical piano training as a child. In the mid-1960s he started playing in rock 'n' roll bands, and at sixteen announced to his parents that he was quitting high school to be a musician. He proclaimed to them: "I know how you and Dad feel about me getting an education, and I won't blame you if you take away the organ and the amp and the van and kick me out of the house. But I am going to be a rock musician and I am going to make it."

*   *   *   *

Despite the unfortunate hand fate had dealt the Grateful Dead in their twenty-fifth year, the band was intent on continuing with the fall schedule, which included East Coast and European tours in September and October. Garcia observed that continuing the tour after Brent's death "was real hard, but the band has been on what might be termed an endless tour since it was formed in 1965, so this is another twist in the road." Jerry added that "both Hornsby and Welnick will continue playing with the Dead until one of them gets sick of it." Hornsby, who also had to consider the schedule of his own band, stayed with the band for about a year and a half, helping the band through a difficult transition period following Brent's loss, and giving Welnick the time to learn the Dead's catalogue of songs and establish himself as the band's keyboard player.

The band's October tour of Europe dovetailed with the release of the live album *Without a Net*, which featured performances recorded at concerts from October 1989 to April 1990. The album was dedicated to Clifton Hanger, the pseudonym under which Mydland had registered at hotels when the band went on tour.

Without a Net was augmented by jazz musician Branford Marsalis, who played saxophone on "Eyes of the World." Marsalis had made a guest appearance on tenor and soprano sax during a concert at the Nassau Coliseum in New York in March 1990. Considered by some critics the best jazz tenor sax player of his generation, Branford's mellifluous saxophone improvisations took the Grateful Dead's music into the realm of jazz, reminiscent of Miles Davis's albums *In a Silent Way* and *Bitches Brew*. *In a Silent Way* changed the course of modern music, for Davis was the first to incorporate jazz sounds with a rock beat and feel, and the follow-up *Bitches Brew* defined the jazz-rock genre. Rather than play traditional melodies, Miles utilized a rock-style instrumentation—electrified guitars and keyboards—to play improvisational jazz-rock pieces based on electric bass solos and vamps against a backdrop of tribal rhythms.

Beginning in the late 1950s, modern jazz players like Coltrane, Davis, and Ornette Coleman made improvisation a key element of their music. Garcia had been a modern jazz fan since Phil Lesh had introduced him to the music of Coltrane and Davis in the early 1960s, and it would be fair to say that the legendary jams of the Grateful Dead owed a debt to these seminal jazz musicians.

Jerry got the chance to play with one of his jazz favorites when Ornette Coleman, whose innovative style of improvisation known as free jazz had been an influence on Garcia, invited Jerry to the recording studio to overdub guitar parts for his 1988 LP, *Virgin Beauty*. Garcia was delighted to participate, and his improvisational talent was evident as he laid down tracks for several songs on the album.

Garcia also got the opportunity to jam with Coleman when Coleman's Prime Time Band opened for the Grateful Dead several years later at the Oakland Coliseum. It was a unique evening of music for Grateful Dead fans when the legendary saxophonist joined the Dead for part of their set. Coleman's eclectic style of improvisation could be incredibly dissonant, and he added a whole new dimension to the music as he drove the band on with his forceful saxophone riffs. Phil Lesh was delighted to have taken part: "One of the great moments of my life!" Jerry was equally impressed with the memorable night of music.

Ever since Jerry had recovered after the diabetic attack that put him in a coma in 1986, he had been keeping his calendar very full. "Almost dying is a good way to get your attention," he revealed. "It's been a whole new life since then." Although playing with the Grateful Dead and his own band would most likely be enough for most other musicians, that was not Garcia's style. Jerry played when the spirit took him, and he soon hooked up with his old pal David Grisman, whom he hadn't performed with in nearly fifteen years.

Grisman recalled, "Jerry came over to my house one day, checked out my home studio, and asked me, 'How about putting out some more Old and In the Way tapes?' I said, 'Frankly, Jerry, I'd rather see us put out something new; we can put out old tapes when we're in wheelchairs.'" The two decided to play some acoustic music and got together with bassist Jim Kerwin and fiddle and percussion player Joe Craven at Grisman's basement studio to rehearse and work out tunes. "Jerry and I knew a lot of the same songs from years ago, and we would just sort of stumble onto these old songs," Grisman related. "We were doing these old whaling ballads such as 'Off to Sea Once More,' 'The Handsome Cabin Boy,' and 'I'm My Own Grandpa.'"

The quartet became known as the Garcia/Grisman Band, and they debuted at John Goddard's Village Music Christmas party at The Sweetwater in Mill Valley on December 17, 1990. Garcia then booked gigs for the band at the Warfield Theatre in San Francisco, where they have played on several different occasions. The music Garcia and Grisman performed was a blend of folk, old-time string band music, bluegrass, and jazz instrumentals. Garcia even broke out the banjo on several songs, the first time he had played the instrument in public since Old and In the Way had stopped gigging.

Garcia's continued passion for acoustic music resulted in the release of *Jerry Garcia/David Grisman* on Grisman's independent record label, Acoustic Disc, in mid-1991. Throughout his career Grisman had been an advocate of acoustic music, both as a producer and as a performer. He had produced bluegrass recordings for Folkways Records, collaborated with acoustic artists Stephane Grappelli, Clarence White, Doc Watson, Richard Greene, and others, and led his own acoustic bands in the 1970s and 1980s.

Disenchanted with the commercial aspirations of mainstream record companies, Grisman decided to found his own company in 1989 to promote the traditional and contemporary acoustic music he felt should be heard by the public. His small label's goal was to produce artistically rewarding music that would be a financial success as well. Garcia's involvement in a recording project on Grisman's label certainly helped the company's bottom line. "Jerry kind of takes care of the profitable part," said Grisman. "His participation has been really important."

Just how important was the rekindling of the musical relationship between Garcia and Grisman for Acoustic Disc? The Garcia/Grisman album of acoustic numbers earned a prestigious Grammy nomination in the Best Contemporary Folk category and sold more than one hundred thousand copies. Grisman also received the Rex Foundation's Ralph J. Gleason Award in recognition for his significant contribution to music. As a member of the foundation's board of directors, Garcia had a say in who would receive the award, and his vote was critical in Grisman being the recipient of the cash grant.

Garcia appeared on another Acoustic Disc release, *Bluegrass Reunion,* which was taped in May 1991 at Grisman's studio and featured renowned bluegrass musician Red Allen on guitar and vocals. The tunes on *Bluegrass Reunion* covered a range of bluegrass music with renditions of songs by the Carter Family, Bill Monroe, and Hank Williams. Garcia thoroughly enjoyed performing bluegrass music again. He admitted, "Ideally I'd have the Dead play two nights a week, play bluegrass two nights a week, play with my band two nights, and on the other day go to a movie."

In the spring of 1991 Garcia and Grisman also participated on an album with Ken Nordine, the originator of "word jazz." Since the 1940s Nordine's voice had been a familiar presence on television and radio; the "King of the Voice-Overs" had hawked a variety of products including Levi's jeans, Taster's Choice coffee, and Amoco gasoline. In the late 1950s Nordine was reading poetry over live music at a Chicago nightclub, and one night his material ran out. He began to improvise, and so was born word jazz. Nordine defined the art form as "talking songs, or spoken lyrics, some of which rhyme, some of which are parables, some of which are fantasies." In 1958 he put out two word jazz albums, and his stream-of-consciousness musings proved popular among the disenchanted segment of American youth, one of whom was Jerome Garcia.

Another fan of Nordine's, soundman Dan Healy, had invited Ken to help with the Grateful Dead's 1990 New Year's Eve broadcast at the Oakland Coliseum. During rehearsals for the live broadcast, Garcia walked by and recognized a familiar sound. "[Jerry] heard Ken's voice coming out of the speakers, stopped in his tracks, and came running into the room. Turns out he was a Nordine freak when he was a teenager too," Healy said. "He grabbed his guitar and came into the room and started noodling around, and Ken started reading, and it just clicked." The eventual result was *Devout Catalyst*, which featured the words of Nordine and the music of Garcia on acoustic guitar and Grisman on mandolin, with a cameo vocal appearance by Tom Waits. Garcia and Grisman laid down some spirited jazz riffs behind Nordine's cool jazz musings.

Jerry continued to work with Grisman, and in 1993 they produced the album *Not for Kids Only*, which was their second collaboration and featured a collection of twelve folk and old-time songs selected from the New Lost City Ramblers Songbook. (Also appearing on the album was Garcia's oldest daughter, Heather, who is first-chair violinist for the Redwood Symphony.) The tracks were laid down in Grisman's basement studio and were performed in a style faithful to the original versions. Some of the tunes were familiar to Garcia because he had played them in folk and old-time groups in the early 1960s. David Nelson noted, "The tune 'There Ain't No Bugs on Me,' which appears on the album, was one of our favorites that we used to do. Garcia, Hunter, and I would fool around with it.

We'd goof on the words, and that's how we came up with 'there may be lobsters on some of you mobsters, but there ain't no lobsters on me.'" With the release of *Not for Kids Only*, Garcia had come full circle in his career.

Not only was Garcia keeping busy with music, he had been devoting more of his spare time to his lifelong interest in art. Though music was his major form of expression, he had never stopped sketching, painting, and drawing. Over the years he experimented with pen and ink, colored pencils, colored markers, watercolor, airbrush, and computer art. Though Jerry had accumulated a portfolio of artwork, he was very modest about it and had never exhibited any of his pieces in public. But a longtime friend, Nora Sage Murray, persuaded him to let her market some of his artwork, and he authorized her to sell prints of his work through her company, The Art Peddler.

In February 1991 Garcia had his first art exhibit at the Weir Gallery in Berkeley, California, which displayed his paintings, drawings, and prints. His works, signed "J. Garcia," showed his versatility in a wide range of mediums: pen and ink, watercolor, airbrush, and mixed media. Garcia's drawings were caricatures that ranged from the whimsical to the macabre, while his airbrush paintings had a psychedelic look to them. An admitted fan of the surrealists, Garcia acknowledged that his work had been influenced by Max Ernst, Paul Klee, and Giorgio de Chirico. All of his works were for sale with prices ranging from $300 for prints to $40,000 for original artwork. For his part, Garcia was unassuming about the sale of his work: "I've always thought of myself as an art student who got seduced by music, but most of what I've done I don't really care for anyone to see, and I've been destroying it as I do it. It wasn't until the last few years that somebody suggested people might want to see some of these things. I said, 'Really? I can't imagine.'. . . I'm glad there are respectable sellers who accept my stuff with some degree of seriousness." When he was asked about the high-ticket prices on some of the pieces he quipped in typical 1960s style, "Don't buy them. Steal them. Steal this art."

After the initial exhibit on the West Coast, the art show went on the road to Washington, D.C. and New York City, concurrent with the Grateful Dead's spring tour of the East Coast. Garcia's artwork generated excitement among fans and critics alike, and additional exhibitions were held at art galleries around the country. Nora Sage Murray was so pleased with the success of Garcia's art that she convinced Jerry to allow a book of his work to be put out. Published by Celestial Arts, it was titled *J. Garcia: Paintings, Drawings and Sketches*, and featured thirty-five black-and-white and forty color images.

While the show was in New York, executives of Stonehenge Ltd., a tie manufacturer, were impressed with Jerry's artwork and offered to manufacture a line of silk neckties using his designs. Though Jerry was hesitant at first, he eventually agreed, and Stonehenge started production of "J. Garcia Art in Neckwear." When the ties debuted at Bloomingdale's the following year, they were a big hit. Retail sales reached $30 million, and such notables as Bill Clinton and Al Gore were seen sporting Garcia's neckwear.

A line of silk shirts imprinted with Garcia's artwork soon

followed. NAK, a company based in Hayward, California, began manufacturing the Jerry Garcia "Art in Sportswear" collection. The colorful shirts cost $45 and had such names as Moon Mountain, Shaman, and Birdland.

Garcia had put out more than thirty albums with either the Grateful Dead, the Jerry Garcia Band, or as a solo performer, and he had written many songs with Robert Hunter. However, the Hunter-Garcia team was never given much recognition within the music industry for their songwriting. In 1991, Arista record producer Ralph Sall attempted to rectify this, releasing in April a tribute album called *Deadicated* that featured fifteen Grateful Dead songs covered by other artists. Sall wanted to expose the mainstream audience to the work of the songwriting teams of Hunter-Garcia and Barlow-Weir. "I really like the songs," he explained, "and nobody knew them. They never got played on the radio. So I got some people who do get played on the radio and tried to prove they were great fucking songwriters." The artists who performed on *Deadicated* were Los Lobos, Bruce Hornsby and the Range, The Harshed Mellows, Elvis Costello, Suzanne Vega, Dwight Yoakam, Warren Zevon with David Lindley, the Indigo Girls, Lyle Lovett, the Cowboy Junkies, Midnight Oil, Burning Spear, Dr. John, and Jane's Addiction.

Bruce Hornsby also felt the songs were unappreciated. "When a general person talks about the Dead, or the press talks about the Dead they always concern themselves with the trappings—the last bastion of hippiedom, that sort of thing. None of that means much to me. What I like about the Dead is their songs. I think they're great songwriters. . . . To me I see [*Deadicated*] as a really significant event because I think that it will draw attention to the fact that these guys are great songwriters. That's a lot of what they are about and they have not gotten their just due as writers."

Robert Hunter was knocked out by the album: "It was like somebody sent me chocolates, roses, and a Jaguar all at once. It was just such a pleasure to hear someone else do the material and to feel that the material did have an independent existence."

Whether or not the public garnered a new appreciation for the Grateful Dead songwriters can't be told. Though *Deadicated* did receive some airplay, which gave the songs more exposure, the album didn't climb very high on the charts. The big splash that Sall had expected didn't occur.

The Hunter-Garcia songwriting team did get more attention in 1991, but from an unexpected source. In August, the first issue of *Grateful Dead Comix* hit the stands. This had been a pet project of Jerry's, who had been a comic book addict since childhood and had been looking for a company to do a comic of the band for several years. Kitchen Sink Comix, a small Wisconsin publisher of high-quality specialty comics and classic reprints, was chosen to publish it. The comic featured interpretations of Grateful Dead songs and included band members as characters in the strip.

The first issue included the Hunter-Garcia songs "Dire Wolf," "Terrapin Station," and "Casey Jones," and the lead strip, "Dire Wolf," had Jerry as the central character. Garcia, who supervised and approved the comic book, said he was delighted with the results. In later issues, the publisher included illustrated anecdotes from the band's history. "It helped that [the band] were personally involved. There's a lot of research to do. We want this to be historically accurate," remarked publisher Denis Kitchen.

The Grateful Dead continued to sell out concerts across the country and were the top-grossing touring band of 1991, taking in $34.7 million in receipts in what music industry analysts considered a bad year for the business. Thanks to their loyal following of Dead Heads, the band had become one of the biggest money-makers in rock history. And more than twenty-five years after they had begun, the Grateful Dead still represented, to longtime Dead Heads and young fans alike, a link to the idealism and freedom of the sixties. Many of the new generation of fans exhibit the same spirit of adventure and rebelliousness that was so much a part of the social upheaval of the sixties. There is a sense of individualism among the younger fans, who are apt to question authority much like the hippies of the counterculture had. The common bond between Dead Heads—whether young or old, black or white, rich or poor—is that they want to be part of a free-form celebration that makes them feel good and enriches their lives.

"The Grateful Dead is one of the last run-off-and-join-the-circus things, and there isn't much like it," expounded Garcia in 1991. "America has been so dull lately. These are the Bush

years, dull stuff and unpleasant, by and large. Doors are clos-
ing everywhere, and the opportunities to do something adventurous and fun have gotten narrower and narrower. The Dead
hasn't changed much from our point of view, but the world has
changed around it."

One change that came as a shock was the tragic loss of Bill
Graham, who died on October 25, 1991, when the helicopter
in which he was flying crashed into an electric utility tower
near Vallejo, California while he was returning from a Huey
Lewis and the News concert he had produced at the Concord
Pavilion. When the helicopter, which was traveling at a low
altitude because of inclement weather, collided with the tower,
the force of the impact threw Graham, companion Melissa
Gold, and pilot Steve Kahn to the ground, killing them
instantly.

News of Graham's death stunned his family, friends, and
associates. Initially, there was concern about the fate of his
company, Bill Graham Presents, but it was announced that all
his productions would go on as scheduled. Bill Barsotti, an official with Bill Graham Presents, said, "We all learned a great
deal from him, and one thing we learned is that the show must
go on."

Though Graham could be a hard-nosed businessman who
rubbed some people the wrong way, he was largely responsible
for bringing a sense of professionalism to the San Francisco
music scene and the rock scene in general. From his annual
New Year's Eve extravaganzas to the numerous benefits that he

staged, he set a standard from which others would be judged. Over the years he developed a close relationship with the Grateful Dead, whom he felt were "on any given night the greatest of them all." He took the time to find interesting venues for the Dead to play at, and labored to create many special productions for the band he loved, so that Dead Heads would get something extra on New Year's Eve, Chinese New Year, Mardi Gras, Halloween, or other such occasions.

Garcia expressed his feelings for Graham: "The thing about Bill is his relationship to us [was] on a lot of levels, like our relationship to each other. It was intimate. There's a certain kind of friendship that you have when there's somebody who understands you, and Bill was there from day one, just about."

Garcia reached a milestone in his life when he turned fifty years old on August 1, 1992. Jerry celebrated by doing what he loved most—playing music. The Jerry Garcia Band was in the midst of a brief Southern California tour when they performed on his birthday to a sold-out audience of 15,000 at the Irvine Meadows Amphitheatre. In typical low-key fashion, not a word was mentioned from the stage about the special event. However, paper masks with Garcia's face on them were distributed by a fan who had made them for the occasion, and a banner in the audience proclaimed "Happy Birthday Jerry."

Though the crowd made several stabs at singing "Happy Birthday," it never came together with enough volume to get an acknowledgment from Garcia. Decked out in sporty red and black sweatpants, Garcia was in good spirits as he performed his usual repertoire of rhythm and blues, rock, pop, and gospel tunes to an audience that was in a decidedly upbeat mood and ready to party. Those who had come to celebrate his birthday were glad to spend one more Saturday night with good ol' Captain Trips.

After the conclusion of the tour, Garcia returned to his Marin County home, where on August 4 he fell ill from a combination of lung and heart problems as well as complications from diabetes. Jerry's ailments could be traced to years of chain-smoking, bad diet, excessive weight, and lack of exercise. Garcia, who at that time tipped the scales at three hundred pounds, was known to have a fondness for chili dogs and milk shakes. A spokesman for the band strenuously denied Garcia's illness was related to drugs, but rumors on the Dead Head circuit persisted that Garcia was once again chasing the dragon.

Garcia was not hospitalized, and he remained at home. Randy Baker, Jerry's physician, reported, "Jerry Garcia's health problems are primarily chronic rather than acute. He has some lung disease related to years of smoking, and this has put some stress on his heart, which has become slightly enlarged. . . . He does have borderline diabetes, which should resolve with weight loss. His current problems are being managed with mild medication, and he is at home and experiencing no discomfort. Jerry has agreed to a program of stopping smoking, losing weight, exercise, and dietary changes. As this is accomplished he should regain good health and continue performing for many years."

Dates for the Jerry Garcia Band and the Grateful Dead in August were canceled, and then the Grateful Dead's fall tour was scrubbed when it became apparent that Garcia's recuperation would take several months. Jerry began to eat right, exercise, and smoke less, and he started to lose weight, get back in shape, and regain his stamina. He became a vegetarian, worked out three times a week with a trainer, and cut down his three-pack-a-day cigarette habit. His new life-style paid off as he dropped sixty pounds and started to feel good again. With his weight down and his energy back, Garcia returned to the stage with the Jerry Garcia Band for a sold-out performance at the Oakland Coliseum on October 31, 1992. An animated and happy Garcia remarked backstage, "I'd forgotten how good it feels to be healthy."

In December, the Grateful Dead started performing again with shows in Denver, Tempe, and Oakland, but the band did not play their traditional New Year's Eve show. Garcia explained, "After seventeen years it had become like the Super Bowl—too much hype and media attention. It was like the music didn't much matter." Instead, Garcia took a trip to Hawaii with Weir, Lesh, and Hunter just before Christmas. Jerry had been going to Hawaii as often as possible to go scuba diving, which he had taken up after he recovered from his coma in 1986.

Scuba diving offered Garcia the opportunity to get some exercise and at the same time enter a different dimension without using drugs. Garcia observed, "Scuba diving satisfies the yearning of going to space; you're in a place where there's no gravity. It kind of takes up the space that drugs left. You dive every day for a month and it really changes your consciousness." During the trip to Hawaii the boys relaxed and hung out together. "We got a chance to remember that we're old friends in addition to being colleagues," said Garcia.

Jerry also had the opportunity to hook up with some old friends when his relationship with Manasha Matheson ended and he began dating women closer to his age. For a couple of months in early 1993 Garcia was seeing Barbara Meier, an acquaintance from his youth, but in the spring he reconnected with Deborah Koons, whom he had been involved with in the mid-1970s. The forty-four-year-old Koons was now an independent filmmaker, and she had wanted Jerry to be involved in a film project she was working on. They rekindled their friendship, and the two traveled to Ireland for two weeks in August where their romance heated up. Jerry had found his match and plans were made to tie the knot on Valentine's Day 1994.

Koons, who was from a well-heeled family, insisted on a traditional church wedding. Invitations were sent out to family and friends, but the whereabouts of the ceremony and reception were kept secret to deflect the anticipated media circus and throng of Dead Heads likely to crash the party. Guests were told to call the Grateful Dead office on February 14 to get the location of each event. The subterfuge worked, and the nuptials were a strictly private affair.

The wedding vows were exchanged at Christ Episcopal Church in Sausalito, California. About fifty family members and friends, including Garcia's three grown daughters, Heather, Annabelle, and Theresa, the bride's parents, and all the members of the Grateful Dead attended the late afternoon ceremony. The bride wore a white wedding gown and the groom donned a dark suit without tie, refusing to wear even one of his own line of J. Garcia neckwear. Steve Parish was the best man. During the ceremony Gloria Jones, vocalist in the

Jerry Garcia Band, sang Stevie Wonder's song "You and I," and David Grisman played "Ave Maria" accompanied by classical guitarist Enrique Coria.

Immediately following the ceremony, a reception was held at the tony Corinthian Yacht Club in nearby Tiburon, where some 250 guests gathered to celebrate with Mr. and Mrs. Garcia. The newlyweds chose an Irish band to perform at the affair, a cheerful reminder of their recent trip to the Emerald Isle. Traditional Irish folk music was played, although there were no reports of the bride and groom dancing a jig. Afterward the happy couple flew off for a good time in sunny Mexico.

9

EPILOGUE

erry Garcia has been a major drawing card for almost a quarter of a century, and he has achieved the distinction of becoming a legend in his own time. His brand of rock 'n' roll has weathered the years—not fancy or trendy, but always a feast for the ears. He is always stretching the limits of his own abilities, and consequently the abilities of his bandmates. As broadcasters love to say about certain sports superstars, Jerry makes those around him better players.

Like some other older rockers, Jerry has held on to his loyal fans from the early years. However, Grateful Dead concerts never seem like old-timers' events, and Garcia's music is played on progressive rock stations rather than on oldies stations. This is because Jerry's repertoire, although rooted in the past, is not static. He still delights in the improvisational jams; still invests time in making authentic-sounding music; and still plays for the joy it gives him, not for the income it provides. Since the music he plays is ever-changing, his fans keep coming to see him, even if just to hear what's new.

And though the furrows in Garcia's brow have grown deeper and his hair has grown grayer, the crowds at his concerts seem to have aged very little. The core of the Grateful Dead— Garcia, Lesh, Weir, and Kreutzmann—have been playing together for thirty years, plenty of time for their original fans to become grandparents. But the number of those early fans is relatively small compared to the legions of listeners they have garnered since *In the Dark* came out in 1987. Thus, a whole new generation of Dead Heads who are still in their twenties has developed.

It is fascinating to witness the popularity of Garcia and the Dead amongst young listeners. Entering a crowd at a Grateful Dead concert in the 1990s is almost like opening a time capsule that was closed in 1970. Teenagers and college-age kids in old jeans and tie-dye shirts are dancing in the aisles; some are high on drugs and most are high on the music. The performance is one long dance concert, as if the old Avalon Ballroom had been magically transported twenty-plus years into the future and expanded to ten times its original capacity. The children of the 1990s are just as happy as the children of the 1960s were to be rocking to the music of the Grateful Dead.

At first glance, this convergence of 1960s icons with 1990s audiences seems incongruous. Garcia and the Dead feature no smoke and mirrors, no fireworks, no coterie of gyrating dancers.

Unless you are close to the stage, it is difficult to make out much movement up there. The band doesn't do a lot of MTV. And you really have to listen to the music and the lyrics. Why are today's vid-kids so taken with these old guys from San Francisco?

Under the surface, though, there are a lot of similarities between the two eras. In the 1990s, America is going through wrenching changes after a period of stultifying conservatism. The youth in the country are dissatisfied with the status quo, and many of them feel that there is little opportunity for them in mainstream society. After a long period of quiescence, there has been an upsurge in social activism among the younger generation. And a number of societal factors—including the advent of computers and the telecommunications boom—have shifted the balance of power from our institutions toward the individual, empowering people to express themselves in heretofore unheard of ways.

This is what the hippie movement of the 1960s was all about, so it makes sense that Jerry Garcia and the Grateful Dead are the musicians of choice for a solid section of 1990s listeners. The music is not cause-specific, although Garcia's songs do sometimes carry messages about war, the environment, and humanity. Rather, it sets a tone that listeners can incorporate into their own lives—a concerned though ultimately optimistic tone. Listeners get the feeling that although life is a heavy-duty trip, they can still feel good about it.

*　*　*　*

Good times are what Garcia has been pursuing ever since he left the straight world at fifteen and decided to pursue his muse. Following in his musician father's footsteps, he took up the guitar and became one of the true innovators in American music. His genius can be found not only in his virtuosity as a guitar player, but in his ability to master a broad range of musical styles with an authority that few musicians can equal. His accomplishments earned him a place in the Rock 'n' Roll Hall of Fame as a member of the Grateful Dead. And in his transition from high school dropout to Haight-Ashbury hippie to millionaire rock star, he has never lost his insatiable desire to play music.

For most people, with age and public recognition come a softening of individualistic attitudes. But Jerry has achieved acclaim and fortune while remaining the nonconformist that he has always been. He continues to do what feels right to him rather than what feels comfortable to others, whether it involves the music he is playing, the causes he is attracted to, or his personal life. In fact, it seems that society has become more accepting of Garcia rather than the other way around. When Jerry sang the national anthem at the San Francisco Giants home opener at Candlestick Park in 1993, he was as American as apple pie. Perhaps this is because many of the hippies of the 1960s are now part of the establishment of the 1990s, and the beliefs and life-style that Jerry represents are more current with today's elite. Or maybe its just because, as Garcia said in his self-deprecating style, "We're like bad architecture or an old whore. If you stick around long enough, eventually you get respectable."

APPENDIX A

AN EARLY
GARCIA SONG LIST

Although lists of songs and performances of the Grateful Dead are readily available (see, for example, *DeadBase*, compiled by John Scott, Mike Dolgushkin, and Stu Nixon; PO Box 499, Hanover, NH, 03755), the following information about the pre-Grateful Dead music that Jerry Garcia was playing, and with whom he was playing, is not so widely disseminated. The titles were culled from tapes made at the performances (dates and venues are included).

July 1961

PLACE   Boar's Head Coffee House, above the San Carlos Bookstall, San Carlos, California

MUSICIANS   Jerry Garcia on guitar, Marshall Leicester on banjo

SONGS   Ellen Smith
Wildwood Flower
Jesse James
No One Will Stand by Me
All Good Times Are Past
Darlin' Corey

June 1962

PLACE   Boar's Head Coffee House, San Carlos Jewish Community
            Center, San Carlos, California

BAND NAME   Sleepy Hollow Hog Stompers

MUSICIANS   Jerry Garcia on guitar and banjo, Marshall Leicester on banjo
            and guitar, Dick Arnold on fiddle

SONGS   Chuck a Little Hill
            Billy Grimes
            Cannonball
            Devilish Mary
            Buck Dancer's Choice
            Little Birdie
            Sally Goodun
            Hold the Woodpile Down
            Crow Black Chicken
            The Johnson Boys
            Shady Grove
            Uncle Joe
            Sweet Sunny South
            Hungry Hash-House
            Man of Constant Sorrow
            Yonder He Goes
            Three Went a-Huntin'

November 10, 1962

PLACE   College of San Mateo Folk Festival, San Mateo, California

BAND NAME   Hart Valley Drifters

MUSICIANS   Jerry Garcia on banjo and guitar, David Nelson on guitar,
            Robert Hunter on bass, Norm Van Mastricht on guitar
            and dobro

SONGS   Little Birdie (Garcia solo)
            Walkin' Boss (Garcia solo)
            Miller's Song
            Deep Elem Blues
            Can the Circle Be Unbroken
            I Truly Understand
            Raging Sea
            Cannonball
            Cuckoo Bird

Man of Constant Sorrow (Garcia *a capella*)
Handsome Mollie
Pig in a Pen
Banks of the Ohio
Gamblin' Man
So Long Buddy
Salty Dog

February 23, 1963

PLACE	The Tangent, Palo Alto, California
BAND NAME	Wildwood Boys
MUSICIANS	Jerry Garcia on banjo and guitar; David Nelson on guitar; Robert Hunter on bass and guitar; Norm Van Mastricht on bass, guitar, and dobro
SONGS	Rolling in My Sweet Baby's Arms
	Jerry's Breakdown
	Standing in the Need of Prayer
	Muleskinner Blues
	Pike County Breakdown
	Come All Ye Fair and Tender Maidens
	We Shall Not Be Moved

May 1963

PLACE	The Tangent, Palo Alto, California
BAND NAME	Jerry and Sarah
MUSICIANS	Jerry Garcia on guitar, banjo, and fiddle; Sarah Garcia on guitar
SONGS	Deep Elem Blues
	The Weaver
	I Truly Understand
	All the Good Times Are Past
	Long Black Veil
	The Man Who Wrote "Home Sweet Home" Never Was a Married Man
	Keno
	Foggy Mountain Top

Summer 1963

PLACE	Monterey Folk Festival, Monterey, California

BAND NAME   Wildwood Boys

MUSICIANS   Jerry Garcia on banjo, David Nelson on guitar,
             Robert Hunter on bass, Ken Frankel on mandolin

SONG   Nine Pound Hammer
             (won Amateur Bluegrass Open Competition)

March 7, 1964

PLACE   The Tangent, Palo Alto, California

BAND NAME   Black Mountain Boys

MUSICIANS   Jerry Garcia on banjo, David Nelson on mandolin,
             Robert Hunter on bass, Sandy Rothman on guitar

SONGS   If I Lose
             Pig in a Pen
             Once More
             Stony Creek
             Two Little Boys
             Salty Dog
             Rosa Lee McFall
             Teardrops in My Eyes
             New River Train
             Love Please Come Home
             Make Me a Pallet on the Floor
             Roll on Buddy
             Darlin' Alalee
             Ocean of Diamonds
             Salt Creek
             In the Pines
             Banjo Breakdown
             Blue Moon Turns to Gold
             She's More to Be Pitied Than Scolded
             Black Mountain Rag

ASTROLOGICAL CHART AND INTERPRETATION FOR JERRY GARCIA

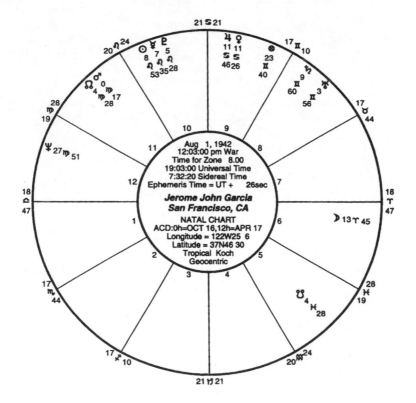

260

General

The most striking factors at first glance are the preponderance of planets in the southern hemisphere (above the horizon). This indicates outgoing, active, intellectual expression and mental objectivity in a general way. Nine out of ten planets grouped like this indicate an extrovert—someone who will be before the public. In addition, the Sun in the Tenth House strengthens the drive to achieve distinction in the chosen career. This placement shows someone who thrives on success and favors positions that call for confidence and leadership.

Stellium

To be more specific, this chart contains a stellium (three planets conjunct, or next to, each other in the same sign and house) in the Tenth House of worldly affairs and professional and career interests. This house deals with a person's public life and achievements and is the house of worldly attainments. The Sun sign, Leo, forms a conjunction with Mercury and Pluto, both in Leo. A stellium like this indicates a major focus of energy. The Sun represents a person's vital life force, the ego, the individuality, the creative powers, and the drive for self-expression. This particular placement indicates someone who is or will be a public, creative figure. The Sun conjunct Mercury strengthens the will to act on ideas. Rather than merely thinking over or talking about plans, the person gives concrete expression to ideas through action. On the minus side, the person can fail to recognize shortcomings and character flaws because the ego influences his thoughts with this aspect.

The conjunct Pluto unites the power of Pluto with the vital life force of the Sun. This aspect gives the person vast powers that can be used constructively or destructively. This person is not tolerant of weakness, either in individuals or in political systems, that allow unfair or intolerable human conditions. Acting in moderation is difficult, for likes and dislikes are intense.

Mercury conjunct Pluto gives deep intellectual insights and broad-

ens the scope of intellectual awareness. This person understands fundamentals and underlying truths, yet can also comprehend broad concepts.
This aspect shows persuasiveness, determination, and curiosity.

Emotions

The Moon in Aries in the Sixth House—the only planet in the northern hemisphere (below the horizon) in this chart—stimulates the emo-
tions. The results are hasty responses and headstrong attitudes that
prompt instinctive rejection of discipline and interference. Patience and
safeguards against mishaps due to haste and rash action is called for.
Physical health depends upon emotional health. Working relationships
fluctuate according to the person's emotional state.

Moon opposite the ascendant shows a person who doesn't like to
be alone—emotional fulfillment is found with and through other people.
The person shows emotional perceptivity to the wants and needs of the
public.

Moon trine the Sun, Mercury, and Pluto produces inner harmony,
which enables the person to function smoothly. Because of the person's
ability to relate to others, this aspect shows someone who can gain
acceptance and achieve success in public life. This person has the gift
of expressing emotional energy in a positive way—with wit, depth, mental alertness, and intellectual versatility.

Personality

This sign on the ascendant (in this case, Libra) has bearing on the total
person: appearance, temperament, attitudes, and personal mannerisms.
Individuality is projected through cooperation with other people; the
personality is focused on and mirrored on those with whom the person
cooperates. This placement's strongest virtue is the ability to see any
matter from the viewpoint of those with whom the person is dealing.
Charm and courtesy come naturally, as do a taste for luxury and an
innate desire for harmony and fair play. Libra rising is refined and peace-
loving, and persuasive in a tactful way.

Strong Miscellaneous Factors

Saturn conjunct Uranus in the Eighth House: This person may feel heavy obligations from business partners—joint financial affairs may not be handled in an entirely open and aboveboard manner. A sudden windfall or an unexpected legacy from a partnership, usually later in life, is indicated.

Venus conjunct Jupiter in the Ninth House: This placement is associated with personal happiness and some good fortune. It indicates that the person is gracious, generous, and extremely well liked. This doesn't indicate much restraint in social pleasures, though. The person probably feels compelled to donate to philanthropic or religion-oriented causes. Artistic interests reflect exceptionally fine aesthetic taste.

Mars in Virgo in the Eleventh House square Saturn/Uranus: The sex drive is suppressed to a degree and is often diverted toward work. This placement shows the person takes the initiative in friendships and group activities. The majority of friends are probably male. This person is attracted to competitive, outgoing people. There is a fear of danger and a dislike of war and the military. Patience and caution are needed as there is a desire for freedom, action, and excitement.

Steve Janofsky

INTERVIEWS

Gene Anthony, January 1994
Jerilyn Brandelius, September 1991
Tom Constanten, January 1989, April 1993, December 1993
Charlotte Daigle, January 1994
John Dawson, August 1989
Phil DeGuere, September 1991
Carolyn "Mountain Girl" Garcia, September 1979
Jerry Garcia, January 1978
Herb Greene, December 1993
Dan Healy, January 1978
Chet Helms, August 1989
Michael Hinton, September 1979
Doug Irwin, June 1990
Jorma Kaukonen, December 1993
William Kreutzmann, Sr., July 1980
Dick Latvala, December 1989
Eileen Law, May 1989
Phil Lesh, January 1978
Stanley Mouse, May 1989
Brent Mydland, September 1979
David Nelson, October 1991, December 1993
Robert Nelson, November 1992
Steve Parish, August 1988
Nora Sage, December 1991
Merl Saunders, December 1993
Nicki Scully, March 1989
Rock Scully, March 1990, June 1990
Owsley Stanley, September 1993

NOTES

Chapter 1

5, 7a, 7b, 7d: Kahn, "Jerry Garcia and the Call of the Weird."
6, 10a, 13, 14c, 18b: DeCurtis, "The Music Never Stops."
7c, 10b, 11a, 16c, 17b: White, *Rock Lives*.
8, 9, 11b: Reich and Wenner, *Garcia*.
14a: Jackson, "Garcia on the Art of Rock."
14b, 15a, 15c, 15d: Barich, "Still Truckin'."
15b: Gleason, *The Jefferson Airplane and the San Francisco Sound*.
16a, 16b, 16d, 17a: Abbott, "Dead Reckoning and Hamburger Metaphysics."
18a: Lake, "Rock 'n' Roll Misfit."

Chapter 2

23, 24a, 47a, 48c, 57b: Reich and Wenner, *Garcia*.
24b, 24c, 24d: Kahn, "Jerry Garcia and the Call of the Weird."
25, 26c, 29a, 29c, 34, 35, 46a: Troy interview of Charlotte Daigle, January 1994.
26a, 26b, 27a: Abbott, "Dead Reckoning and Hamburger Metaphysics."
27b: White, Rock Lives.
28a: Gebhardt interview of Jerry Garcia, 1993.
29b, 54a: Gleason, *The Jefferson Airplane and the San Francisco Sound*.

265

30, 32, 41, 42a, 42b, 43, 49a, 50: Troy interview of David Nelson, October 12, 1991.

33a, 47c, 53: Gans, *Conversations with the Dead*.

33b: Troy interview of Tom Constanten, April 1, 1993.

36a, 36b: Troy interview of Tom Constanten, December 11, 1993.

36c, 37: Gans, "The Pre-Dead Days."

38a, 49b: Troy interview of Jorma Kaukonen, December 5, 1993.

38b, 45, 47b, 54b, 57c: Troy interview of David Nelson, December 22, 1993.

46b: Bothun and Hyde, "Dawn of the Dead."

48a: Donnelly, "What a Long, Strange Trip It's Been."

48b: Groenke and Cramer, "One Afternoon Long Ago. . . ."

51a, 52a, 52b: Jackson, "Ragged but Right."

51b: Juanis, "Dawgwood Revisited."

55: Gans and Simon, *Playing in the Band*.

56a, 56b: Jackson, "Pigpen Forever."

57a: Troy interview of William Kreutzmann, Sr., July 1980.

58: Barich, "Still Truckin'."

Chapter 3

59, 74: Troy interview of David Nelson, December 22, 1993.

60, 64c, 65b, 68, 72a, 72b, 72d, 83b, 85a, 86a: Reich and Wenner, *Garcia*.

61a, 61b, 73a: Gans, *Conversations with the Dead*.

61c: McNally, "When I Had No Song to Sing. . . ."

62a, 63, 76b, 89c, 90: Jackson, "Pigpen Forever."

62b, 86b: Troy interview of Tom Constanten, April 1 and December 11, 1993.

64a, 67b, 71b, 72e, 73c, 81: Lydon, "The Grateful Dead."

64b: Ralph J. Gleason radio interview of Bob Weir, 1969.

65a: Goodman, "Jerry Garcia: The *Rolling Stone* Interview."

66: Gleason, *The Jefferson Airplane and the San Francisco Sound*.

67a, 83a: Glatt, *Rage & Roll*.

70a, 71a: Wolfe, *The Electric Kool-Aid Acid Test*.

70b, 71c, 77a, 80a: Troy interview of Carolyn Garcia, September 1979.

72c: Gans and Simon, *Playing in the Band*.

73b: Jerry Garcia radio interview on KFRC, 1966.

75a, 77b, 77c: Graham and Greenfield, *Bill Graham Presents*.

75b: Greene, *Book of the Dead*.

76a: Troy interview of Rock Scully, March and June, 1990.

80b: Plummer, *The Holy Goof*.

80c, 85b: Babbs and Perry, *On the Bus*.

82, 86c: Troy interview of Jorma Kaukonen, December 5, 1993.

87: Ralph J. Gleason radio interview of John Cippolina, 1969.

88: Troy interview of Herb Greene, December 23, 1993.
89a: Troy interview of Stanley Mouse, May 1989.
89b: Sculatti and Seay, *San Francisco Nights*.

Chapter 4

95: Cohen, *The San Francisco Oracle*.
96a: Sculatti and Seay, *San Francisco Nights*.
96b, 113b: Groenke and Cramer, "One Afternoon Long Ago. . . ."
97, 120: Jackson, "Pigpen Forever."
98a, 136a, 138b: Troy interview of David Nelson, December 22, 1993.
98b, 104, 106a, 107b, 116a, 116b, 119a, 124, 125, 131, 132a, 132b, 133, 138e:
    Reich and Wenner, *Garcia*.
98c, 106b, 107a: Troy interview of Carolyn Garcia, September 1979.
100a, 100b, 112a, 112b, 115: Perry, *The Haight-Ashbury*.
101, 111c: Troy interview of Jorma Kaukonen, December 5, 1993.
103: Gleason, *The Jefferson Airplane and the San Francisco Sound*.
105: Ralph J. Gleason radio interview of Jerry Garcia, 1969.
106c: Scully, "Parties, Parks, Women and Music."
108a: Harry Reasoner interview of Jerry Garcia for CBS news special *The
    Hippie Temptation*, 1967.
108b: "Dropouts with a Mission," *Newsweek*.
110. Selvin, *Monterey Pop*.
111a, 113a: Troy interview of Rock Scully, March and June 1990.
111b: Troy interview of Chet Helms, August 1989.
114: Lydon, "The Grateful Dead."
117, 118a: Troy interview of Jerry Garcia, January 1978.
118b: Dym and Alson, "The Man Behind the Words."
119b: Block, "Garcia on Garcia."
119c: Gans, *Conversations with the Dead*.
121, 128b, 129b: Troy interview of Tom Constanten, April 1, 1993 and
    December 11, 1993.
122a, 122c: Constanten, *Between Rock & Hard Places*.
122b, 122d: Jackson, "T.C."
123a, 123b: Troy interview of Tom Constanten, January 1989.
123c: Hart, *Drumming at the Edge of Magic*.
126a, 126b, 129a: Graham and Greenfield, *Bill Graham Presents*.
128a: Sutherland, "Jerry Garcia Interview."
130: Barclay, "The Woodstock Generation."
134: Stuckey, "Jerry Garcia."
135a: McClanahan, "Grateful Dead I Have Known."
135b, 137a, 138d: Hoskyns, *Across the Great Divide*.

136b, 137c, 138a, 138c: Dalton, *Piece of My Heart*.
137b: Troy interview of John Dawson, August 1989.
139a: Gans and Simon, *Playing in the Band*.
139b: Harrison, *The Dead*.

Chapter 5

140: Itkowitz, "Rapping with Garcia of the Grateful Dead."
141a: McClanahan, "Grateful Dead I Have Known."
141b, 167: Block, "Garcia on Garcia."
141c, 142a, 147, 149, 170: Reich and Wenner, *Garcia*.
142b, 165a, 165b: Jackson, "John Kahn."
142c, 144b, 144c: Sievert, "New Life with the Dead."
143, 144a, 153b, 159, 168a, 168b, 168c: Troy interview of Merl Saunders, December 20, 1993.
145a: Troy interview of Jorma Kaukonen, December 5, 1993.
145b: Troy interview of Tom Constanten, December 11, 1993.
146a: Jerry Garcia interview from *Go Ride the Music*.
146b: Crosby, *Long Time Gone*.
150a, 152b, 152d: Gans and Simon, *Playing in the Band*.
150b: Jackson, *Goin' Down the Road*.
152a, 157: Jackson, *The Music Never Stopped*.
152c: Jackson, "Jon McIntire."
153a: Selvin, "Jamming for the Hell of It."
154, 155b, 158: Grissim, "Garcia Returns to Banjo."
155a, 156: Perry, "A New Life for the Dead."
160, 171: *People*, "Jerry Garcia's Grateful Dead Pass the Acid Test."
161: Troy interview of Jerry Garcia, January 1978.
162: Troy interview of Doug Irwin, June 1990.
163a: Graham and Greenfield, *Bill Graham Presents*.
163b: Troy interview of Phil Lesh, January 1978.
163c: Gans, *Conversations with the Dead*.
164: Brandelius, *Grateful Dead Family Album*.
166: Troy interview of Rock Scully, March and June 1990.

Chapter 6

172, 173b, 176a: Weitzman, "The Grateful Dead: A Look Back."
173a, 176b, 177a, 177b, 177c, 178b, 180c, 184, 185b, 185c: Block, "Garcia on Garcia."
175, 200: Jackson, "John Kahn."
178a, 186b, 187, 188a, 189: Watts, "Dead on the Nile."

178c, 191b: Gans and Simon, *Playing in the Band.*
179: Selvin, "The Grateful Dead Decides to Try a Guiding Hand."
180a: Hall, "True Confessions in Hartford."
180b, 185a: Young, "The Awakening of the Dead."
182: Troy interview of Robert Nelson, November 1992.
183: Troy interview of Jorma Kaukonen, December 5, 1993.
186a, 205c, 206a: Selvin, "Fans Grateful the Dead Are Still Around."
186c: *San Francisco Chronicle,* "The Grateful Dead Play the Pyramids."
188b, 193: Sutherland, "Jerry Garcia Interview."
191a, 195a, 195b, 195c: Fong-Torres, "Fifteen Years Dead."
192a: Troy interview of Brent Mydland, September 1979.
192b: *Grateful Dead Program 1983,* Brent Mydland interview.
197a, 197b: Troy interview of Nicki Scully, March 18, 1989.
198: Lufkin, "The Dead—Just Becoming Alive."
199: *San Francisco Chronicle,* "Grateful Dead Suit Dropped."
201, 213a: Marcus, "Garcia."
203: Jackson and McMahon, "Time Out with Bill Graham."
204a: *San Francisco Chronicle,* "Jerry Garcia Agrees to Drug Diversion Plan."
204b, 206b, 208a, 209a, 211c: Gilmore, "The New Dawn of the Grateful Dead."
205a, 205b: Selvin, "What's 20 Years to the Dead?"
207a, 209b, 210b: Troy interview of David Nelson, October 12, 1991.
207b, 210c, 211b: Troy interview of Merl Saunders, December 20, 1993.
208b: Rense, "Back from the Dead."
210a: Hamlin, "Jerry Garcia Released from Hospital."
211a: Jackson, "Saunders & Garcia: Together Again."
212: Jackson, "Growing Up Dead."
213b, 213c: Jackson, "JGB."

Chapter 7

215a, 222: Troy interview of David Nelson, October 12, 1991.
215b: Rense, "Back from the Dead."
216a: Troy interview of Dick Latvala, December 1989.
216b, 216c: Sutherland, "Grateful Dead: Further Ahead."
217: Goodman, "Jerry Garcia: The *Rolling Stone* Interview."
218a, 218b: Gilmore, "The New Dawn of the Grateful Dead."
218c: Marcus, "Garcia."
219a, 219b: Jackson, "The Album: *In the Dark.*"
220: Jackson, "The Video: *So Far.*"
223: Selvin, "Grateful Dead Guitarist to Make Broadway Scene."
226a: Henke, "Jerry Garcia: The *Rolling Stone* Interview."
226b: Jackson, "Deadline."

Chapter 8

229, 230a: Public Media Center press release.
230b: Waldman, "Grateful Dead Takes a Case to Congress."
231a, 231c: Rosenthal, "Garcia & Saunders Enter a New Age."
231b: Troy interview of Merl Saunders, December 20, 1993.
233a: Henke, "Jerry Garcia: The *Rolling Stone* Interview."
233b, 243b: David Gans radio interview of Bruce Hornsby, December 31, 1990.
234: Dewey, "My Son, The Tube."
235: Millar, "The Grateful Dead."
237a: Lesh, *The Grateful Dead Almanac*.
237b, 239a: Hochman, "What a Long Strange Trip. . . ."
237c, 237d: Juanis, "Dawgwood Revisited."
238: Parrish, "Shaggy Dawg Stories."
239b, 240a: Gougis, "Word Jazz Wiz Nordine Is Back."
240b: Troy interview of David Nelson, December 22, 1993.
241: Mundy, "Random Notes."
242: Morse, "You Too Can Be a Famous Artist."
243a: Selvin, "Dead Songwriters Get life."
244: Gilbert, "Day of the Dead."
245a: Liberatore, "Grateful Dead Enter Comic Zone."
245b: Hochman, "Grateful Garcia."
246: *Los Angeles Times*, October 27, 1991.
247: Jackson, "Remembering Bill Graham."
248: Grateful Dead press release, August 14, 1992.
249a, 249b: Elwood, "It's Good to See You Jerry."
249c, 249d: Svetkey, "Dead Ahead."

Chapter 9

255: Jenkins, "Dream Day—Bonds, S.F. Are Winners."

BIBLIOGRAPHY

Books and Documentaries

Amburn, Ellis. *Pearl*. New York: Warner, 1992.

Anthony, Gene. *The Summer of Love*. Millbrae, CA: Celestial Arts, 1980.

Babbs, Ken and Paul Perry. *On the Bus*. New York: Thunder's Mouth Press, 1990.

Brandelius, Jerilyn Lee. *Grateful Dead Family Album*. New York: Warner, 1989.

CBS News. *The Hippie Temptation*. Television documentary, 1967.

Cohen, Allen. *The San Francisco Oracle*. Berkeley, CA: Regent Press, 1991.

Constanten, Tom. *Between Rock & Hard Places*. Eugene, OR: Hulogosi, 1992.

Crosby, David. *Long Time Gone*. New York: Doubleday, 1988.

Dalton, David. *Piece of My Heart*. New York: Da Capo Press, 1985.

Gans, David. *Conversations with the Dead*. New York: Citadel Underground, 1991.

Gans, David and Peter Simon. *Playing in the Band*. New York: St. Martin's Press, 1985.

Gebhardt, Steve. *Bill Monroe: The Father of Bluegrass Music*. Television documentary, 1993.

Gillett, Charlie. *The Sound of the City*. New York: Dell, 1970.

Glatt, John. *Rage & Roll*. New York: Birch Lane Press, 1993.

Gleason, Ralph J. *The Jefferson Airplane*. New York: Ballantine, 1969.

Go Ride the Music. Television documentary, 1971.

Graham, Bill and Robert Greenfield. *Bill Graham Presents*. New York: Doubleday, 1992.

Grushkin, Paul. *The Official Book of the Dead Heads*. New York: Quill, 1983.

Harrison, Hank. *The Dead Book*. New York: Links Books, 1973.
———. *The Dead*. Millbrae, CA: Celestial Arts, 1980.
Helm, Levon. *This Wheel's on Fire*. New York: William Morrow, 1993.
Hinds, David (ed.). *J. Garcia*. Berkeley, CA: Celestial Arts, 1992.
Hoskyns, Barney. *Across the Great Divide*. New York: Hyperion, 1993.
Hunter, Robert. *A Box of Rain*. New York: Viking, 1990.
Jackson, Blair. *The Music Never Stopped*. New York: Delilah, 1983.
———. *Goin' Down the Road*. New York: Harmony Books, 1992.
Joplin, Laura. *Love Janis*. New York: Villard, 1992.
Lee, Martin and Bruce Shlain. *Acid Dreams*. New York: Grove Weidenfeld, 1985.
McNally, Dennis. *Desolate Angel*. New York: Delta, 1979.
Marsh, Dave (ed.). *The* Rolling Stone *Record Guide*. New York: Random House, 1979.
Nicosia, Gerald. *Memory Babe*. New York: Grove Press, 1983.
Perry, Charles. *The Haight-Ashbury*. New York: Random House, 1984.
Plummer, William. *The Holy Goof*. New York: Paragon House, 1981.
Reich, Charles and Jann Wenner. *Garcia*. San Francisco: Straight Arrow Books, 1972.
Rowes, Barbara. *Grace Slick*. New York: Doubleday, 1980.
Sculatti, Gene and Davin Seay, *San Francisco Nights*. St. Martin's Press, New York, 1985.
Selvin, Joel. *Monterey Pop*. San Francisco: Chronicle Books, 1992.
Spitz, Bob. *Dylan*. New York: McGraw Hill, 1989.
Stevens, Jay. *Storming Heaven*. New York: HarperCollins, 1987.
Troy, Sandy. *One More Saturday Night*. New York: St. Martin's Press, 1991.
White, Timothy. *Rock Lives*. New York: Henry Holt, 1990.
Wolfe, Tom. *The Electric Kool-Aid Acid Test*. New York: Bantam, 1968.

Periodical and Newspaper Articles

Abbott, Lee. "Dead Reckoning and Hamburger Metaphysics." *Feature*, March 1979.
Article on death of Bill Graham, *Los Angeles Times*, October 27, 1991.
Barclay, Dolores. "The Woodstock Generation." *San Francisco Examiner*, May 16, 1979.
Barich, Bill. "Still Truckin'." *New Yorker*, October 11, 1993.
Block, Adam. "Garcia on Garcia." *BAM Magazine*, December 1977.
Bothun, Brian and Monica Hyde. "Dawn of the Dead." *Palo Alto Weekly*, May 12, 1993.
DeCurtis, Anthony. "The Music Never Stops." *Rolling Stone*, September 2, 1993.

Dewey, Jackie. "My Son, The Tube." *San Diego Reader*, March 6, 1980.

Donnelly, Kathleen. "What a Long, Strange Trip It's Been." *Palo Alto Weekly*, May 4, 1988.

"Dropouts with a Mission," *Newsweek*, February 6, 1967.

Dym, Monte and Bob Alson. "The Man Behind the Words." *Relix* 5, No. 1, 1978.

Elwood, Philip. "It's Good to See You Jerry." *San Francisco Examiner*, November 2, 1992.

Fong-Torres, Ben. "Fifteen Years Dead." *Rolling Stone*, August 7, 1980.

Gans, David. "The Pre-Dead Days." *The Golden Road*, Spring 1984.

Gilbert, Matthew. "Day of the Dead." *Boston Globe*, September 20, 1991.

Gilmore, Mikal. "The New Dawn of the Grateful Dead." *Rolling Stone*, July 16, 1987.

Goodman, Fred. "Jerry Garcia: The *Rolling Stone* Interview." *Rolling Stone*, November 30, 1989.

Gougis, Michael. "Word Jazz Wiz Nordine Is Back." *San Diego Union-Tribune*, January 27, 1993.

"The Grateful Dead Play the Pyramids." *San Francisco Chronicle*, September 15, 1978.

Grateful Dead Press Release on Jerry Garcia's health. August 14, 1992.

"Grateful Dead Suit Dropped." *San Francisco Chronicle*, January 1981.

"Grateful Wed," *People*, February 28, 1994.

Grissim, John. "Garcia Returns to Banjo." *Rolling Stone*, April 26, 1973.

Groenke, Randy and Mike Cramer. "One Afternoon Long Ago. . . ." *The Golden Road*, Summer 1985.

Hall, John. "True Confessions in Hartford." *Relix*, 4, No. 6, March 1978.

Hamlin, Jesse. "Jerry Garcia Released from Hospital." *San Francisco Chronicle*, August 2, 1986.

Henke, James. "Jerry Garcia: The *Rolling Stone* Interview." *Rolling Stone*, October 31, 1991.

Hochman, Steve. "Grateful Garcia." *Los Angeles Times*, May 1991.

———. "What a Long Strange Trip. . . ." *Boston Herald*, September 20, 1991.

Itkowitz, Jay. "Rapping with Garcia of the Grateful Dead." *Action World*, October 1970.

Jackson, Blair. "T.C." *The Golden Road*, Summer 1984.

———. "The Album: *In the Dark*." *The Golden Road*, Summer 1987.

———. "The Video: *So Far*." *The Golden Road*, Summer 1987.

———. "Garcia on the Art of Rock." *The Golden Road*, Fall 1987.

———. "John Kahn." *The Golden Road*, Winter 1987.

———. "Deadline." *The Golden Road*, Spring 1988.

———. "Ragged but Right." *The Golden Road*, Spring 1988.

———. "Jon McIntire." *The Golden Road*, Summer 1988.

————. "Saunders & Garcia: Together Again." *The Golden Road*, Spring 1990.

————. "Growing Up Dead." *The Golden Road*, 1992 Annual.

————. "JGB." *The Golden Road*, 1992 Annual.

————. "Remembering Bill Graham." *The Golden Road*, 1992 Annual.

————. "Pigpen Forever." *The Golden Road*, 1993 Annual.

Jackson, Blair and Regan McMahon. "Time Out with Bill Graham." *The Golden Road*, Fall 1985.

Jenkins, Bruce. "Dream Day—Bonds, S.F. Are Winners." *San Francisco Chronicle*, April 13, 1993.

"Jerry Garcia Agrees to Drug Diversion Plan." *San Francisco Chronicle*, March 20, 1985.

"Jerry Garcia's Grateful Dead Pass the Acid Test," *People*, 1976.

Juanis, J. C. "Dawgwood Revisited." *Relix*, December 1992.

Kahn, Alice. "Jerry Garcia and the Call of the Weird." *San Jose Mercury News*, December 30, 1984.

Lake, Steve. "Rock 'n' Roll Misfit." *Melody Maker*, September 14, 1974.

Lesh, Phil. Quote about Ornette Coleman from *The Grateful Dead Almanac*, Winter/Spring 1994.

Liberatore, Paul. "Grateful Dead Enter Comic Zone." *Marin Independent Journal*, August 17, 1991.

Lufkin, Liz. "The Dead—Just Becoming Alive." *San Francisco Chronicle*, July 19, 1981.

Lydon, Michael. "The Grateful Dead." *Rolling Stone*, August 23, 1969.

McClanahan, Ed. "Grateful Dead I Have Known." *Playboy*, August 1971.

McNally, Dennis. "When I Had No Song to Sing. . . ." *Grateful Dead Program*, 1983.

Marcus, Steve. "Garcia." *The Golden Road*, Fall 1986.

Millar, John. "The Grateful Dead." *Stars and Stripes*, October 20, 1990.

Morse, Rob. "You Too Can Be a Famous Artist." *San Francisco Examiner*, December 13, 1992.

Mundy, Chris. "Random Notes." *Rolling Stone*, May 13, 1993.

Parrish, Mike. "Shaggy Dawg Stories." *Dirty Linen*, October 1993.

Perry, Charles. "A New Life for the Dead." *Rolling Stone*, November 22, 1973.

Public Media Center. "Rock Group Grateful Dead Joins Fight to Save World's Remaining Tropical Rainforests." Press release, September 13, 1988.

Rense, Rip. "Back from the Dead." *Los Angeles Times*, April 19, 1987.

Rosenthal, Jim. "Garcia & Saunders Enter a New Age." *Relix*, April 1990.

Schuppisser, Mike. "Hangin' Loose with Bruce Hornsby." *Dupree's Diamond News*, May 1991.

Scully, Rock. "Parties, Parks, Women and Music." *Masters of Rock*, No. 7, 1992.

Selvin, Joel. "Jamming for the Hell of It." *The Night Times*, September 1972.

———. "The Grateful Dead Decides to Try a Guiding Hand." *San Francisco Chronicle*, July 28, 1977.

———. "What's 20 Years to the Dead?" *San Francisco Chronicle*, June 17, 1985.

———. "Fans Grateful the Dead Are Still Around." *San Francisco Chronicle*, December 22, 1985.

———. "Grateful Dead Guitarist to Make Broadway Scene." *San Francisco Chronicle*, August 16, 1987.

———. "Dead Songwriters Get Life." *San Francisco Chronicle*, April 21, 1991.

Sievert, Jon. "New Life with the Dead." *Guitar Player*, July 1988.

Stuckey, Fred. "Jerry Garcia." *Guitar Player*, April 1971.

Sutherland, Steve. "Jerry Garcia Interview." *Melody Maker*, March 28, 1981.

———. "Grateful Dead: Further Ahead." *Melody Maker*, May 13, 1989.

Svetkey, Benjamin. "Dead Ahead." *Entertainment Weekly*, March 12, 1993.

Waldman, Myron S. "Grateful Dead Takes a Case to Congress." *San Francisco Chronicle*, July 12, 1989.

Watts, Michael. "Dead on the Nile." *Melody Maker*, September 23, 1978.

Weitzman, Steve. "The Grateful Dead: A Look Back." *Relix*, April 1976.

Young, Charles M. "The Awakening of the Dead." *Rolling Stone*, June 16, 1977.

INDEX